"No other book does what this book does so well: A husband talks with wives about their husbands' needs, and a wife talks with husbands about their wives' needs. Barb's chapter about a wife's need for emotional intimacy and Gary's chapter about a husband's need for spiritual connection are worth the price of the book. This book will change your marriage!"

Dr. Steve Farrar, chairman of Men's Leadership Ministries and author of *Point Man*

"Each time I've heard Gary speak, my heart has been moved. Yours will be too as you read this book."

Max Lucado, author of *God Came Near*

"Gary and Barb Rosberg are true champions for Christ. Just being around them, talking to them, laughing with them, you sense purpose. I love these folks! I love them not only for the thousands of people they have helped with their timely words, but also for what they have done for my own marriage. Gary and Barbara will challenge you to go to the next level in this great book. May their words take us to higher heights in God."

Randy Phillips, vocalist with Phillips, Craig, and Dean

"What a helpful resource—full of vivid examples and great advice! I believe *The 5 Love Needs of Men and Women* will help any couple have an exciting, fulfilling—and passionate—marriage."

Bill McCartney, president of Promise Keepers and author (with his wife, Lyndi) of *Sold Out Two-Gether*

"The bride-and-groom dream of 'happily ever after' frequently dissolves into a baffling illusion. For many spouses, it is 'unhappily today and tomorrow and tomorrow . . .' The quiet question pulsates: What in the world does my spouse expect? This book distills *the* answers. With clear language and logical sequence Barb and Gary show how marriage can make long-term sense. Newlyweds will cherish their wisdom; older couples will applaud the opportunity to make a much-needed review of their relationship. This book should never just fill up shelf space; these pages must be read, reread, underlined—and practiced."

Dr. Howard G. Hendricks, chairman of the Center for Christian Leadership and author of *Color Outside the Lines*, and **Jeanne W. Hendricks**, author of *Women of Honor*

"I came to the reading of *The 5 Love Needs of Men and Women* totally biased. I not only love and respect Gary and Barb, but I also continue to be impressed with their ministry, America's Family Coaches. So I was not in the least surprised to find them tackling tough marital issues with their characteristic straightforward, down-to-earth, 'Hey, you can do this' practical suggestions.

"As they share their own times of insecurity and uncertainty, readers feel comforted and grateful not to be talked down to. We're all in the same boat, which occasionally threatens to capsize. The Rosbergs' warm, caring, encouraging voices reassure us that in Christ, all things are possible.

"This is one of the finest books I've read about the intricacies and challenges of marriage. Buy an armload. Keep one and give the rest away. The homes of America will be healthier, happier places as a result!"

Marilyn Meberg, Women of Faith speaker and author of *I'd Rather Be Laughing*

"Powerful. Practical. Encouraging. Full of hope. In *The 5 Needs of Men and Women,* our dear friends Gary and Barbara Rosberg have given us an engaging, wonderful resource that will help us to build marriages that will go the distance. The chapters—in which Barbara speaks as a wife to husbands, and Gary speaks as a husband to wives—are heart-felt and practical. You will be moved and encouraged to make your marriage everything that God designed it to be. This book needs to be in the hands of every couple!"

Dr. Crawford W. Loritts Jr., associate U.S. director of Campus Crusade for Christ, and **Karen Loritts**, coauthor of *Leaving a Godly Legacy*

"There have been lots of great partnerships in history. Lewis and Clark. The Lone Ranger and Tonto. Marris and Mantle. But when I think of great partnerships, I think of Gary and Barb Rosberg. I've known and watched these two incredible servants love, bless, and encourage hundreds of men and women over the years, starting with their own daughters. Cindy and I can't think of a couple we'd rather 'counsel' with than the Rosbergs— which is why we loved their book on meeting your spouse's needs so much! You'll also love the wise counsel on loving each other!"

Dr. John Trent, president of Encouraging Words and author of *Choosing to Live the Blessing*

"One of the most important questions in every marriage is: How do we love our spouse? The Rosbergs have *the* answer! *The 5 Love Needs of Men and Women* will enable you to move your marriage to new levels of intimacy, romance, and fulfillment. This is a must-read for every couple who wants a marriage that is all that God intended it to be!"

Dr. Dennis Rainey, executive director of FamilyLife and author of *Moments Together for Couples*

"The Rosbergs expose and explain the often unexpressed needs in the hearts of husbands and wives. With grace and compassion, they offer every spouse the route to a long and happy marriage."

Michael Medved, national radio talk-show host and *USA Today* columnist, and **Dr. Diane Medved**, author of *The Case Against Divorce*

"Listen up! Listen in! Listen well! Gary and Barbara speak a language we all need to hear, one of enlightenment, encouragement, and emancipation. For when we grasp the principles within, we will be freed up to love deeply and well. I personally have listened in not only to Gary and Barb's insightful book but also to their lives. And trust me. They know what they are talking about!"

Patsy Clairmont, Women of Faith speaker and author of *I Love Being a Woman* and *Stardust on My Pillow*

"*The 5 Love Needs of Men and Women* is vintage Rosberg—chock full of very specific suggestions and tools for husbands and wives. You'll be reminded of the needs of your spouse and then given practical steps in meeting those needs. Gary and Barb write honestly regarding the needs we all have in our marriages."

Dr. Stu Weber, author of *Four Pillars of a Man's Heart* and *Tender Warrior*

"This book holds the power to radically impact your relationship. Gary and Barb's extraordinary insight into the love needs of men and women provides an excellent guide to understanding the love of your life."

Dr. Gary Smalley, director of the Smalley Relationship Center and author of *Secrets to Lasting Love*

"With clear understanding of the realities of married life, coupled with a careful exposition of the Bible, Gary and Barbara Rosberg lay out the needs of husbands and wives so that couples can enjoy the highs of marriage and avoid the lows of marital infidelity."

Dr. Tony Evans, senior pastor of Oak Cliff Bible Fellowship, president of The Urban Alternative, and author of *Who Is This King of Glory?*

"*Le•git•ness*—Webster didn't coin the word; Gary and Barb did. In down-home, Iowa farm-boy language, *legitness* means integrity to the core. This couple is the real thing. Their ministry is 'legit.' Their personal, home life is 'legit.' If, after reading this book, my marriage and yours can be half as good as theirs, we better put one of these books in every room in our houses."

Dr. Joe White, president of Kanakuk Kamps, Inc. and author of *FAITHTRAINING*

the 5 Love Needs

of Men&Women

DR. GARY & BARBARA ROSBERG

TYNDALE HOUSE PUBLISHERS, INC. | WHEATON, ILLINOIS

Visit Tyndale's exciting Web site at www.tyndale.com

The Five Love Needs of Men and Women

Copyright © 2000 by Gary and Barbara Rosberg. All rights reserved.

In sharing stories from other people's lives in this book, we have changed their names and some of the details of their stories in order to protect their privacy.

Published in association with the literary agency of Alive Communications, Inc., 7680 Goddard Street, Suite 200, Colorado Springs, CO 80920.

Designed by Justin Ahrens

Edited by Lynn Vanderzalm and Judith Markham

Unless otherwise indicated, all Scripture quotations are taken from the *Holy Bible,* New Living Translation, copyright © 1996. Used by permission of Tyndale House Publishers, Inc., Wheaton, Illinois 60189. All rights reserved.

Scripture quotations marked NIV are taken from the *Holy Bible,* New International Version® NIV® Copyright © 1973, 1978, 1984 by International Bible Society. Used by permission of Zondervan Publishing House. All rights reserved.

Library of Congress Cataloging-in-Publication Data

Printed in the United States of America

05   04   03   02   01   00
8   7   6   5   4   3   2   1

To our children—Sarah and Scott Wolfswinkel
and Missy Rosberg and her future husband

*May you experience the fullness of a great marriage, which comes from
surrendering your lives to the Lord and to one another.*

WE LOVE YOU ALL DEEPLY.
Thanks for calling us Mom and Dad!

CONTENTS

ACKNOWLEDGMENTS

It has been five years since I (Gary) wrote *Guard Your Heart*. In some people's eyes, waiting five years between books is too long. Not for me. For three very important reasons.

First, Barb and I knew the next time we wrote a book, we wanted to write it together. Life is short, and we want to team up as a couple as much as possible to have an impact on families. Barb wrote a very strong and special section in *Guard Your Heart* at the conclusion to the book, showing women how to help their husbands guard their hearts. Yet she has a lot more to say, which you will read in this book.

Second, we had a couple of sweet daughters to finish raising and releasing. God brought those releases within ten days of each other in September of 1999. Ouch! Sarah was married on September 11 to Scott Wolfswinkel. We are thrilled, and we now have a son, whom we love. Missy, our little one, headed for college the same month. We decided that our role as a mom and dad was far more important than writing a book, so we waited. Now that our daughters are released, we are released to write.

The third reason is perhaps more important to you than the first two. We didn't want to write another book until the Holy Spirit had burned into our hearts and spirits something that needed to be said. Our dear friend Dr. John Trent once told me, "The Christian community doesn't need another book by authors who don't have anything to say." We have taken his counsel. We waited until now because we now have something to say. Next to our relationship with Jesus Christ, nothing is more important than marriage. That's why we wrote this book. We want to help you strengthen your marriage and to encourage you to become passionate about helping others strengthen their marriages.

When writing this book, it helped us to surround ourselves with other people who are as committed as we are to putting out the best book possible. That's what we did. And we want to thank those who helped us.

First of all, thank you to Ron Beers from Tyndale House Publishers. When we met you at CBA in 1997, we knew you were the real thing. Your commitment not only to great books but also to great relationships sold us right out of the gate. Thanks for teaming up with us and being so committed to excellence in publishing this book. Thanks also to Ken Petersen and the rest of the Tyndale team. You are the best.

We also want to thank Greg Johnson, our literary agent from Alive Communications, Inc. Greg, you not only steered us in the right direction (to Tyndale), but you also helped provide a strong foundation to this book. It is good to be your friend and your colaborer in publishing books that make a difference.

Lynn Vanderzalm and Judith Markam, you are editors extraordinaire. You kept us on track. You raised the bar of excellence as well as the bar of grace. You are the dynamic duo in our hearts.

Thank you to Dr. Lloyd Taylor of Midwestern State University for helping us with the statistical analysis of our data, and to all the couples who participated in our survey used as the foundation of this book. This book is rich with all of your insight. You are making a difference.

We want to thank Pastor Quintin Stieff for ministering to our family, week in and week out. You shepherd the families at Valley Evangelical Free Church with truth and grace. Thanks for serving all of us so well.

We also want to thank our ministry team at America's Family Coaches. Your commitment to bringing God's truth to families in central Iowa and nationally is distinctive and heartfelt. Your sacrifice has enabled us to spend the time necessary to write this book. May your families and thousands of others be strengthened because of your service. We love you and count it a great honor to serve you.

And most of all, we want to thank our family. Sarah and Scott, we love you and are proud of you and of how God is developing your precious marriage. We hold you up in prayer and cherish you. You have started strong. Now in the power of the Spirit of God, finish strong. Missy, we also honor you and are thrilled you call us Mom and Dad. It is truly a joy to see God using you and shaping you into a remarkable woman. Stay in his grip, kids, and finish strong!

Dr. Gary and Barbara Rosberg
America's Family Coaches

THE LETTER THAT CHANGED A MARRIAGE

Phil called my (Gary's) counseling office to ask if he and his wife could make an appointment. Looking at my jam-packed schedule book, I responded, "This is a really busy time, Phil. It may be a few weeks before an appointment opens up."

"It can't wait a few weeks," he said. "It *has* to be today." Then he added, "Gary, I wouldn't ask if it weren't urgent."

I didn't know Phil well, but I knew panic when I heard it. "If you really need to come in," I said, "stop by at five o'clock."

"We'll be there," he said.

Throughout the day I kept thinking about that phone call and found myself praying for Phil and his wife. The urgent tone of his voice was a red flag, warning me that we were about to step into a battle—a battle for the life of his family.

Several hours later my worst fears were realized as I greeted Phil and Susan in my office waiting room. Susan was weeping, staring at the floor. Phil looked like a man who had just come face-to-face with his worst nightmare.

Once we were all seated in my office, I asked them what they needed to talk about.

"I was going to take the kids to the park this afternoon," Phil said. "Before we left, I was changing baby Annie's diaper. I couldn't find the wipes, so I asked one of the older kids to watch the baby while I looked for some. Then I remembered that Susan sometimes carries a package of wipes in her beach bag, which was stowed in our older daughter's closet. When I reached inside the beach bag, I found a letter. It was a love letter to Susan. The only problem is . . . it wasn't from me."

Phil glanced at Susan for a second, then looked back at me.

"The letter was from another man. He was pouring out his love for *my* wife. He talked about times they were together. Right there in print I began to see my entire life unravel. I couldn't believe it. He talked about her perfume . . . about his favorite dress. *I* bought that dress for Susan. He talked about his memories of hotels and secret lunches. I couldn't believe my eyes. This was my wife, the mother of my kids, he was talking about. But I think the one that is putting me under is that they were even in our bedroom. I go out of town to earn a living for her and the kids, and she is in our bedroom with this guy. All I could do was stare at the letter."

"What did you do next?" I asked him.

"I slid to the floor inside that closet and read the letter over and over again. I couldn't stop," he said. "I knew if I ever stepped outside that closet, I would have to face more pain than I could ever imagine. I knew my life would never be the same. I could hear the kids running through the house, completely unaware that their world was about to change. Finally I gathered enough strength to get up. I could hear Susan on the phone in our bedroom, so I headed down the hallway toward her. As I did, I walked past family pictures representing everything that made sense. Pictures of holidays, white-water rafting, family reunions. . . . It was the longest walk of my life.

"As I walked into the bedroom, Susan's back was to me. Then she hung up the phone and turned toward me. As she did, I looked into her eyes, and all I could say were three words: 'Susan, I know.'

"With that, she fell over onto the bed and began to sob. And then I knew for sure that it wasn't a bad dream. This was really happening. My wife was having an affair. Wrenching pain cut through me from some-where deep inside of my soul. And we both just fell apart."

Oh no, Lord. Not another family, I found myself praying. *Not this couple . . . these little children. Father, give me the words, give me the wisdom.*

"What happened to us, Gary?" Phil asked, tears in his eyes as he looked at me. "We began our marriage with so much love for each other, with such incredible hope for our future together. We were so deter-mined to have a strong, Christ-centered marriage. What happened?"

"Phil and Susan, I am so sorry. Let's talk a bit about your situation," I said. "What is going to happen in the next several minutes is literally going to be a defining moment for the rest of your marriage because you guys are at a crossroads. If you were in a physical crisis as serious as this, I would have a physician hospitalize you. We don't hospitalize couples in crisis, but what I do is give you a safe place to bleed—with the promise that God can sort all this out. It's not too late. He is here, and so am I."

Over the next several minutes I helped Phil and Susan begin to drain the pain. There were tears, outbursts of anger, and times when they were ready to walk out. But they didn't. They stayed and began to face this storm head-on. Then, as I began to sense that they were ready to hear some strong truth, I began to both press them and to give them a vision for what needed to happen to restore their marriage.

"I need to start by asking you some things to bring me up to speed," I said. "Susan, I guess I would like to start by asking how your relationship with this other man got from zero to 100 mph. As painful as this is, Phil needs to hear this, and so do I if I am going to help you. I know it didn't start with a sexual relationship."

"No, it didn't. It started with attention," replied Susan. "Looks. Innocent at first, then playful. Listening. We became friends through a volunteer project we worked on together. I never would have done this intentionally, Phil, I swear. I love you and the kids. I was so confused. It was as if I stepped in innocently and then just got caught up in it. I was just so lonely. You were traveling and totally absorbed in your work. I was trying to juggle the kids, the house, the bills. That project was my only time out, and I think I just let down my guard. It started out with little things. I knew it was wrong, but it felt so good. How could something that felt so good now make me feel so dirty and ashamed? I can't believe this is happening."

"Susan, how could you just lie and lie to me?" Phil asked. "That time I thought you were at your sister's house, you were with him, weren't you? And when you would drop the kids off at different sitters, I thought you were doing volunteer work. What a sham! My whole life is a joke. Nothing is what it appears to be. I know I wasn't paying attention to all your needs, but I just had to get through this busy time at work."

At this point I stepped in once more.

"Phil and Susan, I want you to listen to me. I am not going to soft-pedal the reality of the condition of your marriage. It's a mess. You are in trouble, and everything that made sense when you woke up this morning is now up for grabs. Susan, your lies are now in the light. Phil, you are being broadsided by a freight train you didn't even know was coming.

"Susan, you put down your guardrails. Instead of guarding your heart and being cautious, you gave in to what felt good at the moment. This guy met a need by listening, responding, and spending time with you. The whole nine yards. I believe you when you say you didn't mean for it to happen. People rarely do. But it did. And, Susan, the very things you were giving this other man are the things Phil needs from you. He needs your love, your affirmation, your belief in him. He needs your companionship and your time. He needs you to be his one and only—sexually and with all your heart. He needs you to cheer him on, equipping him for the battles of life.

"And, Phil, you're not off the hook either. You weren't paying attention to the needs of your wife, were you? I know what it's like to have a demanding schedule. You are under the gun at work. Besides that, guys like to go where they are successful, where they know they can accomplish something—and that is usually work. But the time and attention you devote to your work has got to come from somewhere, like from Susan and the kids. Phil, you let your guard down too. The very commitment and energy required to feed your marriage relationship were going to everyone and everything but your wife. To the house, work, church activities, even the yard. Susan needs your love, your heart, your time. She needs you to be the one to encourage her and cheer her on and lead her spiritually. She needs you to be her soul mate, her best friend."

I paused for a moment as I looked straight at Susan and then at Phil.

"Trust me on this, you can't build a marriage unless you are pouring yourself into each other. That is what commitment is all about. That is what the covenant of marriage is all about. That's what a marriage of three is all about: God, a husband, and a wife. You have lost your first love for each other. You both needed to have your needs met somewhere. But you both looked in all the wrong places.

"Now, you both need to be willing to walk right through the eye of this storm, knowing that God will walk with you if you let him, all the way through to the other side. But let me tell you, it is going to be the fight of your life."

As I looked at the heartbroken and heartsick man and woman sitting in my office, I posed the big question: "Phil, what are you going to do?"

"I'll tell you what I'm going to do," he said, looking at me with determination in his eyes. "I'm going to win back my wife."

With that, he turned to look at Susan. "I love you, Susan," he said. "I *want* you. If it takes everything I have, I will win you back."

Susan slowly raised her head and turned toward Phil.

"I am hurt and angry," he continued. "But I want you, Susan. I want our kids. I want our family to heal."

At that point, Susan threw her arms around her husband and held on as if her life depended on it. "After what I have done, you still want me?" Her voice was choked with tears.

"Yes. I want you. You have hurt me. And I know I have hurt you along the way too. I haven't paid attention to your needs. I know my job has consumed me, and I haven't reached out to you. But I love you. Please . . . let's make this work."

WHAT ABOUT YOU?

What is your response to Phil and Susan's story? Are you thinking, *That could never happen to us?*

Before you jump to that conclusion, please understand that Phil and Susan would have said the same thing a year or two earlier. They never dreamed that in their responsibilities to work and family and church, they had unconsciously let go of their commitment to meet each other's needs. They did not see their relationship eroding. They were not aware of the deficits and gaps that left them vulnerable and unprotected. I don't mean to be an alarmist when I say that what happened to Phil and Susan could happen to you. Maybe your affair won't be a sexual one. Maybe it will be an emotional affair or an affair with work or other activities. I've seen it happen too many times to ignore the reality. I also know that it doesn't *have* to happen. You can safeguard your marriage, and that's what the rest of this book will help you do.

Or maybe you read Phil and Susan's story and are thinking, *That's us. Our marriage is disintegrating. I don't see how we can ever have a great marriage. My spouse and I don't talk much anymore. Our sex life is almost nonexistent. We argue more than we ever did before. In fact, I'm not sure my spouse really wants me.*

If you are at that point of discouragement in your marriage, take heart. It may be late, but it is not *too* late. God can restore the most damaged relationship. And we believe he can use the stories and insights and principles in this book as tools to strengthen and heal your marriage.

WHY IS IT IMPORTANT TO MEET YOUR SPOUSE'S LOVE NEEDS?

Meeting your spouse's love needs is one of the most important responsibilities you have in your marriage . . . for several reasons.

Meeting your spouse's love needs is a matter of keeping your vows. When you got married, you promised to love your husband, to cherish your wife, to face the good and the bad hand in hand, together, as one. When you meet the needs of your spouse, you are fulfilling your marriage vows. That's what the marriage covenant is about, as I reminded Phil and Susan. Our culture doesn't recognize, respect, or support the importance of the vows. But God does—as do the men and women who are choosing to live out biblical marriages.

Meeting your spouse's love needs is what God calls you to do. Some of the New Testament's most powerful words about marriage call husbands and wives to the kind of sacrificial love that makes them willing to lay down their lives for each other. God wants husbands and wives to consider the needs of the other as more important than their own. When you meet the needs of your spouse, you are being "God with skin on," a phrase Barb and I use to describe the privilege we have of reflecting Christ's love to each other.

Meeting your spouse's love needs will result in a great marriage. Do you want a great marriage? Do you want an intimate and healthy relationship with your husband or your wife? When you meet the love needs of your spouse, you build the foundation for a great marriage. When you focus on how to meet your spouse's needs, you become motivated to do what God is calling you to do. And when a husband and wife do this whole-heartedly, each loving and focusing on meeting the legitimate needs of the other, the relationship is doubly strengthened. It is no longer a fifty-fifty deal; it is a one hundred–one hundred commitment.

But beware: When our love needs go unmet and we choose to buy into the world's plan of fifty-fifty performance, the results are not pretty.

Neglecting to meet your spouse's love needs could cost you your marriage. Perhaps the bottom-line reason for meeting your spouse's needs is that if you don't, you could end up losing him or her to another man or woman. Or to whatever "affair" your spouse believes will fill that need in his or her heart. You would never think of not meeting your spouse's need for food and water; it's obvious that he or she would die without these essentials. Yet your spouse's emotional, physical, relational, and spiritual needs are so vital, so critical, that if they are not met, your marriage will begin to die. It's that simple. When you meet the needs of your husband or your wife, you guard your marriage against temptation.

At the heart of the urgency Barb and I feel for this issue of meeting love needs is our deep commitment to marriage and family—ours as well as yours. For the first ten years of my adult life, I worked with imprisoned men and women whose lives were marked by broken relationships and devastated families. For the past sixteen years, in over twenty-five thousand hours of counseling, I have worked with thousands of couples who have come into my office to try to repair their damaged relationships. All told, then, for the past twenty-six years I have lived "below the waterline" with hurting people, listening to the pain of their hearts. Now, together, Barb and I speak to couples all across the country about how to keep their marriages strong and rooted in biblical truth. They all ask the same basic question: "How do I have a great marriage?"

I think most of you would agree that our culture has no answers to that question. And just being Christians doesn't make a marriage great.

Pollster George Barna tells us that Christian marriages are ending in divorce at an even higher rate than non-Christian marriages (27 percent vs. 23 percent). These statistics indicate that just showing up in church isn't going to build a healthy, biblical marriage. We must be more than hearers of the Word; we must be doers of the Word. That's what the New Testament writer James meant when he said, "Remember, it is a message to obey, not just to listen to. If you don't obey, you are only fooling yourself" (James 1:22).

You need to know your spouse's heart and needs, and then sacrificially step away from your own selfishness and learn—really learn—how to meet those needs. You must build your life on a foundation that is going to stand the test of the storms—a rock-solid foundation that will not shift under pressure. That is the rock that Phil and Susan held on to for dear life.

At the end of the Sermon on the Mount, Jesus says, "Anyone who listens to my teaching and obeys me is wise, like a person who builds a house on solid rock. Though the rain comes in torrents and the floodwaters rise and the winds beat against that house, it won't collapse, because it is built on rock. But anyone who hears my teaching and ignores it is foolish, like a person who builds a house on sand. When the rains and floods come and the winds beat against that house, it will fall with a mighty crash" (Matt. 7:24-27).

Houses don't do well on sandy foundations. Neither do relationships. Marriages built on the rock of Christ Jesus not only start strong but also finish strong.

WHAT ARE YOUR SPOUSE'S LOVE NEEDS?

Human nature is strange. Something in us assumes that if we treat our spouse the way we would like him or her to treat us, we are meeting our partner's needs. But when it comes to needs, the Golden Rule does not always apply. Why? Because in many cases a husband's needs are different from a wife's needs. That is most evident in areas like sexual needs, but it is true in other areas as well.

If I asked you if you are meeting your spouse's love needs, you would probably answer yes. In reality, what many of us are really doing is just assuming our spouse wants what we want, and so we act on that. Often we really don't *know* what our spouse's needs are. And if we don't know what the needs are, we can't possibly meet them effectively.

To help us understand the unique love needs of husbands and wives, Barb and I surveyed more than seven hundred couples. We presented them with a list of twenty needs and asked them to rank, in order of importance, what they needed from their spouse and what they thought their spouse needed from them.

The complete results of that survey can be found in the appendix, but here are the top five responses:

HUSBANDS' TOP FIVE LOVE NEEDS	WIVES' TOP FIVE LOVE NEEDS
1. Unconditional Love and Acceptance	1. Unconditional Love and Acceptance
2. Sexual Intimacy	2. Emotional Intimacy and Communication
3. Companionship	3. Spiritual Intimacy
4. Encouragement and Affirmation	4. Encouragement and Affirmation
5. Spiritual Intimacy	5. Companionship

How do these love needs align with your own? Do any of these needs surprise you? Does the order of priority surprise you?

Barb and I have a good marriage. In fact we have a *really* good marriage. There are times when we are convinced that we have the best marriage on the planet. We'll look each other in the eye and say, "What we have could not get any better." Then there are other times when we know we haven't arrived yet. But armed with our love for each other and the necessary information tools, we keep working to make our marriage the best that it can be. We want a *great* marriage, and that is our desire for you too.

I love watching and interviewing couples who have been married fifty years or longer. Barb and I try to have a golden-anniversary couple on our radio show once a month, and when we do, we just drink up the wisdom. One of the things I ask them is this: "What do you have to say to those of us who are not as far along on the journey? What works? How have you done it?" Their answers almost always include the needs our surveyed couples ranked the highest.

"Gary and Barb, we take time every day to listen to each other and learn what the other experienced that day."

"We love to spend time with each other. We just enjoy being each other's best friends."

"It is a little embarrassing to say on radio, but Barney taught me a long time ago that when I meet his sexual needs, he feels valued. When I listen to him and encourage him, he feels respected. When he prays with me, I feel so safe. When I spend time with him, he feels like a million bucks!"

"Mildred taught me a long time ago that my voice of belief in her is the only real voice, next to God's, that she really needs to hear. So I learned to speak. Yep, we have been married fifty-four years, and I think the marriage is going to take, don't you, Barb and Gary?" The twinkle in this man's eyes almost knocked us off our chairs!

Unconditional love. Encouragement. Companionship. Sexual and spiritual intimacy. Sound familiar? Look again at the top five love needs of men and women. They are all there. Not all couples married fifty years or more are living out great marriages, but many of our parents and grandparents really get it and want to pass it on.

In the following ten chapters we will explore each of the love needs listed earlier. I will talk to wives about the top five love needs that husbands have because I think I can offer wives some unique insight into how men think and feel. Barb will talk to husbands about the top five love needs that wives have because she can speak authoritatively about how women think and feel. Then in the final two chapters of the book we'll switch, and I will talk to husbands, and Barb will talk to wives. By combining our voices, we hope to offer you the best possible opportunity to understand your spouse's needs and to learn how to meet those needs.

You may choose to read all of the chapters of the book, or you can opt to read only the ones that you feel apply specifically to you. I recommend that you read them all, though, because if you are a husband, you may find that I did not do a good job of describing your needs to your wife. If that is the case, then you can clarify what I have said so that your wife understands you. If you are a wife and you feel that Barb does not adequately describe your needs to your husband, you can augment what she says so that your husband has a clear picture of your needs. In this way, the book will become a springboard for your own personal discussions and actions.

We also encourage you to study this book with other couples in your home or in a Sunday school setting. Instead of adding questions for group study at the end of each chapter, we opted instead to include questions throughout the chapters. Use these as the basis for your discussions of the unique needs that husbands and wives have. Then spur each other on to meet your spouse's unique love needs.

Our goals in this book reach beyond helping you understand and learn to meet your spouse's love needs. We also want you to understand why it's important to meet those needs. And we hope that the stories and principles we share will inspire you and motivate you to a lifelong commitment to love your spouse in ways that neither of you dreamed possible. But most of all, we hope you discover that in meeting your spouse's love needs, you are "putting skin on" God's love. Marriage really is a relationship of three: God, a man, and a woman. The world doesn't get that, does it? And sadly many Christian couples haven't quite grasped that profound truth either. But when a husband and wife truly begin to understand the significance of a marriage of three, relationships begin to flourish.

God has used the intimacy of the marriage relationship as a metaphor to describe his love for us. As a husband or a wife, you can demonstrate what God's love for your spouse looks like; you can be God's voice and arms of love and care. What a privilege!

THE REST OF THE STORY

Now, are you wondering what happened to Phil and Susan? Well, for several months after their first meeting in my office, they came for counseling and explored the causes of their disintegrating relationship. At that point they had a long road ahead of them, but since they moved when Phil's job took them to another state, I did not see them for some time.

Then, not long ago, Phil and Susan called me. They had heard I was going to speak at a conference in their hometown, and they asked if I would spend a night in their home. I said yes, eager to see them.

As I pulled into their driveway on the first evening of the conference, I looked at their beautiful home and wondered if the lives of the people on the inside would look as good as the house. When I rang the doorbell, a little girl, dressed up in her Sunday best, answered the door. The curly-headed blonde looked up at me and asked, "Are you Dr. Gary?"

"Well, yes, honey, I am. And what is your name?"

"I'm Annie. You get to stay in my room tonight."

With that proclamation, little Annie, who had been a baby when Phil and Susan first came to my office four years earlier, welcomed me in. And there on the staircase stood Phil and Susan, hand in hand with the rest of their family.

What a picture! Just the sight of them made the tears begin to flow. They were tears of gratitude to a God who gives us second chances. Tears of thankfulness that Phil had the humility to forgive his wife and rebuild his family. Tears of joy that as Susan and Phil learned how to understand and meet each other's needs, they began building a marriage that is not only surviving but radiant.

That is the joy and oneness that Barb and I desire for every marriage.

TAKE A STEP TOWARD MEETING YOUR SPOUSE'S LOVE NEEDS

So where do you start? Well, first of all . . .

1. How committed are you to meeting your spouse's love needs?

2. Take some time in the next two days to discuss with your spouse what his or her love needs are. One of the ways you can begin that discussion is to make a list of what you think are your spouse's top five love needs.

3. At the same time, make a list of your top five love needs. (If you are not sure that the needs listed on page 8 are your needs and if you want some other ideas, turn to the appendix on page 235 for the list of twenty needs we used for our survey.)

4. Then sit down with your spouse and say, "I want to learn what your

love needs are so that I can meet them more fully. I've made a list of what I think your top five love needs are, and I want to discuss those with you. But what is more important to me is what you think are the most important love needs that you need me to meet." Then begin to discuss his or her needs. If your spouse asks you what your love needs are, you have your list ready.

Part 1

Understanding and Meeting
Each Other's Love Needs

CHAPTER 1

UNCONDITIONAL LOVE

A HUSBAND'S #1 LOVE NEED

"You mean you will love me no matter what?"

Gary talks to wives

Unconditional love and acceptance. Isn't that what every one of us searches for as we risk letting other people get close to us? When we open our hearts to another person, our bottom-line desire is to be accepted and loved the way we are, warts and all. We want to be able to drop the mask and be safe. We want unconditional love. We want the real thing. Deep. Lasting. Resilient.

In our national survey, a majority of both men and women told us that unconditional love is their number one love need from their marriage partner. No doubt many would expect the number one need for men to be sex and the number one need for women to be communication, but that was not what we found. Instead, as different as men and women can be, both agreed on this one truth: We all need to be loved unconditionally by our spouses.

When my wife needs my unconditional love, it simply means that she needs me to love her and receive her no matter what. For richer or for poorer. In sickness and in health. You remember the vows. Unconditional love is the commitment that says, "I will stay with you no matter what. I will always love you. I will affirm you and support you." Acceptance means, "I will receive you even in the midst of tough times."

Barb and I have found that our love for each other is glorious in the good times—the vacations on the beach, the memory-making experiences with the kids, the times of deep intimacy together with Jesus Christ. It's easy to love in the good times. But when our marriage comes under intense testing, we need *unconditional* love. Love that won't quit. We need to know we are accepted even when we come up short, even when we can't see beyond our own pain and failures.

You've had those times; I know you have. Times of crisis. Times of unbearable stress. Times when, in your heart of hearts, you wonder whether your husband will draw close to you and love you without question or whether he will turn his back and reject you.

Let me share one of my experiences with this kind of crisis. It was a time when I really needed to hear Barb say, "I'm here, Gary. I'm not leaving. I'm here for you. *No matter what.*"

My crisis began with a phone call to a business client from another state. During the call, I had to take a strong stand on an ethical issue. And the result of that stand was that at the end of the call, I had lost half of my income for the year.

Half of my income!

That phone call sent me into a tailspin, and I knew I needed help to come out of it. More than that, I needed a safe place, a place where my heart, spirit, and soul would be loved unconditionally. No strings. No exceptions. No limits.

I reached for the phone and called Barb. "Something has happened. I just need to know, Barb, that no matter what I have to tell you, you will support me. That we are going to be okay. That the Lord and you will stick by me."

"Gary, you don't even need to qualify it. Yes, I'll support you. And God promises never to abandon us. What happened?"

"Barb, I need to talk to you right away, but I can't do it on the phone. I'll be home in ten minutes. Please, just clear the decks."

When I hung up the phone, I knew my safety net was in place—whether or not I deserved it. I could tell by the tone of Barb's voice that she was mine and I was hers and that we both belonged to God. I knew that regardless of what I was about to tell her, *that* wouldn't change.

Still, as I drove home, fears pelted my heart. As a man, my roles as provider and protector—the two roles every man feels he *has* to fulfill—were in jeopardy. I felt like a failure, and I was afraid that I might have put the welfare of my family at risk. So I started to second-guess myself. *Maybe we could have worked something out. Should I have taken such a strong stand with this client? What if I misunderstood what he was saying?*

Then I thought about the ramifications for my family: *How am I going to make up for this significant loss of income? What will Barb and the girls say? What are we going to have to sell to keep ourselves afloat?*

At that point God's Spirit began to shove away some of my lingering doubts. I knew that he would provide for all of our needs and that I had made the right decision by confronting the issue. But I still needed to look Barb in the face. I needed to connect to her and know that she thought I had done the right thing. I needed to know that she loved me, that nothing would change between us.

As I walked through the back door, I must have had "that look" on my face because Barb immediately grabbed me and held me. "No matter what, Gary, I am with you," she assured me. "Please, sit down and tell me what happened."

It was one of those "God with skin on" moments, when we needed to reassure each other that we are secure, safe, and one with each other and with the Lord.

"Barb, I talked to ——— on the phone. You know that I have sensed something is wrong, deeply wrong, in our business relationship. As a result, I haven't been sleeping, concentrating, or focusing on the ministry. You and the girls haven't gotten my best over the last few days. I've had such deep conviction in my spirit that I needed to confront this guy about his business practices, but I knew that if I did, I would run the risk of losing the contract. Today I called him and asked if I could talk something out with him. Within a few minutes we agreed that we couldn't work together any longer. As quickly as that, our business relationship was over. I know it was the right thing to do, but it is really going to hurt us financially."

"Gary, I am so sorry," Barb said. "You must feel both overwhelmed and scared at the same time."

"I don't know what I'm going to do. What if this means we have to sell the house? I keep wondering if I could have handled it differently."

"Honey, how can I help you most right now?" she said.

"You are doing it, just by listening."

Even as I was saying all this, I was searching her eyes for her *real* response. What a relief I felt when I saw no panic, no fear. Not even disappointment. Instead, her eyes told me the same thing that her words did: "I'm so sorry this happened to you. But it will be all right. We are going to be okay." With each fear-driven comment I poured out, Barb responded with an encouraging nod or a touch. The circumstances hadn't changed: We were still going to lose a substantial portion of our income for a time. Yet because of Barb's response, everything *was* different. I knew that I wasn't alone; and I knew that between the Lord and my wife, I was secure.

When I finished telling her why and how I had made the decision to sever the business relationship with this person, Barb looked me in the eye and quietly but confidently reminded me of the truth that often escapes us in the heat of pressure, stress, or trouble. "Gary, God owns the cattle on a thousand hills. He will provide for you and for our family," she said. "And no matter what happens, I will stay close to you." And then the words I can never hear often enough: "I'm proud of you, Gary. You did the right thing."

I remember looking at her and thinking, even as the tears rolled down my cheeks, *You mean you love me . . . even now?* And I can't begin to explain the impact her response had on me. Her words, her touch, her look all affirmed my worth as a man and helped me regain my confidence that I was a husband deserving of her respect.

That was unconditional love and acceptance at its finest. And let me tell you, it doesn't get any better than that for a man. When the wife God has given him reminds him that she will always be there for him, that's when he knows the power, real power, of unconditional love and acceptance.

UNCONDITIONAL LOVE STARTS WITH GOD

Barb's response that day became a defining moment in our marriage. But that moment was possible only because, years earlier, Barb and I had been introduced to the One from whom all unconditional love emanates. Let me back up a little. . . .

I grew up in a good home, a moral home. It was a home that was culturally Christian but not biblically Christian, although it wasn't until I was in college that I learned the difference. In fact, I was sitting in a fraternity house when I learned the difference. I was listening to some guys from Campus Crusade for Christ talk about a personal relationship with Jesus Christ, and I immediately realized two things. The first was that I couldn't "do life" without God, and that his love was there for the asking. All I had to do was ask. It was up to me to humble myself and confess to God that I needed him in my life. The second thing was that he loved me—me, Gary Rosberg—enough to send his Son to live a perfect life on earth and die a sacrificial death for my sins. I knew that God loved people. But I had no idea until that night that he loved *me*

with that kind of sacrificial love. These two truths may seem elementary to you, but they sent shock waves through me.

Why hasn't someone told me this before? was my first response. My second response was to try to disprove the resurrection of Jesus Christ.

I was dating Barb at the time and falling in love with her. She was a brand-new Christian herself. After five months of intense study, wrestling with God, and at times almost torturing Barb and the guys God sent into my life with countless questions, I accepted Jesus Christ as my Lord and Savior. What finally convinced me? It was the simple yet overwhelming truth that God loved me unconditionally. Completely. Without reservation. Unequivocally. Just as I was. No matter what.

The apostle Paul reminds us, "But God is so rich in mercy, and he loved us so very much, that even while we were dead because of our sins, he gave us life when he raised Christ from the dead. (It is only by God's special favor that you have been saved!)" (Eph. 2:4-5).

That describes *agape* love. His great love. His mercy. His grace. These words took on a whole new meaning as I began to come to a true understanding of just how much God really does love me.

And that is the heart of Christ's love for me: He truly loves me without limit. He loved me before I trusted him. Before I knew him. Before I even existed. He loves me even though I fail him miserably, even though I come up short emotionally, spiritually, and relationally. He loves me even though I don't deserve it, which is much of the time. He loves me even though it would be easier not to love me when I disappoint him in my thoughts, words, actions, and deeds. He loves me even though my heart is full of pride and my thoughts are self-centered.

Bottom line? He loves me, no matter what. He accepts me, no matter what. And that's how I know what unconditional love is—because I've been to the Source.

UNCONDITIONAL LOVE CHANGES LIVES

But that's God, some of you may be thinking. How does unconditional love and acceptance operate practically on a human level?

Matt and Melanie

Let me tell you how it worked, on both levels, for Matt and Melanie. Two summers ago, Matt got on a bus with a group of men from his church and headed to a Promise Keepers conference. His wife, Melanie, and his kids were thrilled and excited; they had been praying for Matt for several years, and now those prayers might be answered. And they were. Matt made a personal commitment to Christ at the conference and returned home with a new, redeemed lease on life. He began meeting weekly with a men's Bible study and accountability group, and he was growing spiritually.

Then Matt started getting negative vibes from the guys at the office. "What happened to Matt? Isn't he taking this religion thing a bit too far?" On top of that, his parents voiced concern that he had gone off the deep end, that perhaps he was being too extreme.

Over the next few months Matt's faith commitment began to diminish, and he returned to old patterns: excessive work schedules, meeting with the gang for drinks after work. By caving in to the belief that he could "manage" his own sin rather than be transformed by the power of the Holy Spirit's work in him, he drifted further and further from his walk with Christ and his reenergized marriage.

Melanie's hopes for a distinctively Christian marriage and family were folding before her eyes. Yet she knew she had made her own commitment when she took her marriage vows, and that meant loving Matt in spite of her fear of losing all that she held dear. Her staunch Christian friends echoed this truth. "Love him unconditionally," they encouraged her. "You've seen God work in Matt. You know it's possible. Don't give up. Ever."

So Melanie continued to love her husband, even though he did things that disappointed her deeply or when he behaved in ways that made it difficult for her to love him.

Matt is very aware of Melanie's love for him, and he realizes that he often doesn't deserve it. Thankfully, he is beginning to show signs of returning to his commitment to follow Christ.

Patty and Jeff

Jeff grew up on a farm with three brothers, and Jeff's dad always made time for fishing, hunting, and playing sports with his boys. Jeff loves to hunt, and he looked forward to sharing the experience with his own son, Zachary. Jeff's wife, Patty, however, grew up in the city and didn't share Jeff's passion for autumn days in a cornfield with a rifle. Besides that, she was worried. She thought Zach was too young and inexperienced to go on a hunting trip. "He's shot his new gun only a few times at the rifle range," she told Jeff. "Please don't take him out. Not yet. He isn't ready."

Jeff dismissed his wife's fears. She just didn't understand what an important family tradition this was for father and son.

So Jeff and Zachary headed for the woods on a Saturday morning, and they had a great day. Zach even got his first deer. As Jeff drove home that night, he knew that he and Zach had drawn closer because of the shared experience and the time together. He began thinking of ways that he might continue to deepen the relationship with his son.

Suddenly, an oncoming car crested the next hill at high speed and swerved into their lane. Jeff survived the terrible crash. Zach was killed instantly.

It has been three years since the accident, and although Patty knows the accident was not Jeff's fault, she is still haunted by the voices that continue to ring in her mind: *If only they hadn't gone out that day. If only Jeff had listened to me. If only . . .* The pain of their loss and the pressure on their marriage often seem unbearable. Yet God continues to call Patty to love her husband—no matter what. And she is. Meanwhile, Jeff himself is just beginning to feel some relief from his own guilt and pain. God is pumping new life into their relationship, and much of it is due to Patty's unconditional love for Jeff.

Marge and Ben

Ben is another man who knows what it means to be loved no matter what. After twenty-three years in his career, Ben was worn out, exhausted from trying to climb the corporate ladder. One morning he happened to catch a television infomercial that promised him all the luxuries of life if he would just attend an upcoming seminar in a local hotel. So Ben went to the seminar—and was promptly overwhelmed with the potential of the program as he watched the videos and studied the brochures. He and Marge had always discussed any expenditure over one hundred dollars. But that day he caved in to his greed and withdrew all their savings as well as cashed in their retirement fund to invest in this get-rich-quick enterprise. It was such a sure thing. It had worked for so many.

Months later Ben's life was one huge mess. He had quit his job, believing that if he devoted all his time to this new venture, he would surely reap the rich rewards the videos and glossy brochures promised. Unfortunately, that's not what happened. He was out of a job, their credit cards were maxed out, and Marge had to go back to work full-time for the first time since before they'd had children.

Despite all this, Marge didn't give up on her husband. When she discussed her fear and anger and frustration with her pastor, he told her, "Marge, you've come smack up against one of those 'in sickness or in health' realities. But you are called to love Ben *even if* . . . That's the kind of love Christ exhibits for us—*agape* love. It's the real thing, Marge. It is love without limit." With strength and commitment that Marge admits come solely from God, she took her pastor's words to heart.

And Ben responded. He found a new job with a Christian employer, and the nature of the work made him feel truly useful for the first time in years. He and Marge downsized their home, sold their boat, and made serious inroads into paying off their creditors. Ben replaced his desire to get rich quick with a renewed vision and commitment to live and finish life well. When I asked him what made the difference, he said, "Christ and Marge. It is that simple. I have learned that God really does love me. Marge taught me that. She accepted me *even when* I had messed up. And she showed me the kind of unconditional love and acceptance that I never knew existed. I really got caught up in my greed. Now the simple things make more sense. A walk with Marge. An evening at home. Time with a few close friends. The Word of God each day. And an honest day's work. I am beginning to feel whole again."

Matt, Jeff, and Ben have, through tough and painful experiences, learned what a difference unconditional love and acceptance can make. From Christ and from their wives.

Now, let me ask you a tough question. Has your unconditional love ever been put to the test? Have those vows that you took on your wedding day to love your husband in good times and bad ever been put through the crucible of painful reality? If so, just like Barb and Melanie, Patty and Marge, you have been called to love your husband unconditionally. No matter what.

Every family struggles with hard times, broken promises, unmet expectations, financial setbacks, betrayals. When you face such difficulties, call on God's strength so that you and your husband can walk through the pain together and emerge the stronger for it. Stronger individually and stronger as a couple.

THE POWER OF UNCONDITIONAL LOVE AND ACCEPTANCE

Unconditional love is powerful stuff. By way of example, let me tell you what happened inside me when Barb showed me unconditional love. If

Matt and Jeff and Ben could talk with you, they would probably say some similar things.

Barb's response helped me feel safe in the midst of a lightning storm. Her love allowed me to be honest. It established a comfortable environment for open communication between us. Her love reminded me that I wasn't ultimately in charge—the Lord was. It reminded me that her commitment truly was for bad times as well as good. It confirmed for me that even though my decision was going to put our family at risk financially, it was the right decision.

When I share the story of that memory-making day, people often ask me, What would have happened if Barb hadn't responded with such grace and encouragement? What if she had responded with anger and told me I had made a stupid decision? What if she had panicked and withdrawn? What if she had turned her back on me? What if she had said, "Gary, I told you so. You never should have gotten involved with that guy"?

Don't misunderstand. Barb certainly had to deal with her own share of fear and uncertainty during that turbulent time in our life. But if she had rejected me or, maybe even worse, been neutral and unresponsive to me, I would have felt lonely and isolated. Her rejection would have built a wall that would have weakened our intimacy and trust.

WHAT YOU CAN DO TO MEET YOUR HUSBAND'S NEEDS

Your response, initiative, and connection to your husband are crucial to the health of your marriage and family. Your expression of your unconditional love and acceptance is the very force that will drive you together in the midst of the testing times in your marriage. Your standing with him in the painful times as well as the good times is one of the primary elements of a great marriage.

At times this means putting aside your own needs in order to meet his. It means resisting your tendency to be selfish and self-protective. But if you love unconditionally in the hard times, you and your husband will become one in the kind of intimacy the Lord desires for you. If you don't, you will end up living like two immature children, each trying to get your own way and resenting the other person when you don't. You may still be married, but you will miss out on the joy of a great marriage.

Your husband desperately needs to know that you will accept him no matter what. Even when he fails or makes poor decisions. Even when he feels crummy about himself or disappoints you. Your love is a make-or-break reality. Your inability or refusal to love will cripple him and tear him apart. Your unconditional love and acceptance will build him up and free him to go on.

Okay, this all sounds good in theory, you may be saying, *but how do I live this out in the nitty-gritty of real life? What does it look like?* Before we get to that and discuss some practical ways you can demonstrate unconditional love, let's focus one more time on what we said earlier in the chapter: *Unconditional love starts with God.* We cannot lose sight of that. Our ability to give costly love comes from God's unconditional love for us.

Just think about your own relationship with God. Because you are convinced of his grace toward you, your faith has meaning and foundation. After all, each of us knows the condition of our own heart; we know what we've done to offend God in word and deed. Yet as believers we are able to start anew each day with God, repenting for sinful lapses and being assured of his forgiveness. Perhaps in a similar way we need a daily clearing away between husband and wife.

This becomes especially important for those of you who are in situations right now where the need to demonstrate unconditional love is a daily concern or struggle. You may be living with a hard-hearted husband. Or perhaps your dreams and desires have been put on hold while you support your husband so that he can fulfill his dreams. Your husband may have wounded or betrayed you. Or you may be married to a man who is spiritually passive, not serving you as God has instructed him to do. But whether you are in the midst of a crisis, living with an ongoing circumstance, or just responding to the normal routine of married life, giving your husband the security of your unwavering love requires at least five elements: showing grace with his weaknesses; affirming him whenever you can; helping him feel safe; taking time to connect; and studying your husband.

Show Grace with His Weaknesses

All of us need grace. But we need it most when we are truly aware that we don't deserve it—when we have failed, when we have made mistakes, when we have been selfish, when we have sinned.

If your husband has failed you or disappointed you or sinned against you, then he needs your grace. And when you express grace to your husband in his areas of weakness and sin, you love him as Jesus loves him.

Let me ask you, where does your husband need an extra dose of grace right now? Where does one of his weaknesses need a covering of grace from you, his wife?

- If he has sinned against you, forgive him. Over and over.
- If he has violated your trust in some serious way, show your love by getting help from a pastor or professional Christian counselor.
- If he is experiencing failure, let him know that you will stand with him, no matter what.
- If he is experiencing a pressure point in his life, perhaps at work or in a decision he must make, encourage him with understanding.
- If he is going through a dangerous passage of life and drifting from his moorings, remind him that God and you love him and that both of you are with him even during these times.

Affirm Him Whenever You Can

Mark Twain once said, "I can live a whole month on one compliment." Just think about the life we can bring to a marriage with an ever flowing stream of affirmation.

Strengthen your husband with comments such as

- "I am proud of you, honey."
- "I love the way you love me when you . . ."
- "When I saw you with one of the kids this morning, I was so encouraged that you . . ."
- "Yesterday when you told me you loved me, it meant so much to me. Thank you for expressing your love."
- "Thank you for providing for our family."
- "You are one of God's richest blessings to me."
- "When you receive me even though I hurt you, I feel safe and secure in your love."

Hearty affirmation is a key ingredient in unconditional love. It's like a magnet: It draws us in; it attracts us.

If you have a hard time verbalizing your affirmation to your husband, think about when you first met him. What drew you to him? What opened your heart to him? What about him made you tingle inside? What would you have said to him then?

Now, as you have matured in your marriage, what do you appreciate about your husband? How would you express this? Write your thoughts down on a piece of paper. Here are some examples:

- "I appreciate the way you stand up for me with the kids."
- "I appreciate how hard you work to provide for our family's financial needs."
- "When you participate in _____ [some family activity], it makes me feel secure."
- "I love to watch you interact with people who don't know the Lord."
- "You are so patient with our difficult neighbors."
- "I appreciate that you are active with other Christian men."
- "When you touch me with an encouraging touch, it makes me feel loved."
- "I am proud of you for not being part of the negative attitude at work, even though you are surrounded by it daily."
- "I am proud of you when you persevere in the face of discouragement."
- "I appreciate that you initiate prayer with me and tell me what God is teaching you in his Word."

From your own responses, make a list of at least five statements that you can grab onto and begin to repeat to your husband. Someone once told me that it takes eight to ten affirmations to balance out the impact of one negative remark. Do you affirm your husband eight to ten times more frequently than you criticize him?

Take your list of affirmations and begin to repeat these to yourself each day. Then repeat them to your husband each day—even if he has disappointed you. *Especially* if he has disappointed you.

Help Him Feel Safe

When I know that Barb understands me, I feel safe. When I don't feel understood, my insecurity increases. Normally, a man won't recognize it in these terms. He won't think, *My wife doesn't understand the pressures I'm under at work and how it affects the way I feel about myself. So I'm going to find a way to compensate. I'm going to lash out at her and the kids. After all, I have to control something.* We husbands don't know how to tell you this, so instead, we blow up. Or we bury ourselves in some excessive behavior. Or we search for *something* we can control. Some men overwork or overeat. Others turn to alcohol or other drugs, or to pornography. Some men become obsessed with hobbies and sports.

If you see any of these patterns in your husband's behavior, something is missing in your relationship. I am not saying you are responsible, although you may be contributing to the patterns, but something definitely is missing and needs to be addressed.

Where do you start? Get alone with him and assure him that you are not intending to criticize but that you are committed to him and want to help him work through any patterns that could be undermining the security of your marriage. As you do this, you begin to lay the groundwork for healing to begin. At some point, couples or individuals who are struggling with excessive behavior may need to seek the outside help of a professional Christian counselor and/or a pastor. But first you need to approach your husband to begin the process.

How do we husbands know we are beginning to be understood? In two ways:

1. When you are truly interested in our mundane life to the point of fascination.
2. When we try to "fix" something and we know that you understand that we are just exercising the part of our masculinity that needs to "make things better."

Just as you feel understood when we listen to your *feelings,* we feel better when you listen to our *ideas.* For example, Barb lets me know that she appreciates my good intentions even though she sometimes checks me on my timing. It usually sounds something like this: "Gary, I know you are trying to make things right. And I know you have good insights. But right now I need you to listen to my feelings about this. After that, I would be happy to hear what you think I should do about it." I truly can receive that message because she isn't saying, "Gary, you're wrong." She is just saying, "Your good input is too early." I can accept the fact that my timing is lousy as long as I don't feel completely inadequate as a husband.

Sound familiar?

Take Bob and Sherry for instance. They're having an after-dinner conversation, and she's describing a painful disagreement she had with her mother on the phone that day. *Another* disagreement. There have already been two this week. As Bob listens, he has the solution to the problem on the tip of his tongue. He can't wait to fix the situation so Sherry will feel better and they can get on with the rest of the evening. All day long he fixes things, and this is a no-brainer: *Just don't call your mother so often since she upsets you so much.* Makes perfect sense to him. Subconsciously Bob is operating on the assumption that if Sherry valued and understood him, she would know how important it is to get his insight so she could solve this problem.

Instead, Sherry is focused on her own (unconscious) need to be listened to, encouraged, and hugged. She needs her husband's support and approval. Now, those are real needs, too, but I'm talking to *you* about men. (Barb will hit the guys on this in her chapter.)

Each day couples like Bob and Sherry make subtle choices that either *strengthen* their spouse or *feed* their insecurities. Just as your husband shows you how valuable you are when he listens to your feelings (strengthening you), so you make him feel valued when he knows you have understood him and listened to him.

I'm not real proud of us men on this point, but my experience in my ministry and at home bears it out: When we sense that our opinion is not being enthusiastically received, we feel frustrated and rejected. Then we start to clam up or to get angry. And when this happens often enough, it can destroy the security of the relationship. For a marriage to become a great marriage, husbands and wives need to learn to partner with each other, accentuating each other's strengths and helping to compensate for each other's weaknesses.

Take Time to Connect

As unbelievable as it may sound, the first few minutes you and your husband connect at the end of the workday is critical.

When I was growing up, I saw this modeled positively by my own parents. When we kids heard Dad drive into the garage after work, we would yell, "Dad's home!" We would rush to greet him at the back door, and he would ruffle our hair or hug us. But then, for the next sixty minutes, we would disappear (most of the time) while he and mom sat and talked. Sixty minutes!

Barb and I have carried that tradition into our own home. Within minutes of greeting each other at the end of the day, we are sitting in two mauve-colored chairs and talking—just the two of us. We talk about the kids, we review Barb's day and my day, we discuss the highs, the lows—everything! Sometimes these are deep discussions, but often they're just newsy, connecting talks. And this connection sets the tone for the rest of the evening. It reminds us we are teammates who are absolutely committed to the same game. There's no competition between us, no fear of hearing a sermon instead of gaining a sympathetic ear. I'm not trying to fix her problems (not always, anyway), and she's listening to me. We're two weary people reconnecting to each other and, most important, tearing away the layers of the day. Our souls get revived.

When this doesn't happen consistently, the atmosphere can become colder than a Dairy Queen blizzard. We get out of sync, disconnected, and that leaves room for coolness and selfishness to grow. I've tried to imagine what would happen if there were no connection between us for a week, a month, a year. Guess what? I don't have to imagine too hard because I see the grim reality walking into my counseling office every week. Couples who are hanging on desperately, hoping their marriage will survive, when it all could have been prevented by an hour a day . . . thirty minutes . . . even fifteen!

Unconditional love occurs only in the context of communication and true connection.

Think about your own relationship with God. When do you feel most secure, protected, loved, understood? It's when you've had a rich time of prayer, when God has spoken to you personally through his Word, and when you've reached the heart of the Father in worship. And when this connection happens every day, not only do you feel secure as a Christian, but you also develop a mature relationship with God, where *everything* is possible.

That's the way marriage is designed to work.

Study Your Husband

One of the best ways for you to know how to meet your husband's need for unconditional love and acceptance is to *know* your husband. This means you must become a student, getting to know your husband inside and out.

As a man, I can't figure out sometimes how Barb knows things, but *she just knows.* The kids may be hurting, hiding something, having problems with a friend, or isolating themselves a little because of some insecurity or conflict. And Barb just knows. Our household isn't unique in this. When a husband and father senses the kids aren't around as much as usual, he may think, *Good. Now I can get some work done or watch the game or read the paper.* When a wife and mother senses this kind of distance from the kids, she gets concerned. You need to use that same womanly sensitivity to pick up on what's going on with your husband—which means not only reading his moves but also his moods.

Men often don't know how to verbalize what they are feeling. So it's essential for you to use your instincts when you're trying to understand what's going on in our heads. Timing is always important, even when dealing with the most even-tempered male. So learn to *read our moods.* If you do, you'll soon know the answer to these kinds of questions:

- If you bring up a sensitive issue at the end of the day, is your husband going to enter into the discussion, withdraw during the conversation, or lash out at you?
- When your husband gets home from work and you are telling him about your day, will he be more likely to give advice or to do what you really need and just listen?
- If you get a disturbing phone call from your mother on a Saturday afternoon and your husband is out working in the garage, is he going to be tender and attentive to you, or will he be distracted by the tasks at hand?
- When does your husband get cranky?
- What tends to diminish your husband's sense of value and worth?
- Does your husband get more irritated when he's hungry or fatigued?
- Your husband seems to be unusually short-tempered. Is he upset with you, or is he stressed out about something at work?

A buddy of mine recently boasted, "My wife can read me like a book." Think about that statement. You go to a bookstore, hoping that among the myriad of books on the shelves, you'll find a treasure. You pick up several, read the jacket copy, thumb through a few, and wonder if what is inside measures up to all the marketing on the outside. Will the content be as beautiful as the cover? Finally you make a selection, take it home, and curl up in your favorite chair. Suddenly, the characters become friends; the story becomes part of you. You're reluctant to put it down and wish it could go on and on.

Change a few words, and this could describe a great marriage. The relationship starts off with an attraction to the outward, visible features—looks, personality, charm, sense of humor. But it's when you really see what's inside, when you come to know each other in the deepest sense as husband and wife, that you truly delight in each other and become one.

Grace. Affirmation. Safety. Time. Study. All are keys to unconditional love and acceptance. Here's a checklist to help you begin to measure how you are doing in each of these areas:

- Where do I need to show some grace, real grace, to the man I married? Where do I need to let go and let God do his thing with him?
- Who needs my words of affirmation more than anyone in my life? Is it easier for me to affirm my kids and my friends than it is for me to affirm my husband?
- What are we doing to build safety into our marriage so we can take the risks to love unconditionally?
- When was the last time we took time to go deeper with each other? Are we making time to connect with each other daily?
- Am I studying my husband? Do I know his strengths as well as his weaknesses? Am I helping to build on the former and strengthen the latter so that I can best become one with him?

These are tough questions. Building a great marriage is not easy. As Barb says, true love doesn't always take place on a romantic balcony. Sometimes it takes place on a battlefield. Let me tell you about a husband and wife who know all about the reality of unconditional love in the tough times.

UNCONDITIONAL LOVE AT ITS FINEST

Brian worked hard and came from a long line of hardworking men— good, stoic, midwestern stock. His dad and grandfather before him had both prided themselves on a work ethic that bragged, "You may be smarter than I am, but you will never outwork me." Yet under pressure, that strong work ethic looked more like a stubborn streak that both hurt and scared Brian's wife, Karen.

Karen's greatest fear was that Brian's refusal to take care of himself would leave her without a husband and their children without a father. She had good reason to fear. Both Brian's father and grandfather had died in their fifties from heart attacks. At forty-eight, Brian had high cholesterol and ate high-fat foods at his power lunches. He hadn't been on their home treadmill for months, and he habitually canceled his annual physicals, insisting, "I'm just too busy at work to get there." Karen had done everything she could to take care of her husband. She had pressed him to see the doctor. She had bought the treadmill. She cooked healthy foods for him at home, although she had given up trying to control his eating patterns at work. Bottom line: Brian wasn't taking care of himself, and it was driving her nuts. They'd had more than one argument about it.

Brian knew Karen's nagging (as he sometimes called it) came from her love and concern for him, but he was unwilling to change. He just couldn't be bothered. Then he started having some mild chest pain, and he got scared. He didn't tell Karen. For one thing, he didn't want to worry her; for another, he didn't want to admit to himself that something might be wrong.

Then one night his chest pains became more intense, pushing him from his denial to the point of blurting out, "Karen, I need to tell you something. For the last three weeks or so, I've been having some chest pain. I think it's probably just heartburn, but . . ." Somehow, letting her into his fears relieved some of Brian's anxiety.

While Karen was thankful that Brian had leveled with her, she became even more fearful. She begged him to go to the hospital immediately. He didn't want to do that, but he promised to call the doctor the next day. In desperation Karen said, "If you have a heart attack and die, the kids and I will always know it was your fault. You are deliberately choosing not to take care of yourself. I am so frustrated, I don't know where to turn. Please do something."

But it was too late. While climbing the steps to his second-floor office the next morning, Brian had a massive heart attack. He didn't die, but he faced a long recovery. And he would never be the same again.

Karen had feared this very thing for a long time, and here it was. In an instant, her life had changed. With one child in college and the other getting ready to go, she faced major adjustments. She worked day and night, caring for Brian, being a mom to their kids, and trying to bring order and stability to a household in crisis. In her heart she felt she had been left holding the bag because of Brian's negligence, yet she loved her husband and wanted to take care of him.

Their style of living changed dramatically. Brian was unable to return to his high-powered job. With his earning potential greatly diminished and their savings depleted, Karen was forced to take a job outside the home.

She was faced with a choice. She could resent Brian for his stubbornness and careless behavior, which had brought them to this point, or she could forgive his failings and love him unconditionally with a Christlike love. Should she give him the love he didn't deserve? Or should she wall off her heart and go through the motions of marriage, never releasing him from the pain his actions had brought to their family?

She chose to love him unconditionally. Karen faced the truth that as long as she withheld love and forgiveness from Brian, her own anger and resentment would imprison her. In her brokenness and obedience, God met her and gave her the courage and humility to love her husband no matter what—regardless of the results of his actions. She took the high road, returning a blessing for an insult (see 1 Peter 3:9).

Karen's self-sacrificial love modeled Christ's love for Brian, and he responded. He came to grips with the pain he had caused her and their family, and he began to love her with the same kind of sacrificial love.

This once culturally successful family had become something much more significant: they had become a model of Christ's love for each other. Their marriage took on a whole new dimension as they served each other and loved each other unconditionally. Things that used to seem so important—golf-club memberships, exotic vacations, large stock portfolios—were replaced with times together in prayer, simple pleasures like a walk around the block, and the kind of intimate understanding and connection they had never known.

Make no mistake, Brian and Karen had to make major adjustments in their lifestyle. But they made them well. Why? Because they followed Christ's example of loving each other with an *agape* love. And Karen set the pace.

Unconditional love is the real thing. The genuine article. It is the kind of love that is given when it isn't deserved. Jesus models it, Paul writes about it, and our Father gives it to us.

Will you love your husband unconditionally, the way Karen loved Brian? This is the number one love need men have in their marriages. This is the way a great marriage is designed to work. God said so.

CHAPTER 2

UNCONDITIONAL LOVE

A WIFE'S #1 LOVE NEED

"I need you to love me with Christlike love."

Barb talks to husbands

Nothing in Joe's wildest dreams could have prepared him for what he was about to hear from his wife.

"What's bothering you, Leslie?"

"Nothing." A cloud descended over her face, and she pulled away from him.

It was just a simple question. The same question Joe had asked her dozens of times during their thirty-five years of marriage. And her response was always the same: Leslie's words said nothing was wrong, but her moodiness and distance told him otherwise. When this invisible switch flipped on inside her, Joe felt uneasy and helpless.

Maybe a walk would help. "Let's go for a walk," he said. "It's such a beautiful day."

The weather was perfect, a cool, crisp October afternoon. The sun beat down on them, warming their skin. Joe loved being with his wife. He held her hand as they walked, hoping that the sun would penetrate the cloud in her soul.

He tried again to reach her. "Can you talk with me about what's bothering you?"

"It's nothing, Joe."

"Look, I'm trying everything to make you happy today. A walk through the park, time alone as a couple. I thought that you would like it, but I can't get anything back from you. I can't get through to you. You seem so cold."

Cold. You're right, Joe. I am cold. I'm frozen by my past. I'm also terrified. How do I tell you about the memories that haunt me? I've prayed that I would forget, but I can't. If I told you, you would leave me. You could never love me if you knew. Nobody could love me. It's my secret, and I have to keep it that way.

As Leslie battled her inner thoughts, she began to cry.

Oh great, she's crying again, thought Joe. *All I wanted was for this to be a good day. Now what do I do?*

"Let's sit down a minute," he suggested.

They sat on a park bench nestled beneath the red-leafed maples and golden oaks. The wind stirred dry leaves at their feet as Leslie continued to weep.

"What is wrong, Leslie? I'm sorry if I sounded harsh or abrupt, but when you are hurting this much, I want to help. But you just clam up, and I can't get through to you. Leslie, I've known you for thirty-seven years, and I can see that whatever is causing you this pain is getting worse. What is it?"

"I love you so much, Joe, and I know you love me as much as you know me," Leslie whispered, wiping her tears.

"As much as I know you? I've known you since you were seventeen and moved into the old house at the end of the street. What do you mean, 'as much as I know you'? Honey, please tell me what's wrong. You can tell me anything."

Silence ensued for what seemed like an eternity as Leslie struggled with whether or not she should finally tell Joe. After what had happened two days earlier, she knew she didn't have much time. Circumstances might decide for her.

God, please don't let me lose Joe. Not now. Not after all these years.

Joe waited patiently, sensing his wife's inner battle.

"Oh, Joe. I love you so much, but I am so afraid."

Joe squeezed her hand tightly. "It's okay, honey. Take your time. You are safe with me. I love you more than any other person on the face of the earth could love you."

Leslie blew her nose on her handkerchief and took a deep breath before she continued. "Joe, I know you do, and that's what I'm afraid of losing. I'm afraid you won't be able to love me after you know who I really am."

"I will always love you," Joe whispered softly, not wanting to break her willingness to speak.

"When we first met, you gave me the kind of love and respect I had never known before. I now know that I can't live without that love, and I'm so afraid of losing it.

"I've been running all my life. When I moved to our neighborhood as a kid and met you, I thought I could start over. I *was* starting over, Joe. I was running from something terrible in my past. I was too ashamed to tell you. You see, I had a baby." Leslie started to sob again.

Joe let out a breath and closed his eyes. "Oh, sweetheart, I'm so sorry. What a heavy thing for you to carry all these years." He put his arm around her, kept his head down, and prayed silently, giving her the chance to continue.

"I was fourteen when it happened. My parents were devastated and so ashamed of me. Their main concern was that no one find out about the pregnancy, so they sent me to live with my aunt Edna for six months."

Joe rubbed her shoulder, silently encouraging her to say more.

"The baby was a girl. I held her for only a few minutes and then surrendered her to the nurse. I never saw her again."

"Oh, Leslie, what a hard thing that must have been for you to do. What a horrible loss," Joe said tenderly.

Spurred on by his comfort and understanding words, Leslie took a deep breath and raised her head a bit. "After I met you, you became everything to me, and I was terrified that you could never truly love me if you really knew me. I have lived a lie all these years by not telling you. I had hoped to keep up the lie for the rest of my life. But that hope died two nights ago." Leslie dropped her head again and hesitated, wondering if she had the courage to tell him the rest.

"It's okay. You can tell me."

"Two nights ago I got a phone call. It was my daughter, Joe. She's been searching for me, and now she's found me. What am I going to do?" she cried.

Joe started to cry too. He wrapped both of his arms around his wife, and together they wept over the deceit, the wounds, and the scars of the past.

He held her head to his chest and rocked her, whispering in her ear, "Whatever is ahead, you've got me at your side. I am never leaving you, honey. We're going through this together, and we will be better for it. I will always love you. No matter what. I will never leave you. Never."

Soothed by her husband's words and strengthened by his unshakable love, Leslie began to relax. Still, the fears echoed within her: *Can I trust his love? Will he really stay?*

Sensing that his wife needed reassurance, Joe began to talk about what he was feeling. "I am not ashamed of you, Leslie. I would not be honest if I didn't say that I am hurt that you didn't tell me before this, but I forgive you. God will get us through this. You don't have to be afraid any longer, sweetheart. I'm not leaving."

Leslie lifted her head and looked into Joe's eyes for the first time since they sat down. "Joe, I can't believe you would love me after knowing this about me. I feel so exposed, so guilty, so unworthy."

"You are guilty and unworthy. So am I. We're both sinners saved by grace. But if what we believe about God's love is true—that he loves us even though we don't deserve it—then we must believe that he can help us love each other even though we've done things that are wrong. Do you believe God has forgiven you?"

"I can't tell you how many hundreds of times I have confessed my sin and asked him to forgive me. I know the Bible says that he does, but I don't feel it. I just feel dirty."

Joe took her in his arms again and held her tightly for several minutes. "God has forgiven you, Leslie. And so do I." Then he began to pray. "Lord, we really need your help. Release Leslie from this heavy burden she has carried for so long. Help her to accept your forgiveness and your love. Help her to believe in my love for her. I commit myself anew to loving her unconditionally for the rest of our lives. Fill my love with your own. Help us know where to go from here. Amen."

In the days and weeks that followed, Joe and Leslie shared Leslie's story with their adult children. And as Joe modeled his love for Leslie, the children followed their father's example. They encouraged their mother and comforted her as she revealed her past pain to them.

One night as Leslie and Joe got into bed, she said, "Joe, you know my greatest failures. Yet your love covers me. I feel clean and accepted. I don't feel the disgrace anymore. I never dreamed that I could feel this safe."

"You are safe, sweetheart. And you're free. You're no longer a prisoner of your past. Something has always held us back as a family, and now we know what it was. This is like a second chance for all of us."

Released from her fear, Leslie was able to begin to have some contact with the daughter she had given up for adoption.

The destiny of an entire family was changed because one man loved his wife unconditionally.

THE POWER OF UNCONDITIONAL LOVE

Every wife's life story is different, but every wife shares this same need for unconditional love and acceptance. That became clear to us when a majority of our female survey respondents said that the need for unconditional love and acceptance was their number one love need.

That's not surprising when you think about it. We all need love, but we need it most when we deserve it least—when we have sinned against someone, when we have made poor choices, when we have failed. In these situations ordinary love must become extraordinary love.

Imagine your spouse loving you completely, without even hesitating over your mistakes. Sounds just like Christ, doesn't it? It is. That's the core of unconditional love, and *he* is the exclusive source of it. Unconditional love *covers* your mistakes, and the results take a couple deeper in their relationship.

Joe's love for Leslie mirrored God's love for us. It was while we were still sinners—when we didn't deserve God's love—that he showed his love to us by sending Christ to die for our sins (Rom. 5:8).

I remember when I first felt the power of God's unconditional love for me. It was during my sophomore year in college when I realized that I was close to failing two classes. I had no one but myself to blame for the situation; I had simply spent more time with my friends than I had with my homework. But I couldn't bear telling my parents, who were sacrificing financially to put me through school.

I was so ashamed of myself, so sick at heart over disappointing them. I had failed to meet their hopes and expectations. I longed for my parents' approval, and I wanted them to be proud of me, but my grades reflected only a very immature daughter. I felt as if I had a huge sign on my back, weighing me down, and on it was the verdict: *guilty*. Can you relate to what I was experiencing? No matter what we've done, our guilt and shame have a way of making us feel weighed down and awful.

Sensing my heavy heart, my brother, Barry, got me to talk about my discouragement. Barry was a new Christian, and he encouraged me with words about how God's grace covers our worst mistakes and how his love for us is unconditional—he loves us even when we are guilty.

That night, as I wrestled with my inner feelings and Barry's words of spiritual direction, it was as if the forces of good and evil were in a battle over my soul. And it was in that dark hour that I began to see and believe that God loved me even though I was so unlovable. I heard God proclaim, *Barb, I love you so much that I sent my Son to die for you. Because of his death, I declare you not guilty!* That night I first tasted God's unconditional love. And in the years since then, God has reminded me again and again, in many ways, of his unconditional love for me—especially through the times my husband has loved me when I didn't deserve it or when I was actually hurting him.

When you love your wife unconditionally, you reflect God's love to her. Like Leslie, your wife needs this kind of love most during times of pain. She needs you to surround her with your presence, your tenderness, and your desire to help her heal. Such fiery trials offer you an opportunity to put your own feet in the coals along with her and show your wife that you love her no matter what. Grab these opportunities to show your complete trust and devotion to her. Make use of those times to love your wife in the way God would love her. God's Spirit is in you. Rely on him to teach you what to say, how to say it tenderly, and what to do. Lean on his understanding to become "God with skin on" to your wife.

Unconditional love has the power to transform your wife. Just as it transformed Leslie. Just as it transformed Julie.

Julie tried raising five boys single-handedly while her husband, Frank, traveled the road as a salesman. Most days she survived the battle but at night fell into bed exhausted from the endless demands made on her. Waves of discouragement washed over her. In the darkness her fears would mushroom. Julie was afraid that Frank would abandon her. After all, her dad had. After her parents had divorced, her dad had taken off, leaving his wife and children to fend for themselves.

During the long hours of the night Julie worried that Frank would bail out on her too. By the time Frank returned from his business trips, her fear would have grown to such proportions that she was often short-tempered with him, yelling at him at the slightest provocation. Once she even threatened to leave *him*.

Whether or not she realized it, this toxic pain was destroying their trust in each other.

Frank was frustrated by his wife's outbursts, which he felt were irrational, but he did not retaliate. Then one day, in a frenzy, she blurted out all her fears: "I know you'll leave me just as my father did when I was eight!" Suddenly Frank got a glimpse of the root of the problem: Julie was living and reliving the abandonment of her childhood, in constant fear that the man she loved would leave her just as her father had.

Frank decided that he would love his wife back to security. He rearranged his schedule so that he could spend time alone with her every week for two months. He canceled a weekend ball game, got his sister to baby-sit, and took Julie to the art museum instead. Sometimes they would just have lunch together, walk in the mall, or do the grocery shopping.

Frank's loving persistence and decisive action communicated to Julie that he recognized the many responsibilities she was shouldering when he was gone. When they were alone, he would encourage her to talk. He would lean forward in his chair and say, "Tell me about your day, Julie." Then he would *listen*. As he did, he learned more about issues that stemmed from her father's abandonment, the ensuing loneliness, her desire for Frank's companionship. Frank began to care in new ways about his wife's concerns. Understanding his wife's loneliness, he tried to phone her more often when he was back on the road.

Instead of blaming his wife for her angry behavior, Frank chose to love her unconditionally. And Julie blossomed in the sunshine of that love.

As both Frank and Joe discovered, when you choose to love your wife unconditionally, that love will reap enormous rewards in your marriage. It will, in fact, transform your marriage.

When I look back at all Gary and I have gone through as a couple, I realize that our marriage has been strengthened the most when he has loved me in spite of my failures and my weaknesses. Through these painful times, God has forged in us a love that will last a lifetime. We have become bonded together in such a way that nothing can separate us. Experiencing the deep joys of Gary's unconditional love for me has made me eager to give back to him the same kind of love he has given me.

If you have children, you will discover, as Joe and Leslie did, that your unconditional love for your wife will also have a great influence on them. As your children see you love their mom unconditionally, they will have a model to follow in their own marriages. Thus, the effect will be passed from generation to generation.

WHEN DOES YOUR WIFE NEED YOUR UNCONDITIONAL LOVE?

How would your wife complete these sentences?

- Would my husband love me even if I . . . ?
- I need my husband's love especially when I . . .
- I don't deserve my husband's love because I . . .
- My husband would never love me if he knew . . .

If you can complete those sentences with some confidence, you have made a good start toward meeting your wife's needs by being aware of situations that require your unconditional love. How you show that love is the next step, which we will discuss later. For now, let's concentrate on understanding her need.

If you cannot complete the sentences listed above, then you can do two things: Read the following sections, and then ask your wife to help you complete the sentences as they apply to her.

Love at Her Greatest Point of Pain

Points of pain vary from woman to woman. Maybe your wife's greatest area of pain is something she did in the past, something that still haunts her. Like Leslie, your wife may need forgiveness and patience and a safe place to heal. Perhaps she cannot forget a relationship that she feels she ruined or some incident she perceives as a failure on her part.

Or maybe the pain is something that was done to her in the past. If your wife experienced neglect or abuse or abandonment in childhood, she needs your unconditional love as she moves beyond the damage done to her. If she has been belittled, causing her to lack confidence, she needs to know that you will love her no matter what.

Your wife's pain may stem from physical problems, hers or someone else's. If your wife has chronic health problems or if she is a caretaker for someone who does, she needs your patience and encouragement. Your willingness to stand with her will boost her emotional stamina.

Your wife may be struggling with loss. It could be a miscarriage or the death of a parent, a change in career or the loss of a friend, a move to a new location or a move to a new church. Planned or unplanned, changes have a way of catching up with a woman, making her feel as if the rug has been pulled out from under her. At such times, she desperately needs your emotional connection as you share the pain with her.

Love at Her Greatest Point of Vulnerability

For many women the desire to please is a point of great vulnerability. Most women have a deep need to please others. That's just the way we are wired. We need to connect with and relate to people as we fulfill our goals in life. We are stimulated by tasks that involve people. And part of our connection with people is pleasing them: We are fulfilled by knowing that we have pleased others, that we have made others happy, that we have done the job well. The problem is that trying to please others can take precedence over everything else. When that happens, it can sometimes seem as if there is a sea of faces in an audience and we are expected to please every one of them. This is a demand we women can so easily impose on ourselves—and it is a goal we can never attain.

We work hardest to please the people we are accountable to: our husbands, our children, our parents, our close friends. Yet we can't please everybody all the time without self-destructing. This is where your unconditional love can make a real difference.

You can encourage your wife at this point of vulnerability by reminding her that she is really living her life before an audience of One and that the true source of her fulfillment is her relationship with the Creator. He created her, planned her life purpose, and fashioned her to please him. That is the "God-shaped vacuum" that she is seeking to fill. She must not define herself by how well she pleases others but by how she brings delight to the Lord, by pleasing an audience of One.

Far too often, however, women look into the faces of people in their lives to fill this need, placing too much pressure on themselves and experiencing devastating disappointment when they do not meet their own or others' expectations. Instead of trying to please God, they put themselves in the precarious position of being people pleasers.

Many women work so hard at trying to make a good impression on everyone that they end up pleasing no one, including themselves. Sometimes that tendency pushes women into overcommitting themselves to too many activities, leaving them overwhelmed and at risk for health problems. If you see these tendencies in your wife, assure her that you love her just the way she is. Remind her often that God delights in her. Your unconditional love may help her to stop trying to fulfill other people's endless demands on her and to rest in God's plans for her life.

Fear of failure can be another area of vulnerability for women. If fear is immobilizing your wife to the degree that she's afraid to try anything, she needs to know that you will love her even if she fails. She needs to know that you love her regardless of her performance. Your unconditional love will melt her fear and free her from the internal expectations she is piling on herself.

If your wife is like most women, she spends a lot of time comparing herself with other people, often judging herself inadequate. She secretly fears that others are better, stronger, wiser, or more beautiful than she is. This can drain away her contentment and confidence. She needs your unconditional love to cover those hidden insecurities and assure her that she is a blessing to you. Remind her that she is God's gift to you! Remind her of all that she brings into your life.

Unconditional love provides a climate of safety and security in which your wife can accept herself as she is.

Love at Her Greatest Point of Failure

I hope that you think your wife is the most wonderful woman in the world. I hope that you are her greatest cheerleader and encourager. But you probably are also the person who sees her faults most clearly. Not because you are critical of her—at least I hope you are not—but because you know her more completely than any other person does.

The important question, though, is this: What do you do with what you know about her? What do you do when you see your wife's faults? Do you magnify them? Do you withhold your love until she corrects her flaws? Do you use what you see to hurt her?

Or do you see all of her human flaws and weaknesses and choose to love her in spite of them? Do you choose to love her even if she doesn't change? That's unconditional love.

WHEN YOUR WIFE'S NUMBER ONE LOVE NEED ISN'T MET

Mark is a successful businessman; he's a high producer for his company and is well rewarded for his hard work. His job requires a great deal of travel, and when he is not traveling, he chairs several boards. Mark is always on the go, always pushing ahead, always seeking new opportunities for what he terms "significance" in his life.

Mark's wife, Sally, is just the opposite. She seems stuck on hold. In fact, she may even be going backward. She spends hours watching television, and when Mark does come home, she seems aloof and disinterested in what he is doing. Their conversations revolve mainly around the family calendar, the kids, and immediate issues that need to be resolved. Annoyed by this, Mark has withdrawn even more into his own interests.

What Mark doesn't see is that while he has been devoting himself to his job and his other activities, he has been neglecting his wife and her needs. Sally feels that Mark doesn't value her as highly as he values his work. In his absence, she has turned to the soaps, talk shows, and shopping networks for companionship.

Mark has a choice here. At some level he is aware that his wife is shriveling. He can continue to be annoyed and push her further away, or he can look beyond her "flaw" and discover that at the heart of it is her need to be loved. If Mark is willing to give Sally time and real attention, he will see her blossom into the woman she is meant to be. He will also see their marriage become the vital relationship that it should be.

Your wife is God's special gift for you to enjoy throughout your whole life. She has love and tenderness and so much more to offer you. But a woman who doesn't receive unconditional love and acceptance from her husband will shrivel and withdraw. If her emotional needs aren't being met by her husband, as Sally's weren't met by Mark, this love and tenderness has nowhere to go. It dries up and leaves both husband and wife empty. In a worst-case scenario, Sally may start to look to other men for the time and attention she doesn't get from Mark.

Dave has had bitter experience with the worst-case scenario. When his wife confessed that she had been having an affair with her boss, Dave's response was, "Do you want a divorce?" He never talked with her about the affair. He never wrestled with her over the issue, never tried to save their marriage. He merely gave in.

After I heard his story, I asked Dave, "Why didn't you fight for your marriage? Did you ever think that maybe she confessed what she had done to test your love for her? Did it occur to you that maybe she was trying to find out if your love was conditional or unconditional? When she was at that low point in her life, she probably longed for you to love her absolutely and fight for your marriage. Maybe she never wanted the divorce. Maybe she was only asking to be loved unconditionally. At that moment of your wife's deepest failure, you had an opportunity to show her what God's unconditional and forgiving love looks like. I wonder how she would have responded if you had."

Dave's face reflected his deep regrets as he realized that he had missed an opportunity to try to salvage his marriage. Instead, he had turned and walked away.

When Mark and Dave married their wives, each committed before God to be the exclusive man to cherish and uphold his wife. And those marriage vows included adjusting daily activities to continue to meet her needs as well as showing her the continuous and real love of God.

Where does it say that? Well, Ephesians 5:25 contains this humbling mandate: "You husbands must love your wives with the same love Christ showed the church. He gave up his life for her." Your first action is to follow Jesus Christ, who showed us what authentic, unconditional love looks like. He was selfless. He willingly exchanged the comforts of heaven and his position of royalty for the form of humanity; he became one of us in order to serve us—godless and guilty men and women.

MEETING YOUR WIFE'S NEED FOR UNCONDITIONAL LOVE

Once you understand your wife's unique love needs, you can begin to learn how to meet them. Although all women are different, we have several common areas where we need unconditional love and acceptance.

Encourage Her

When your wife fails or disappoints you or others, your first response—your words—will determine whether she folds under the pressure or rises above her circumstances. You can show her unconditional love with phrases like

- "I will never leave you or turn my back on you."
- "I don't care what you have done; we can work through it."
- "I love you, and my love will never be something you have to earn."
- "I forgive you."

The power of unconditional acceptance during a time of hardship or failure can heal a woman's wounded soul. Because these soulful messages connect your heart to hers, they can literally feed and nourish your wife . . . and your marriage. Such encouragement heals broken hearts. It soothes the aching aloneness that gnaws at a person's spirit.

Ultimately, it's up to you to provide your wife with a sense of permanence and safety in your marriage—no matter what comes your way.

Stand with Her

When your wife feels as if she is a failure or when she is discouraged that she isn't growing, your ability to stand with her for the long haul will give her the strength to become stronger.

Every woman struggles with insecurity from time to time. When that happens, she has to decide whether the problem she is struggling with will shake her up and hold her captive or whether she will get control of it. The worst thing a husband can do is use this kind of situation to exert control over his wife. Sadly, Gary and I have seen many men do exactly that. Instead of "coming alongside" their wives and helping them get through the difficult period, these men become controlling, leaving their wives feeling devalued.

Gary is awesome during those times when I am struggling and can't get my bearings. He uses them as an opportunity to step closer to me and to find out what is going on inside me. As he does this, he gently and comfortingly expresses his unconditional love for me, assuring me that he will love me no matter what.

You can show your wife your unconditional love by saying things such as

- "It's okay. I'm here."
- "I can't pretend to know what you're feeling. Tell me what is upsetting you."
- "I don't understand what you've been through, but I sincerely want to. Help me by telling me what you are thinking. Is something from the past troubling you? Tell me about it."
- "Let me pray with you. Together we'll explore what steps need to be taken."
- "We will get through this together."

Your ability to stand with your wife during times of real trials has the power to dissolve fear. Why? Simply because she doesn't have to face life alone. Do you want to know what true wisdom looks like? Then drop whatever you are doing and tune in to the issue at hand. Turn off the TV and turn to your wife. Look squarely at her, lean forward, and listen. Feel what she feels to the best of your ability.

Your wife needs your undivided attention. Your unconditional love in this area lets her know that she is of primary importance to you. Beyond that, your compassion gives her the fortitude that she needs; she is upheld and sustained by the knowledge that she won't have to go it alone.

Compliment Her

When your wife feels insecure and self-conscious, you can compliment and affirm her. All women want to look good and feel good about themselves, but when women look in the mirror, they tend to notice what's wrong with them rather than what's right. That tendency can rob your wife of joy. So here's what you can do to show her unconditional acceptance and affirmation:

- Tell her specifically what you love about her. Let her know how much she excites you, how good she looks, how nice she smells.
- Use affirming words. If you can do it creatively, compliment your wife at least three times a day. It's easy. Just begin each sentence with, "You are . . . ," and comment on her hair, the softness of her skin, the loveliness of her face, the attractiveness of her outfit, the special things you love about her.
- Be sensitive. Most women are touchy about aging issues, weight gain, and body changes. When your wife feels discouraged about her appearance, say things such as:
  —"You are all the woman I will ever need."
  —"I know you are discouraged by your body, but remember that I think you are beautiful."
  —"I love your body because it's yours."
  —"You never look bad to me."
  —"Your complaining can't get me to look the other way. You still are the most beautiful woman I have ever seen."

Compliment your wife on who she is. Her actions and character are as important as her looks. Express your unconditional love with words about

- her skill at managing things, such as your home or her job
- the way she counsels other women who come to her for advice
- how she patiently handles the kids
- the fruit of the Spirit that you see in her life
- how well she treats your side of the family

- her perspective, which gives you additional insight into people and situations
- the way she gives up things in her life so that you can pursue your dreams
- her ability to be kind even when others are rude
- her spiritual growth

Respect Her Opinion

When your wife is expressing her opinion, love her by listening. Validate what she says with comments such as

- "That's a great idea."
- "You did a good job in a hard situation."
- "Tell me more. I need to understand."
- "I wish I could have thought of that."

Such positive statements reinforce and affirm the presence that she is in your life.

When your wife says things that you may disagree with, before trying to "straighten her out" or "fix her thinking," express your unconditional love by being willing to hear her out and ask questions. That kind of acceptance and understanding will allow her to process her thoughts, unload her anxiety, and respond positively to your response.

Talk with Her—and Listen

When your wife needs to talk, it's essential for you to create a safe environment for her. Don't minimize how important your role is. Set the tone by

- turning off the football game or putting it on mute (no glancing at the score)
- telling your kids that you and Mom are taking some time to talk and that you need ten uninterrupted minutes together
- not answering the phone if it rings

Initiate discussion times between the two of you. Remember that practice makes perfect.

Your ability to love your wife unconditionally depends to some degree on the depth of your relationship. Set the stage for the moments when your love will need to move from the ordinary to the extraordinary by maintaining an open atmosphere of sharing between the two of you.

Remember Leslie and Joe? Joe persisted with Leslie about their need to talk. He took her for a walk. He encouraged her to say what she felt and provided a safety net of unconditional love. As a result, Leslie was finally able to share her deepest fears and feelings with him.

As we will discuss more fully in other chapters, women need to verbally process their thoughts and ideas more than men do. You can create a safe environment for your wife to reveal herself to you fully by taking time to talk with her and assuring her that you will listen. Practice these things regularly:

- Set up regular times to ask her about her thoughts and dreams, hopes and fears.
- Listen with care when your wife expresses a hope or a dream. Ask her to tell you more about that hope. Ask how you can help her fulfill that dream.
- Resist the temptation to fix the problem when your wife describes an embarrassing situation she's had. Assure her of your love for her, even if she did something that made her (or you) look bad.
- Call her in the middle of the day to find out how her day is going.

When your wife is confident that you are listening to her and that you understand her (or are trying to), she will have a soul-deep intimacy with you.

Be Tender with Her

Do you find it hard to love your wife when she is cranky and irritable? We realize it's impossible for you to understand fully what women experience with their monthly mood swings and fluctuating energy level. We'll cry for no apparent reason or change our minds erratically; we ache; we snap at everyone for small irritations. All of the physiological factors—the cramping, bloating, and sluggishness—cause most women to feel irritable. Some change personalities altogether!

When "that time of the month" hits for your wife, stand back and let her express her feelings. Anticipate her menstrual cycle, and recognize that her hormones are affecting her emotions.

What should you do?

- Make a special effort to be extra tender and sensitive to your wife. No matter how hard we are to live with, our need for tenderness is ever present.
- Be prepared for her to magnify problems. One day I was sitting on the floor weeping over milk that had gotten spilled on the carpet. (I was actually crying over spilled milk!) Gary looked down at me and said quietly, "This is the bad time, isn't it?" Did he put me down or laugh? No, he handled the problem, then went above and beyond. He stepped up his fathering duties so I wouldn't have to face additional pressures.
- Don't take her moodiness personally. After the inner storm has passed, she'll feel embarrassed about how she overreacted. She may even apologize if she acted in a manner that was not Christlike.

Spend Time with Her

When your wife's days are full of hard work and the unending needs of family, when she is pouring out more than she is taking in, she needs time with the most familiar, trusted, comforting man in her life. You won't believe how refreshing that can be for her. Make that time together happen.

- Cut back on your involvement in some of those sports activities during the week. Tell the guys that time is reserved for your wife.
- Give up one golfing or hunting outing a month and spend the time with her.
- Set aside specific times at the beginning of each month to be with your wife. Tell her, "We've got a new month. Let's plan our calendar together."
- Replace an "extra" meeting that you usually go to, and serve your wife by giving the time to her. Spend it doing something she loves to do.

Serve Her

The first time Gary spoke to the men at a Promise Keepers conference, I went with him so that I could support him and pray for him.

The arena was a vast sea of men, thousands of them, and Gary was electric that night, preaching with fire. Then, toward the end of his message, I was shocked to hear these words: "I'm going to ask my wife,

Barbara, to come up here on the platform and join me. She didn't know I was going to ask her to do this."

As those words swirled inside my head, someone escorted me up the black metal stairs. Just as I thought my knees were going to buckle and give way to fear, a man pulled out a chair for me. I didn't dare look to the left. I knew I would surely die if I saw sixty thousand men looking at me.

So I fixed my eyes on Gary, waiting for my next cue. Why did he call me up on stage with him? Our eyes met, with mine screaming, *What now?* Then I sensed the words *"Trust him"* resounding in my heart.

Before me stood my husband with his Bible in hand. As he began to read from Scripture, I realized he was reading from the Gospel of John, "'No,' Peter protested, 'you will never wash my feet!'" (John 13:8).

Fear engulfed me again. Feet? Whose feet? Oh no, nobody's washing my feet!

All I could do was trust Gary, my soul mate. My most trusted friend. A man of integrity. A man who walks what he talks. So I watched and waited as he knelt in front of me and removed my shoes. I trusted him as he took my feet and began washing them. Tears rolled down his cheeks as he showed me the depth of his love for me.

I watched as he pulled his handkerchief from his pocket. This was the same handkerchief he hands me during sad movies. The one I cry into when our younger daughter Missy plays "Memories" on the piano. The one I wept into until I had no more tears to shed when I said good-bye to Sarah, our older daughter, as she left for her freshman year of college. With that handkerchief he wiped the tears from his eyes and the water from my feet. And in that moment I felt as if we were the only two people in the stadium.

Then Gary stood to his feet before that quiet crowd of awestruck men. And with the strength of a warrior and the tenderness of a lamb, he challenged them to go to the next level of love for their wives and asked them to kneel while he prayed. Throughout that arena, men dropped to their knees, demonstrating publicly that they wanted to go home and love and serve their wives.

Do you have any idea how a woman feels living with a man like this? Gary's willingness to serve me—as he demonstrated not only in that moving moment at a Promise Keepers rally but also in the everyday moments of our marriage—convinces me on the deepest level that no matter what comes our way, no matter what flaws I have, no matter what I might do to disappoint him, he will love me unconditionally.

Take the risk. Ask God to help you love and accept your wife uncon-ditionally—in the midst of her pain and vulnerability and weaknesses. Love her even if she annoys you, even if she disappoints you, even if she doesn't deserve your love. Love her with the kind of love that Christ shows to you.

Lavish her with an extravagant love—one that isn't conditional.

CHAPTER 3

INTIMACY—MEN SPELL INTIMACY S-E-X

A HUSBAND'S #2 LOVE NEED

"Sex is a deeper need than you think."

Gary talks to wives

D an and Melody could be the poster couple for God's creative design. Melody's idea of intimacy is sitting on the love seat with Dan, a couple of cappuccinos beside them, a roaring fire in front of them, no kids around them, and plenty of time for a good, long heart-to-heart talk. While Melody can certainly become sexually responsive in this setting, she first needs to sense the security of Dan's commitment and love.

Dan's idea of intimacy is to move past the cappuccinos and light their own fire. The first time the two of them really discussed this matter of intimacy, Dan said, "I know you like all that romantic stuff, hon, but what happens when, out of nowhere I, you know, look at you, the woman I love with all my heart, and, well, *get the urge.*"

Like one particular Sunday. After church and lunch, Dan paid some bills, watched a little ESPN, and shot baskets with one of the kids. Then he walked into the kitchen and saw Melody walk by and . . . that was all it took. He got the urge.

Meanwhile, Melody looked at Dan and thought, *I know what that look in his eye means. But there's stuff we need to do today, and besides, we keep telling each other we're going to take a walk on that new nature trail near the house.* And suddenly she was running through a list of all the things she wanted to do yet that afternoon: plant some flowers in the flower box out front, take a walk together, and maybe visit her mother.

But Dan had one thing on his mind. So at about six o'clock when they were having dinner, he began sending Melody little "blinky eye" signals. It was his courting dance.

One of the kids looked at him and said, "Dad, do you have something in your eye?"

Dan's challenge—and he took it as a challenge—was not only to get Melody on track but the kids distracted. A few minutes later he kicked off his shoe and began rubbing Melody's ankle with his toe.

His six-year-old daughter made a face and said, "Mom, do you smell something?"

By the time Dan and Melody went to bed, she was ready to strangle him for being so single-minded. In Dan's zeal to get the kids tucked in early, Melody's plans got interrupted, and she was frustrated that they never took a walk.

Similar scenes get played out every weekend in countless homes. No matter how many times I hear couples lament their differences in the counseling room or at conferences, it's the same story: Men spell intimacy S-E-X, and women spell it T-A-L-K.

Why is this? Why does a woman think about sleep, errands, the kids, the house . . . while her husband is thinking about sex? Let's start with the one truth that is foundational: God created us differently. "God created people in his own image; God patterned them after himself; male and female he created them" (Gen. 1:27). What this means is that we are just plain different.

But here's the good news: That's God's design. He created you as a woman with all the incredible, unique gifts and needs that you bring into your relationship with your husband. And he created your husband with all of his unique gifts and needs. Including his need for sexual intimacy.

MEN AND WOMEN ARE WIRED DIFFERENTLY

When it comes to expressing intimacy, men and women are wired differently. Think about it. At the end of a long day, Dan walks through the door completely shot. Weary though he may be, however, before long he has "that look" in his eye. He may have had a marathon of meetings or built an engine on the assembly line. He may have been forced to slay a few megabytes on his computer or frame a house all day in subzero temperatures. Yet regardless of how he spent his day, he has the uncanny and amazing ability to shift gears immediately. All it takes is one touch, one word, one single eye-to-eye contact.

At the end of Melody's day, she often wants to hug only one thing when she goes to bed: her pillow. Not only is she exhausted from the stress of the day's work schedule, the kids, and the home front, but she's also worried about all that she has to do tomorrow. And if she could escape all that, what does she crave? Some time alone and a relaxing bath. Time just to sit and enjoy her home and her husband. That sounds wonderful.

What was God thinking when he created husbands with very little energy for communication and enthusiasm to spare when it comes to . . . the urge?

Let's be honest: You've experienced this transformation firsthand more than once, haven't you? No matter how rotten a day your husband has had or how much pressure he's under, when he gets that feeling . . . well, he gets that feeling. But it's not just about feelings; it has a great deal to do with our male chemistry.

It's not surprising that the men we surveyed cited sexual intimacy as their number two love need. God created males with a strong sex drive. Scientific study of sexual desire indicates that our sex drive is generated in our brain and that sexual desire can occur without any stimulus from outside of our body. The limbic system of the brain contains centers that enhance or stimulate sexual drive, and other centers that, when activated, inhibit it. We also know that testosterone, the primary male hormone (also found in women), plays a major role in a man's desire for sex.

Men also have the uncanny ability to compartmentalize their lives. We live in "boxes." We have a work box, a church box, a friend box, a sports box, a sex box, and so on. The sex box is always on the periphery of our lives, ready to be opened at a moment's notice. We may be worn out from work, preoccupied with pressures, or even struggling with conflict in our hearts, but we readily place each of those problems in a different (much smaller) box, separate from sex. We forget all the other boxes when we become sexually aroused.

Women, however, tend to tie all of these boxes together. Or perhaps a better way to say it is that when one box is open, they are all open. That's why open and vulnerable communication is so important for a woman. That's what helps her sort out all the rest and relax into physical intimacy.

Perhaps the most important fact you need to know is that a man finds much of his own masculinity in his sexuality. This is part of our maleness; we can't erase it. Although percentages differ from man to man, no less than 50 percent and up to 90 percent of a man's self-image—his "feeling like a man"—is locked up in his sexuality.

Ninety percent! (I wanted to say it again in case you thought that was a misprint.) Sex, passion, pleasing the woman he loves . . . that's what makes a man feel like a man. Consequently, when a man experiences sexual rejection from his wife, even if it is for a completely understandable reason, he may shut down, pull away, or—worst-case scenario—do something morally stupid.

When a wife withholds sex, for any reason, her husband feels emasculated. To be sure, other factors can also contribute to this feeling: when a wife is overly critical; when she compares her husband to other men; when her number one home-improvement project is her husband.

When a man begins to feel that he can never meet his wife's expectations, he will then, often unconsciously, quit meeting *her* emotional needs. And guess where that leads? No talk, no sex. No sex, no talk. It's a vicious cycle.

You may be thinking, *You guys sure do have tender egos.* Well, you're right! That's why the way you connect with us makes all the difference.

UNDERSTANDING YOUR HUSBAND'S NEED FOR SEXUAL INTIMACY

Recently, I was talking with a group of men about marriage, kids, aging, and balancing our busy lives. It was one of those times when you could sense that the Holy Spirit was moving and we were about to experience some honest discussion.

Bruce was the first guy to brave it when he said, "Tina and I are struggling a little. Do you guys ever feel as if you aren't quite clicking in the sexual area like you'd like to?"

Instead of raucous laughter (the way most of us would have responded in our adolescent days), his question was greeted with something entirely different. Each of the men glanced around, and then you could see a kind of nonverbal permission to go deeper pass from man to man.

"I've been waiting for years for a godly man to bring up this issue, but I was beginning to think no one ever would," said Tim. "I love my wife. I love sex with her. But something really bugs me. She never initiates it. And if I tell her I would like her to, she makes me feel like a dirty old man. Is there something wrong with me?"

You could sense the mood shift as the questions and comments began to get more personal. It's tough for men to talk about their feelings, but because these guys wanted answers and, I believe, truly wanted to honor their marriages, things got gut-level honest.

"Is it okay to feel that I'm not always the best lover?"

"I lost an erection the other day. I never thought it would happen to me. I felt like such a failure. I know this happens to men sometimes during stress or fatigue, but I just felt as if *I* had failed, not my plumbing."

"I think my wife sees me as some wild-eyed sex machine when I want to make love to her. I admit that occasionally I want to have sex to relieve some tension, but other times I just want a fulfilling lovemaking time with all the passion, and I get nothing back in return. You guys ever been there?"

"Now don't get me wrong. I love my kids. But before we had children, we were so spontaneous with sex. Now my wife is worn out from being a mom, I'm stressed out about money, and it seems as if we never have the time or energy to make love. To be really honest, I feel that I have been replaced by my own kids in her heart. How do you guys do it all? I mean, how do you balance out being a husband, dad, son, friend, and employee? I can't figure it out. And every time my wife and I try to talk about it, the phone rings, the baby cries, or I have to head off to work. Does it ever get any better?"

"I think I have a different problem altogether. My wife is more interested in sex than I am. Lately, dealing with the death of my mom and problems at work, I just don't care anymore. Sex is the last thing on my mind."

I know this is probably not what women think goes on in the locker room, but these men are authentic believers and concerned husbands trying to find answers to tough questions about a fundamental part of their lives and a crucial part of the marriage relationship. As they talked, they covered the key issues that I see in counseling situations with regard to men and sexual intimacy:

- A husband needs his wife to initiate sex.
- A husband often struggles with feelings of inadequacy or failure.
- A husband gets discouraged when his wife does not express her passion for him.
- A husband feels as if he's not important to his wife when she doesn't take time to make love.
- A husband becomes concerned when life situations (such as depression, grief, and loss) interfere with his interest in sex.

- A husband feels loved when his wife receives him and responds to him sexually.

Most of us men don't like to talk about sex with anyone. That includes our friends *and* our wives. As kids we eagerly shared our ignorance about the subject with our buddies, but as men—real, godly men—we often don't know what to say or how to say it. It is true that some insecure men will joke about their sex lives, even at times overstating reality. But rarely will a husband approach his wife and say, "Let's talk about our sex life." We don't want to admit to ourselves, let alone verbalize to someone else, that we might have a problem. We want the sexual aspect of our life to take care of itself. But after years of counseling couples, I can tell you, it rarely does.

For one thing, men aren't sure what "normal" sexual desire is. Since we don't even know where our desire comes from (besides the fact that God put it there), knowing what's normal in marriage is even more complicated.

Psychologically, of course, there is a strong connection between our sexual interest and our psychological health. If we are stressed or depressed or going through difficult life-stage cycles, our sexual interest may diminish. Between our brain, our hormones, and our emotions, a lot can influence our sex drive and our sexual relationship in marriage.

Usually, however, it isn't the "internal" problems men are most worried about. It's you.

Why has it been months or years since you've initiated making love?

Why, when there are no obstacles to intimacy on a Saturday morning, do you choose to do laundry or clean the bathrooms instead of cuddling up next to him?

Why, evening after evening, is there no spark in you for him?

Why have you once again rebuffed his overtures when you're in bed at night?

These are the questions that are dividing marriages across the land. Some couples divorce because the hurt and neglect have gone so deep. But many Christian couples simply endure emotional distance. Men who love God, their wives, and their children are going through intense struggle, trying to figure out what's going wrong.

Unless both partners agree, sexual infrequency (once a week or less) should be a cause of major concern in any marriage.

WHEN YOUR HUSBAND'S NEED FOR SEXUAL INTIMACY IS NOT MET

By the time I see men in my counseling office, their sexual frustrations have led to real problems in their marriages.

Lyle, for example, told me that he had gotten to the point where he had given up on even having a healthy sexual relationship with his wife, Lauren. Early in their marriage they had had a vibrant sexual relationship, but as time went on, Lauren showed less and less interest, and Lyle felt rejected. Instead of communicating about their hurts and their needs, they both withdrew. Now Lauren seems to have her love needs met by her relationships with the kids, and Lyle just repressed his . . . or so he thought. But then they began to surface in all the wrong areas. He found himself fantasizing about one of the women in his Sunday school class. Sometimes those thoughts were sexual, other times romantic, but regardless of the content, they always caused guilt.

Roger said he simply got mad and withdrew from his wife, Michelle, when she rejected him. Roger had a high sexual need and blamed Michelle not only for not meeting his needs but also for undermining the intimacy of their marriage. Michelle had been sexually abused as a young woman and had never worked through the pain. She felt frozen and trapped between her fear of understanding her abuse and her lack of desire for a husband who didn't honor her hurts and work through them with her. Roger knew they were in a downward spin, but he couldn't figure out how to change it, so he fed the situation with self-destructive behavior and a growing rage. He began to eat excessively and put on a great deal of weight, which made him even less attractive and further diminished his own self-image.

When a man's sexual needs are not met in marriage, he responds in one or more of three ways: He feels rejected. He shuts down. He looks outside of marriage to have his needs met.

He Feels Rejected as a Person

Greg grew up in a home where any affirmation he received was tied to his performance in school or in sports. His dad applauded his athletic performance; his mother praised his academics. Yet he often found himself in a squeeze play between the two. If his grades began to slip, his mother would not only criticize him but would also withdraw her affirmation of him. If he devoted more time to his studies and was not doing as well in one of the three sports in which he lettered, his dad would scream at him from the stands and withhold the "attaboys" all young men need. From this experience in his formative years, Greg learned one thing: "If I do well, I am loved and affirmed. If I don't perform, I am rejected." He carried this standard of behavior into his marriage with Kim, and when they began to have sexual problems, he simply felt rejected and withdrew. Because his parents had never encouraged him to talk things through or provided an environment in which he felt safe to do so, Greg had no practice in verbalizing what he felt.

Often when a man's needs are blocked, he will feel rejected and will isolate himself rather than express his frustration and verbally connect with his wife. Many men won't even risk opening up about their feelings of rejection because that only subjects them to fear of further rejection. For men like Greg, whose fear of rejection was learned early on from his parents, this pattern of performance = acceptance must somehow be broken. If this pattern is not changed, then he will become self-protective and will simply shut down and pull away.

He Shuts Down or Pulls Away

Some men, when their need for sexual intimacy with their wives is not met, will just shut down emotionally. They begin to withdraw from their wives and isolate themselves. Here are some of the signs:

- He won't go to bed when you do for fear of another round of rejection.
- He'll quit trying to romance you with flowers or dates because you've sent out the message that when he does that, he only wants one thing.
- He'll work longer hours so he won't have to think about the emotional distance between you.
- He'll absorb himself in recreation, activities with the kids, or TV—anything to numb the pain of expectations never fulfilled.

What do wives do when this happens? Sadly, most welcome the relief. They figure that they've successfully "trained" their husbands to be satisfied with infrequency. "He's gotten used to my sexual clock, and everything is now as it should be." Some wives rationalize that "sex isn't like food or air. He doesn't actually *need* it."

Jim is a good example of a man who often has higher sexual desire than his wife does. Early on, their sexual relationship was vibrant. After a number of years, however, children, work stress, and financial problems have come into play. The result? Their sexual intimacy is infrequent. Yet Jim's desire remains strong.

"I want and desire sex more than the weekly or sometimes monthly times I have with Amy," says Jim. "But I just can't seem to get her to respond, let alone initiate."

Their vast difference in sexual rhythms is causing conflict not only within Jim but also between Jim and Amy. Jim is becoming increasingly frustrated, and this only fuels the everyday conflicts. When Jim expects and needs sexual intimacy and it doesn't happen, he often ends up making Amy pay by withdrawing the very thing *she* needs from him— emotional support. His emotional distance only exacerbates their marital conflict. Their marriage is in a downward spiral.

He Looks Elsewhere to Get His Needs Met

When a man feels rejected or isolates himself, our enemy, the prince of darkness, is right there, ready to provide an alternative that will ruin not only a man's family but also the generations that come after him. I'm not being melodramatic here. This is happening all the time.

Some men turn to other women. Larry, in his longing for intimacy, began an emotional relationship with a woman who worked in the office of one of his clients.

Larry's wife, Ruth, was a perfectionist. She was demanding and critical of Larry. Not surprisingly, her attitude began to affect their marital intimacy. She pushed, and he ran—into the arms of another woman. It seemed so innocent at first; the other woman was kind and understanding, and they had great conversations. But business talks soon led to private lunches, and before long the two had consummated a sexual relationship. Now two families—his and hers—are being torn apart.

Other men turn to a perverse fantasy life and pornography. With the Internet, this is now even more readily available in the home. Men used to have to step outside the home to search out pornography at a magazine rack or a bookstore, but not anymore. As one man shared with me recently at a men's conference, "Now sin comes looking for you. It's right there for the taking on my computer screen, twenty-four hours a day. I used to have to go after it. Now it is chasing after me and consuming me. And I can't seem to stop."

Arnie spends hours late at night surfing the Internet, looking at pornography. He claims it started out as just curiosity, but it has become an obsession.

Arnie's wife, Louise, grew up with a mother who told her repeatedly that men want only one thing: sex. Louise carried this distorted perspective of God's design for a healthy sexual relationship into her marriage. She could take sex or leave it, she told Arnie. In fact, she seemed more inclined to leave it, spending more time with her romance novels than she did with him.

As Louise withdrew, Arnie began acting out through the use of pornography. Because he had never established effective spiritual boundaries in his life, he was soon in a free fall, feeling totally out of control. He is ashamed of his behavior. But he rationalizes that since he doesn't have a vital sexual relationship with his wife, he deserves to have his needs met in other ways. He has developed a pattern of masturbation that only perpetuates his self-disgust. Yet he feels trapped in his inability to express his real needs to his wife.

While husbands are certainly responsible for their own moral decisions, a wife plays a key role in keeping her husband from desiring to meet his God-given sexual needs in a place other than their marriage. She is the person chosen by God to fill those needs. That doesn't mean she's a sex slave; it means she has the privilege of being the sole person to meet her husband's sexual needs and to have him meet hers as well. Thus, you play a vital role in your husband's contentment.

MEETING YOUR HUSBAND'S NEED FOR SEXUAL INTIMACY

When I speak to men at conferences or in the counseling room, I encourage them to recognize that our focus on physical needs makes us look as if that's all we think about. In fact, the typical male *does* think about sex throughout the day. That's not all we think about, of course, but understanding this about your husband is key in learning to meet his need.

When I am counseling a woman in this sensitive area, I often challenge her to recognize that sexual intimacy is a very real and vital need for her husband. And when she responds to him sexually, she affirms him far beyond anything she could imagine. This, then, results in a reciprocal response on his part, as he is increasingly motivated to meet *her* deep needs for affection, nonsexual touch, and tenderness.

Recently Barb and I were talking with a young couple about this major difference between men and women. "I can't explain it, but I know it's true," Barb said to this young bride. "We, as women, will often respond sexually when our need for tenderness and affection is met. Our husbands, on the other hand, often respond tenderly after their sexual needs are met. Yes, we are opposites, but it is in those differences that God brings us together to honor one another and to meet each other's needs. I have been married to Gary for almost twenty-five years, and it is still a mystery to me, but I know it is true: When I listen to his needs and step closer to him sexually, he is greatly affirmed. Then he can't wait to give me the tenderness I need. We both just need to look out for ways to serve each other."

Talk to God about the Issue

One of the best places to begin is to be honest with God and directly admit to him what he already knows: The sexual aspect of your marriage may need some review.

For some couples, of course, the sexual relationship is the only aspect of the marriage that **is** working. This fact always surprises me in the counseling room, but it's true: About 10 percent of the time couples who still enjoy great sexual relationships have marriages that are in deep trouble. Typically, though, couples who are struggling with conflict, disappointment, lack of communication, isolation, and pain report that their sexual relationship really is a barometer of the problems in the marriage.

For those of you in healthy marriages with a vibrant relationship, perhaps a little encouragement will help in this section. For those who are hurting, let's get deeper so we can find some answers.

Start with Your Own Heart

The next place to look is your own heart. Let me ask you a few questions:

- What is blocking you from enjoying the sexual aspect of your marriage?
- Is there hurt between you and your husband? Is there unresolved conflict? Is there lack of forgiveness?
- Are you bringing past pain from other relationships into your marriage bed? Are past sexual experiences or family difficulties keeping you from enjoying a healthy sexual relationship with your husband?

If the answer to any of these questions is yes, then you will find that until you clean up your own heart and pain, it will be nearly impossible for you to have a healthy, active sexual relationship with your husband. Women who have unresolved emotional pain have difficulty taking the risk and opening their hearts and bodies to their husband.

I was counseling Ron and Lisa, and quite honestly we were stuck (a counseling term for when you stop making progress). No matter how hard Lisa tried to pull down her wall of self-protection, Ron couldn't break through. She would allow him only so close, then she would withdraw—until one day when he took a deep breath and then a deeper risk.

"Lisa, do you think your fear of giving yourself to me, I mean totally to me, could have anything to do with what you told me when we were dating?" he asked. "Can we let Gary in on it so he can help us?"

"I don't know if I can," Lisa whispered. "I'm so ashamed."

Then Ron looked into her eyes and with a genuine, affirming tone said, "I know, honey. But I'm here, and nothing we talk about will ever change my love for you."

Now we were all taking some deep breaths. I knew we were about to venture into an area of some kind of trauma. Abortion perhaps. Or maybe sexual abuse or abandonment. A couple's sexual relationship is directly related to the experiences they bring into a marriage or to those that occur outside the marriage bed. These wounds can be healed, but stepping through the pain of our hearts is the only path that leads to that real healing. Only then can God begin the cleansing process.

With Ron's support and encouragement to go deeper, Lisa allowed the Holy Spirit to work. She finally began to deal with the emotional consequences of aborting a baby when she was in high school.

"I was so scared," she told us. "I was only fourteen, and I thought that giving myself to my boyfriend sexually was the only way I could keep him."

Lisa's story is painfully familiar. But as she began walking through all the bad memories, she also began to walk into the light of God's grace and forgiveness. This restoration process took several months, but as the emotional barriers began to fall, so did the physical barriers.

With her husband's love and support, Lisa explored those painful memories and faced them. As she did, she began to drain the pain and experience healing. She had carried shame for many years as the enemy continued to whisper his lies: "Ron will never love you if you tell him the truth." But as her heart began to feel alive again, she knew she could take that risk with Ron. The level of intimacy between this couple grew deeper and deeper as they drank together of the well of honesty. Ron assured her that she was new and clean in his eyes, and his unconditional love offered her patience and support. He showed up for counseling with her and—very important—took a vacation from sex during this time when Lisa needed to heal.

The root of every conflict is the condition of the heart. If our hearts have become hardened by painful memories or broken relationships, it will be difficult for us to have a healthy and intimate sexual relationship in marriage. Why? Because before two bodies touch, two hearts must touch. And before two human hearts open up to each other, our relationship with Christ needs to be open and transparent. This necessitates confession, brokenness, and facing up to the issues of the past. A healthy marriage is truly a marriage of three: husband, wife, and Jesus Christ. And when a man and woman submit to God's work in their lives—breaking down the hardness of their hearts—God brings them together in a union that is not easily broken (Ecclesiastes 4:12 reminds us that "a triple-braided cord is not easily broken").

As you bring the issues of your heart to God and ask him to cleanse you, he promises to forgive you. "If we confess our sins to him, he is faithful and just to forgive us and to cleanse us from every wrong" (1 John 1:9). And as you receive his forgiveness, he brings you into intimacy with him. When that happens, your heart is prepared for the intimacy of the marriage relationship with your husband.[1]

Learn What Satisfies Your Husband

Since 1988 Barb and I have traveled across the United States, teaching FamilyLife marriage conferences for FamilyLife (a division of Campus Crusade for Christ). One of the main points we try to communicate during these conferences is the absolute necessity of becoming a student of your spouse—emotionally, spiritually, relationally, and sexually.

What do I mean by this? Simply this: Study your husband. Learn everything you can about him: his sexual rhythm, his needs, and how you as his partner in a lifetime marriage can move toward meeting those needs as God strengthens your marriage.

The mystery—and beauty—of a healthy sexual union is the desire to

---

[1] If this is an area of need in your marriage, I suggest that you take a look at my book *Dr. Rosberg's Do-It-Yourself Relationship Mender* (Wheaton, Ill.: Tyndale, 1995) to learn how to close the open loops of unresolved conflict.

be known at the deepest, most intimate level. Do you know—or care—what pleases your husband sexually? What signals does he give, indicating his desire to have a sexual experience with you? What is his sexual rhythm? How frequently does he need to feel sexually understood and satisfied?

Some men admit that they desire sex on a daily basis. For others, it's once a month. For most men, it is somewhere in between.

Do you know what it is for your husband?

Some women pick up a magazine from the grocery store rack, read an article to get the national average, and then try to apply that statistic to their marriage. I probably don't have to tell you that this isn't your best source of information. Other women talk to their female friends, but that's not a good source either. Each marriage relationship is unique. So the best source for finding out what is normal for your husband is *your husband.*

How do you find out? Two ways: watch him and ask him. Be observant. You know when he is feeling amorous. He sends you signals. Some men do it coyly, but most are pretty obvious. But go beyond observation. At the right time and place, simply look him in the eye and *ask.* Most guys don't expect their wives to read their minds (not all the time, anyway). They also don't expect perfection. But they do expect understanding and attention. Show interest in his sexual life and sexual satisfaction.

Is he acting frustrated and short-tempered? Perhaps he needs to connect to you intimately to help him relieve the tension he may be experiencing. Be alert to his love needs and signals by observing his comments and actions. He may be initiating a desire to experience marital intimacy with you through nuances that only you and he know. If you don't have your antennae attuned, you may miss his signal and may miss meeting this very real need. Ask him some of the following questions, which will reflect your desire to be a student of your husband:

- "What would show you that I am interested in your sexual needs?"
- "How often do you need sexual intercourse?"
- "What satisfies you most about our sexual relationship?"
- "What do you need me to do more often?"
- "What do you need me to do less often?"
- "What does it mean to you if I initiate sex?"
- "If I am not ready for sex at the same time you are, how can I show that in a way that doesn't make you feel rejected?"

If a wife doesn't satisfy her husband in the area of sexual intimacy, most men—even Christian men—will eventually begin to malfunction. So if a wife doesn't know what it takes to satisfy her husband, it is essential that she find out.

If a woman knows her husband's sexual needs but can't meet them for a period of time, a husband has the capability to offer the grace she needs. If you are ill or under emotional stress or in the midst of dealing with past sexual pain or other issues, then a brief vacation from sex is often appropriate. *But only for a time.* Scripture is clear: "Do not deprive each other of sexual relations. The only exception to this rule would be the agreement of both husband and wife to refrain from sexual intimacy for a limited time, so they can give themselves more completely to prayer. Afterward they should come together again so that Satan won't be able to tempt them because of their lack of self-control" (1 Cor. 7:5).

If your husband is struggling in some area of his life, then you need to love sacrificially by putting *your* needs aside for a time. There are times when your husband may not be initiating sexual intimacy or responding to your sexual needs. He may be experiencing physical pain (chronic pain or problems after surgery), emotional pain (depression or anxiety), or stress. If a man has encountered loss in his life, he can experience either an increase in his desire for sex or a decrease in his need for sexual intimacy. It is not uncommon for men to experience either intermittent times of impotency or long-term problems with loss of obtaining or maintaining an erection. Recent research and medication have accelerated the treatment of this condition, and a visit to a physician can be invaluable, but your response to your husband during these times is vital. Again, the best rule of thumb is *to know your husband.* Know his spoken and unspoken needs.

Husbands and wives must always be willing to sacrificially forgo their sexual need for a higher goal during tough times . . . as long as there is plenty of communication and understanding. If there is pain or conflict, then take the time to clean it up. But you cannot go without sexual intimacy for too long without harming your relationship. As time goes on and the needs of either a husband or wife aren't being met, the neglected spouse can be tempted to develop alternative ways of meeting this need. Although this is never an excuse for the sin of meeting sexual needs outside the marriage, the risks for a couple are too great to ignore.

Commit Yourself to Meet His Needs

Your husband's sexuality is so entwined with his masculinity that as you reach out to him and meet his need for sexual intimacy, you will affirm his God-given masculinity. As Barb has done that in our marriage, she has stirred within me the passion and ever-increasing commitment to outserve her. So as we conclude this chapter, I challenge you to commit yourself to meet your husband's needs in this area of sexual intimacy. But don't just limit this commitment to the silence of your own heart; tell him of your deep desire to encourage him sexually. Tell him! And then do it![2]

Now, let me offer some suggestions of ways you might demonstrate your commitment to sexual intimacy with your husband:

- Call your husband during the day and tell him that he is your one and only and that you can't wait to have an interlude with him at just the right time!
- Leave him notes (always in discreet places: his briefcase, suitcase on trips, lunch bag, personal planner) to stir the passion.
- Remind him that you are committed to meet his needs just as you need him to commit to meet your needs of intimacy, both emotionally and sexually.
- Ask him where you need to be a better student of him and where you both need to "go back to school" in the development of your sexual relationship. This will stir some great discussion!
- Don't forget that few things affirm your husband more than when you initiate, initiate, initiate times of sexual intimacy.
- Tell him that when you see him serve you by spending time with the kids, it draws you to him and you can't wait to spend some tender private time with him later!
- As you see him growing in his spiritual life in prayer, reading the Word, and sharing spiritual insights with you, bring him in on this secret: that as his wife you feel nurtured and secure in his spiritual leadership and this makes you want to draw close to him sexually.
- Flirt and play with your husband. Barb and I have been married since 1975, and we are more playful now than we were as newly-

[2]This desire and commitment do not mean that you must participate with your husband in sexual activity with which you are not comfortable. Husbands and wives must communicate clearly with each other about their own desires as well as their own comfort level and boundaries when it comes to sexual intimacy. But I always encourage couples to have these discussions outside of times of sexual intimacy.

weds. When people comment about this, we often say it is because we are safe with each other and are committed to building the foundation of our marriage on the Rock. This allows us to be playful and have fun and enjoy each other. As you strengthen your marriage and mutually serve each other, increase the flirting.

- Stir the romantic fires of your marriage! Barb and I enjoy romance more and more with each passing year of our marriage.
- Remember that your husband responds to visual stimulation. Use your imagination in the security and privacy of your marriage relationship on this one!

IT'S NEVER TOO LATE

Marty and Lila had been married for over fifteen years. Early in their relationship the sex was great. Lila would tell her close friend, "He can't keep his hands off me when he comes home." Lila was both flattered and bothered by the fact that Marty seemed to sexualize much of their relationship.

When they started a family, however, like most of us, they found that sex began to take a backseat to child rearing, work, and just plain daily life. Lila wasn't really concerned about their more and more infrequent lovemaking. Sometimes, in fact, at the end of a long, tiring day, she was relieved that Marty just rolled over and went to sleep. But she did miss what she thought of as "the romance" of their early married life and wistfully wondered if they would ever experience a vibrant relationship again. To fill that need, she began reading romance novels and living vicariously through the heroines. Instead of making time for intimate moments with her husband, she found herself fantasizing about tall, dark, handsome strangers.

Marty also missed the relationship they had had in the early days of their marriage. He missed both the sexual intimacy and the spontaneity of their lovemaking. Granted, he didn't always have the energy at the end of a long, stressful day at the office. But often he felt pushed away, isolated by Lila's preoccupation with the kids and the house and even her women friends—she always seemed to have time for them. And when he did reach out to her sexually, more often than not she was not responsive to his advances.

Marty found himself pulling away and distancing himself from true intimacy with Lila. When the guys in his accountability group asked if he was "clean," he would say yes, but he wasn't being honest. As his job took him on the road, temptation came knocking. After too many nights alone and without the guardrails of a healthy marriage, Marty compromised his wedding vows. It started with watching adult movies in the hotel and then spread to surfing pornography sites on the Internet. Curiosity soon became full-fledged moral breakdown.

As the pornography stopped meeting his needs, he began visiting "gentlemen's clubs" while he was on the road. The dilemma, he had convinced himself, was that his sex life would never get any better at home—and since he had gone too far already, it was easy for him to step into a series of sexual encounters. He mistakenly thought that a lack of sex was the reason his heart felt so empty. All of the compromises made him forget that he could never be satisfied outside of an intimate, obedient relationship with Jesus Christ . . . and an honest and open relationship with Lila.

The whole thing exploded the day Lila found a credit-card slip from a massage parlor. After she filed for divorce, they ended up in my office, looking for one last chance to save their marriage.

"How can it get this bad?" How often I've heard that question. And the answer won't be found in the "blame game." This kind of pain is the consequence of the hardening of two hearts toward God and each other. When that happens, anything is possible. This marriage seemed destined to end in tragedy; another home going the way of destruction. But Marty and Lila beat the odds.

How?

It started with Lila.

God broke her heart and convicted her that she had to love and forgive her husband. Even though she had every right to be angry and walk away, she followed a biblical principle that has stood the test of time in countless relationships: "All of you should be of one mind, full of sympathy toward each other, loving one another with tender hearts and humble minds. Don't repay evil for evil. Don't retaliate when people say unkind things about you. Instead, pay them back with a blessing. That is what God wants you to do, and he will bless you for it" (1 Pet. 3:8-9).

Some of you may be saying, "Now wait a minute, Gary. Are you telling me she took him back? He didn't deserve anything but a fat alimony bill. He deserved to be out on his ear. God even says that a woman or man whose spouse has committed adultery can be released from that marriage."

You're right. Marty didn't deserve Lila's forgiveness and her willingness to take him back. He deserved to be out on his ear.

But God had a different plan.

As Lila went to God in her brokenness, asking him to do a work in her heart, Marty saw something so supernatural in her response that he couldn't resist God's desire to work in his own life.

The Holy Spirit convicted Marty of the deceit and lies in his life, and Marty faced up to the truth: He had isolated himself not only from Lila and his children but also from God. As his "sins found him out," he recognized that he had a choice. He could either continue to feed his lust and live a life of deceit, or he could confess his sinful heart to his heavenly Father and begin to experience the grace and forgiveness that can come only from our Lord. Thankfully, Marty chose to let God have his way with him. Humbled and broken, Marty began seeking God's healing in his life.

Then, together, Marty and Lila began to work through the painful steps of facing up to what went wrong. Lila recognized her own responsibility in the breakdown of their relationship. While Marty was 100 percent responsible for his sinful choices and actions, she was responsible for her neglect and rejection and indifference to him. She also saw how she had turned to unhealthy avenues of romantic fantasy to meet her needs.

Lila's willingness to take Marty back was truly an expression of unconditional love and acceptance. She also committed herself to understanding Marty's needs for sexual intimacy and learning how to meet them.

Marty and Lila still have a long way to go, but they are living proof that God is the God of second chances. And third . . . and fourth and . . . He proves himself faithful over and over again.

A fulfilled and vibrant sexual relationship is part of God's plan for a great marriage. That's why when a man and a woman are committed to oneness in their marriage, their sexual relationship only gets better. A vibrant sexual relationship is the result of a healthy and fulfilling spiritual life and marriage.

So enjoy your husband! Affirm him. Reach out to him. Study him and his needs. Communicate your love and passion for him. And experience deep pleasure in the safety of your marriage relationship.

Do you need to have the joy of sexual intimacy restored in your marriage? Take the first step. Meet your husband—not halfway, but all the way. (And to all you husbands who are sneaking a peek at this chapter, you do the same. That is what servant leadership is all about.)

God's design for marriage is always the best.

CHAPTER 4

INTIMACY—WOMEN SPELL INTIMACY T-A-L-K

A WIFE'S #2 LOVE NEED

"Come closer to me."

Barb talks to husbands

K en is a former air force pilot. He knows what he wants and maps out a plan to achieve it. Today is no different. On his way home from work he's driving along, feeling pretty good, whistling and dreaming about his "love pilot" plan.

I'll pull into the garage, walk in the house, and loosen my tie. I'll drop the briefcase, unwind a bit, have sex with Debbie, change into sweats, shoot some hoops, grab the remote, catch some news, and then close my eyes for a few minutes before dinner.

When Ken got home, he walked in the back door, Debbie looked up, and their eyes met. His eyes pierced hers with "the look."

All day long Debbie had been chasing to keep up with two preschool boys. Her conversations had centered on a fictional purple creature named Barney, and she had dealt with several catastrophes: the belt on the washer had broken, the boys had spilled grape juice on beige carpet, the cat had scratched one of the boys, and Ken's mother had called to say she was coming to visit for a week.

That "look" in Ken's eye was the proverbial straw that broke the camel's back. It put Debbie over the edge! Ken was no longer the companion and confidant she had looked forward to all day. He was now . . . *the enemy!* His look, that twinkle in his eyes, sent any number of possible messages to her: "Let me have every bit of the energy you have left." "Let me take everything you have—and leave you with nothing." "Let me be like everyone else and stand in line and take, take, take."

Debbie threw her hands in the air and yelled, "No, not now!" Then she stormed out of the kitchen and went to the living room to sit alone for the first time all day. Normally she was a strong and resilient person, but today she winced back tears. Her fuel tank registered way below empty.

There goes the ultimate plan of the love pilot, thought Ken with a sigh. But instead of accusing Debbie of overreacting, he walked into the living room and sat down beside her on the sofa.

"Tell me about your day, Debbie," he said as he gently reached over and put his arm around her.

"I had no idea that parenting the kids would be so hard, Ken. I am so tired of Cheerios and applesauce. I miss talking to adults and having a conversation that isn't interrupted by arguments and coloring books. The house is pitted out. I go from room to room picking up, but I am barely out of sight when they pull out more stuff. I never feel on top of it."

What Debbie needed at that moment from Ken was the safety of being able to unload some of the stress that had been building within her during the day. And because Ken knew his wife so well, because he knew that at that moment she needed connection with him, he sat and listened. As she unloaded, he focused totally on her. Then, after she had talked most of it out and was quieted, he kissed her on the forehead and told her to relax. Then he went into the kitchen, rolled up his shirt-sleeves, unloaded the dishwasher of clean dishes, and then reloaded it with the dirty dishes sitting on the counter.

When he was done, he peeked out from the kitchen and said, "Debbie, I know you've had a full day. Just sit for a while. I'm going to take the kids outside to shoot some hoops."

Ken's keen sensitivity and willingness to step in and share the household chores not only validated Debbie's need but also lightened her load. She got some time to herself to refill her empty tank.

After dinner Ken was still tender, making sure she was doing better. "How are you feeling? Can I get you anything?" he asked at one point. He took her hand and said, "I know how hard you work for our family, and I want you to know how much I appreciate all that you do for the boys and me. You may not think this, but I know that you are the best mom in the world to our boys. I love to watch you with them."

Debbie hugged Ken and said, "Thanks, honey."

When the ten o'clock news came on later that night, Ken shut off the TV, got out of his recliner, locked the door, turned off the lights, and plowed up the stairs to crash before another day of work. But as he opened the door to their bedroom, he saw the glow of soft candlelight and Debbie smiling at him from beneath the sheets.

"The night is young, Ken," she said.

Ken wasn't tired anymore.

So, do I have your attention, guys? While men listed sexual intimacy as their number two love need in marriage, women indicated that emotional intimacy was their second most important love need.

MEN AND WOMEN ARE WIRED DIFFERENTLY

As Gary said to your wife in the last chapter, men spell intimacy S-E-X, and women spell it T-A-L-K. How true is that for you? If you are like most men, when you hear the word *intimacy,* you think of a passionate physical experience. But when your wife hears the word *intimacy,* she thinks about emotional connection and communication.

God has wired men and women quite differently. Your sex drive is connected to your eyes; you become aroused visually. Your wife's sex drive is connected to her heart; she is aroused only after she feels emotional closeness and harmony.

You compartmentalize sex from everything else in your life. Your wife sees everything connected to everything else.

You feel less masculine if your wife resists your sexual advances. Your wife feels like a machine if she doesn't experience sexual intimacy flowing from emotional intimacy.

The word *intimacy* comes from a Latin word that means "innermost." What this translates into for us in the marriage relationship is a vulnerable sharing of our inner thoughts, feelings, spirit, and true self. Both men and women need to feel secure in this sharing and confident of their spouse's support. This support is achieved through listening, empathy, prayer, or reassurance. Generally, this sharing and support must be in place before a woman will share herself physically in sexual closeness.

As we said earlier, people view intimacy differently. For example, Steve's view is that intimacy is all sex. When he looks at his wife, Jill, his motto is "Let's just do it." Jill's response to Steve is "Don't even think about it." She insists that Steve understand and respect her heart and mind before he initiates sex.

For Brenda, pursuing intimacy with Stewart is a rich experience when they truly open up with each other and share their deeper thoughts. The first ten years of their marriage were rather rocky because Stewart didn't understand how Brenda was wired. He thought she looked at intimacy the same way he did. It's only recently that Stewart has understood how fulfilling talking time is for his wife.

Carla is a strong personality, an extrovert. She thinks of intimacy as sex with her husband, and it upsets her that John always wants to talk. Carla can easily come across as controlling and critical. That's why John has a strong need to talk as a preparation for times of intimacy; communication with her creates safety in the marriage, softens her control, and gets them on the same page. The way John thinks is representative of how most women view intimacy, which may help you understand your own wife's needs better.

Men are by nature compartmentalized creatures. Figuratively speaking, you view your work, your family, your hobbies, and your recreation as separate boxes. You eat breakfast in one box. You have disagreements with your wife in another box. You spend your workday in a box. Men go through their entire day with each box standing alone, unconnected.

Women are totally different! We go through the same activities, but each box has an invisible, emotional thread connecting them all together. And all those boxes are open. Our emotions are connected to our thoughts, to our hearts, to our minds, and to our bodies. When one box is affected, there is a chain reaction that ultimately affects our spirits. For example, if your wife has had a rough day with the kids or a coworker, her emotional tank will be depleted. As a result, her physical energy may be shot, and she may need to withdraw to regroup. Her parenting or workplace box is connected to her emotional box, which is connected to her energy box, which is connected to her relational box.

Have you noticed how quickly your wife can recall a disappointing event that happened three years ago? That's also why she can remember exactly when you last gave her flowers. A woman's life events are carefully threaded together.

UNDERSTANDING YOUR WIFE'S NEED FOR EMOTIONAL INTIMACY

Promise Keepers and several other groups have done an outstanding job of educating men about the differences between men and women. Men generally leave these rallies knowing that women have needs that are exclusively female, and many of these men are committed to meeting their wife's needs. The problem is, they know their destination, but they lack a map telling them how to get there. By the time you finish this chapter, I hope you will hold the Rand McNally of emotional intimacy in your hand and in your heart. But first I want you to hear what some women have to say on the subject.

Gary and I were conducting a week-long marriage conference on a cruise ship when I casually invited the women to join me one day for an informal discussion of emotional intimacy. The next morning every one of the women showed up.

"How does it affect you when your husband doesn't recognize your need for emotional intimacy?" I asked.

One woman offered, "When my husband walks in with that 'look of love' in his eyes—"

"Look of love or lust?" another woman interjected.

Everyone giggled to release the stress of talking about this delicate topic. Then the first woman continued.

"My initial response is disappointment: *Oh, all he wants is sex.* I feel disappointed because I know my emotional needs won't get met."

Emotional intimacy is so rich, so fulfilling for a woman. It doesn't replace the need for sex, but for her, the emotional need is as intense as the physical need. And when that need is fulfilled by her husband and sustained through thoughtful T-A-L-K time, it is much easier for her to move more quickly into a sexual mode.

But what if that doesn't happen? You may not realize it, but when you show disappointment that your wife doesn't respond to you sexually, you send a nonverbal message that she may hear as this: "Oh no. You mean I have to listen to you before I use you?" That may sound crass, but that's how your sexual advances may make your wife feel. A woman has a God-given need to connect emotionally, but if that need is either not recognized or is cavalierly dismissed, she feels that her husband is only using her to gratify his sexual desires.

"I want my husband to treat me like one of his customers," said another woman in the group. "He is a top salesman, and he gives his customers the best service you can imagine. When he does that for me, when he shows interest in what I'm saying and looks directly into my eyes as he tracks my conversation, I feel incredible!"

"Yes," chorused the women, nodding and voicing their agreement.

One woman whose husband is a travel agent said, "My husband's mind is sharp. He works with hundreds of people, and yet he can tell you which of his clients prefer aisle seats and which prefer window seats. I sometimes wish he'd remember my preferences that clearly!"

Everyone agreed that after a full day's work both men and women are weary and exhausted. But when a husband seems to reserve all his attention for his work and shows no attention to his wife, she feels unloved. When that happens, instead of having a loving and sexually responsive wife, he will run the risk of being at continual odds with her. He will get wrath instead of warmth.

Stop giving your wife leftovers at the end of the day, and begin treating her with the kind of attention you reserve for your best customers. The results may astound you!

Ever have a conversation with your wife in which you are mumbling, "Yes, dear. . . . I understand, honey. . . . Uh-huh, sweetheart," but if she asked you what she just said, you would be hard-pressed to tell her? A woman's need to talk has become a standard sitcom joke, but it is not a joke. For many women, talking is a way to work through thoughts, feelings, ideas, and problems. It's the way we're wired, and it's solid wiring. Sure, just like your wiring, it can short-circuit sometimes. But overall, it's a positive way to express and process her thoughts and emotions. Be wise: Listen to her and draw her out. It will draw you closer as a couple.

Sometimes listening and processing issues may seem anything but logical to you. Like the times when what starts as a quiet discussion about a family issue becomes tense. Although both husband and wife may agree logically on what the problem is—not enough family time, for example—they may approach the issue from two different emotional sides. He wants to get in there and solve the problem quickly. When he won't listen and try to understand her perspective, her face flushes, she gets butterflies in her stomach, and her emotions begin to swell. Angry and hurt, she lashes out, and he retaliates in kind. He decides the confrontation is getting them nowhere, so he turns to leave. She collapses in tears on the edge of the bed.

This is not some imaginary scenario. Kate and Doug were in this very spot. And when he turned to leave, she yelled, "Doug, come back here! We're building a wall between us, and we need to work things out—now!" When a woman hurts, she wants to feel understood and, therefore, connected to her husband.

And do you know what Doug did at that point? He turned around and without saying a word walked over, lifted Kate off the bed, and held her in his arms. What did she do? Kate held on for dear life! She knew that at that very moment they were fighting to guard the wholeness that results after two hearts join on the other side of pain.

Too often couples give up when they are in conflict and remain in chronic isolation. That particular day as Doug and Kate held each other, they felt emotionally spent. But once they got beyond the hurdle and communicated—that is, truly listened to each other and understood each other—they experienced the most intense emotional intimacy any couple can share.

Emotional intimacy doesn't come when one side caves in or when you finally agree. For a woman, it comes when her point of view is validated, listened to, understood. This connects with the deepest part of her soul.

Let me recap here.

- Your wife needs to experience emotional closeness.
- Your wife needs to feel listened to and understood.
- Your wife needs to feel as if she is your top account.
- Your wife needs your undivided attention.
- Your wife needs you to demonstrate your respect for her as a person.
- Your wife needs to feel a cut above other people.
- Your wife needs to know that she is valuable to you.

WHAT HAPPENS WHEN YOUR WIFE'S NEED FOR INTIMACY IS NOT MET?

If you do not meet your wife's need for emotional intimacy, you will leave her vulnerable. She may withdraw from you or may not feel free to respond to you sexually. Ultimately, she may begin to look elsewhere to have her needs met.

She Will Withdraw

One indication that your wife may be starved for emotional intimacy is that she may withdraw.

"What's wrong, honey?" Jerry asks.

"Nothing," she replies.

What did I do now? he thinks to himself. *What is happening to us?*

Jerry knows that invisible wall all too well. The wall Mary builds one brick at a time when their relationship hasn't been his priority. This usually happens following a flurry of activities. He's gone too much or gets distracted by other issues, and the two of them don't make time to talk. Mary starts withdrawing to that place inside her that is guarded and formal.

Chances are good that Mary is hurt by her husband's lack of connection with her in talk time. She doesn't know where to take all those real issues that need to be addressed, so she stuffs them all inside, buries them alive, if you will.

When you sense your wife's wall going up, you know that something is very wrong. From a woman's perspective, it means that her husband is not a harbor of safety but a threat. This pattern of withdrawal can do significant damage to a relationship. And if this remains unaddressed, over time you can end up as two strangers coexisting under the same roof, sharing meals and the same bed but walled off from each other emotionally.

Take a look at the guy in the mirror and ask the hard question: "What have I said or done to contribute to the wall my wife has built?"

Much of the time a woman will withdraw to protect herself if she is threatened by something you are doing or if she is feeling verbally attacked. When your words are positive, they strengthen the very foundation of your marriage. But if your words are critical, harsh, and destructive, your wife will retreat to protect herself. If you are using retaliation to hurt her, if you are belittling her, you are throwing bricks at her and bruising her heart; she may then take those bricks and continue to build the wall.

Take the lead and address the pain. Become responsible for the tone of the relationship, and get back on course, especially if you are guilty of contributing to the pain.

If you see any of the following danger signals, your wife may be withdrawing, isolating herself, protecting herself from being hurt:

- Is your wife acting distracted?
- Does she maintain a distant relationship with you?
- Is she spending more than the usual time at work or in other activities?
- Is she too busy to be intimate with you?
- Does she avoid spending time alone with you?
- Do the children seem to be a higher priority for her than you are?

A woman can hide behind a wall, or she can flee by staying busy with a full personal calendar that doesn't have your name on it. When a woman seems cold and emotionally frozen, some men will make the mistake of trying to get her to snap out of it by "setting her straight." I assure you, this is no way to win your wife back. If you intimidate her by rage, anger, or demands, she will withdraw even more. She will stay locked up and frozen.

She Will Not Feel Free to Respond to You Sexually

A second indicator that your wife's emotional needs are not being met is that she may not respond to you sexually. Husbands tend to interpret their wife's resistance to their sexual advances as rejection. Often her resistance is not rejection, however, but an indication that she may not feel safe or that she can't get beyond a conflict the two of you are having.

Mike is a workaholic who wins at work. He thrives on conquest, whether it is people or deals. Fifteen-hour days consume him. He's proud of the lifestyle he has provided for his wife, Peg. After all, he has achieved the American dream of having it all: a large home in a gated community, a three-car garage with two new cars, his-and-her snow-mobiles.

But what defines success in industry doesn't define success at home. The work that provides all the toys is nothing other than the "other woman" in Peg's eyes; work is the mistress that is robbing her of her husband's focus and attention. She's been squeezed out of his daily planner.

When the doors of the master bedroom suite close them off from the rest of the house, the two people inside are closed off from each other as well. Mike may conquer at work, but he's not winning with her. If he truly cared about her, he would be as eager about spending time with her as he is about spending time at work. Most days he is so spent by the time he gets home that he doesn't have the emotional energy to satisfy her heart needs, and Peg responds by rejecting his sexual advances.

Mike tries to buy her affection, taking her to the finest hotel rooms when they travel, letting her spend all the money she wants, but he gets little in return. He feels as if he's "romancing the stone." What Mike doesn't realize is that more stuff doesn't satisfy a woman's heart. What Peg needs is a connected relationship with *her husband*. She loves him and wants a life connected with him. She does not want to be the woman on the outside of all the deals. If a man wants great sex with his wife behind the bedroom door, he needs to work on the way he relates to her outside those doors.

She May Look Elsewhere to Have Her Needs Met

A third consequence of your wife's unmet need for emotional intimacy is that she may become involved with another man. This is a worst-case scenario, but it does happen. If a woman is not understood and cherished, if her need for emotional intimacy is not met, she becomes vulnerable to other men who show interest in her thoughts and emotions.

If another man makes your wife feel comfortable and safe by validating her thoughts and sharing her emotions, you could be headed for trouble. In all likelihood, this man will be someone she encounters in ordinary daily life: your best friend, a neighbor, her boss, or a fellow associate. It will start out very innocently with a few conversations here and there. The more compassionate or empathetic he is, the more dangerous it becomes.

Rusty and Ann are both professing Christians; in fact, they met at work. Which is where the trouble started.

If we were to go back a year and warn them of the ruin that comes from unguarded hearts, both Rusty and Ann would arguably have boasted, "Well, that will never happen to us! We are Christians. We swear it could never happen to us!" But it did.

It all began so innocently one day when Ann was emotionally vulnerable and began to connect with Rusty, a man she was comfortable talking with at work. This connection of understanding felt so wonderful that she found herself wanting to access more and more of this spiritual man's mind. Yet this would never have happened if Ann's need for emotional intimacy was being met by her husband. She didn't even know she was at risk.

Ann and Rusty worked together in an office where the atmosphere among the employees was fairly congenial. People were open about their problems and willingly encouraged one another. But Rusty was a man who stood out from the others. He truly cared about the people he worked with and went out of his way to make sure they were doing okay. He was straightforward and outgoing, and Ann loved listening to him. She was drawn to his personality and gradually became infatuated with him because he was such a neat Christian. She missed that in her own husband, who was a nominal Christian and a noncommunicative spouse. He rarely expressed warmth and love, and he never prayed with her. In fact, one reason Ann had taken the job was that it gave her a chance to talk to other Christians.

One day Rusty found Ann crying. He put his arm around her and consoled her. Then he prayed for her. He, of course, had no way of knowing that Ann's husband wasn't meeting her basic emotional needs. So what happened over the next few minutes caught Ann totally off guard. As Rusty was praying for her, he was touching her vulnerable heart. His words, his warmth, his touch, and his spirituality ignited something inside Ann. She felt *emotionally intimate* with him as he accessed her unguarded heart spiritually, emotionally, and physically.

Ann began thinking about Rusty a lot. As she was dressing for work in the morning, she thought about what would make him attracted to her. She couldn't wait to get to work and talk with him. She would go to his office about the smallest problem to get his attention. She loved those times of emotional engagement and confidential sharing with him, and she used any excuse to get more of him. She would respond to him by reaching out and touching him, patting his arm as they talked.

Rusty thought he was untouchable by any woman other than his wife—until Ann started reaching out to him in such tender ways. Her charm made it such a gray area. After all, they were just friends; he was just ministering to her.

How can such a thing happen to Christians? "Above all else, guard your heart, for it affects everything you do," Proverbs 4:23 warns us. In satisfying your wife's love need for emotional intimacy, we guard each other's hearts. A woman can form emotional attachments more easily than a man can. And when a woman has an unguarded heart, before she knows it, she's developed an emotional bond with someone other than her husband.

Don't let pride and arrogance tell you that what happened to Rusty and Ann could not happen to *you*. The label of "Christian" isn't going to hold your marriage together for you. We Christians must surrender everything that gets in the way of following God wholeheartedly in our marriage. Begin by becoming alert to the red flags that may indicate your wife is finding her emotional needs met by another man. Then work hard to protect your marriage by making sure you are the one to meet your wife's emotional needs completely.

HOW CAN YOU MEET YOUR WIFE'S NEED FOR EMOTIONAL INTIMACY?

Nothing satisfies a woman's emotional need like her connection with her husband. She trusts you to stand by her no matter what—when even closest family members may not be able to be there for her or understand. And friends may come and go in her life, but you are her constant companion; you are always there for her.

By way of example, I wish you could sit in my living room at the end of the day and watch my husband in action. Gary comes in the door each night eager to talk. No kidding, he really does. No matter what his day has been like, he always saves some energy just for me. He greets me with a warm kiss and then tells me about his day—conversations he's had with the staff, phone calls and decisions, what he's been thinking about. Some nights we may sound like the six o'clock news reporting about our day to each other: who did what, when it happened, where they were. But no matter what, we engage with each other, listening and responding.

We wives flourish as we emotionally engage with our husbands and know that you are really listening. We love being in the spotlight of your attention. But you men love it just as much. Often Gary will walk in the back door, swing his sport coat around and around over his head and yell, "Baby, your handsome dog is home. Let's talk!" He'll have me doubled over with laughter, and then he takes advantage of the moment, tickling me. And I've got to admit that laughter relieves all the stress of a bad day for both of us.

We treasure our sharing time at the end of the day, and it sets the tone for the entire evening as we stay connected. When Gary shows me his continual love and active presence, when he openly shares with me about anything and everything, I see his devotion to me. And I am so attracted to him.

Your wife will be able to take on most of the assaults the world has to offer as long as you are at her side, and your desire to be that close companion will motivate her to give the same to you—100 percent.

A woman is eager to hear about the smallest details in your life, from what you ate for lunch to what you would lay your life down in defending. She wants to know what you're thinking and how you think, and she wants you to do the same for her. You want to keep the chemistry in your relationship with your wife? Ask her what she thinks! Women love a conversation that volleys back and forth. Open up and articulate what you're thinking about, and you'll be amazed at how exhilarating it is for her. When she sees you growing and developing, she is challenged to do the same.

Remember how you felt when you first dated the young woman who is now your wife? How you called her during the day just because you were thinking about her, because you just wanted to hear her voice? You went out of your way to drop in and see her at work or the dorm. You weren't distracted when you talked with her. In fact, the two of you could sit and talk for hours. You actually heard everything she said. In fact, you were eager to discover her thoughts and opinions. Conversation was so easy. You told her everything.

Emotional intimacy was easy then because your hearts were always connecting. And that's the secret, the bottom line: Two hearts have to connect to experience emotional intimacy. That's the way Gary and I begin our day, before we even crawl out of bed. Gary's the morning person in our house, so he's usually awake first. I'm still half-asleep when I hear him whisper, "I love you, Barb. . . . I need you, Barb." But what gets me every time is when he says, "Baby, baby, baby!" It makes me laugh every time he says it, bringing joy to my soul, and that's when I start telling him I love him! We begin each day this way.

Try it. Before you crawl out of bed in the morning, give your wife a heartfelt "I love you." Then, during the day call your wife from work. You won't believe how many points a simple phone call will score. It makes a woman feel loved and honored that you would take time from everything else to let her know you're thinking about her.

June's husband has a high-stress middle-management job for a large utility company. Yet he takes time at least once a day to call her. Sometimes it's to tell her what's happening with him. Sometimes it's to check up on her day. And sometimes it's just to say, "I'm here for you. I love you."

This kind of connecting, of taking the time to tune in to each other, builds security and intimacy in a relationship. It's part of what makes a great marriage.

Your wife has an intense drive to be emotionally transparent with you. She needs to know everything about you. Not so that she can possess or control you, but so that she can experience true oneness with you. That's what intimacy is on the deepest level: when you let her get into your soul and you get into hers, when together you reveal who you are to each other, when you talk about everything and anything, when you share your opinions and perspectives.

When a woman feels secure and safe enough to fully disrobe emotionally with her husband, that's as good as it gets. And I'll give you a clue: If your souls undress before one another, your bodies will follow.

If you provide this kind of intimate emotional environment for your wife, your life will never be the same! But in order to do that, you have to do several things.

Listen to Her

Overload. I'm sure you know the word—and the feeling. Few of us escape it in today's world. You're busy; your wife's busy. This rapid pace often separates couples simply because there's no time to connect, or at least they don't *make* the time to connect.

One sure way of connecting is to offer a listening ear. The emphasis here is on listening, not fixing. Truly listen to the messages your wife sends you. Don't just hear them—listen to them. What are they telling you? Are you hearing the same comments over and over again? Do you always argue about the same things? Wake up, these are unresolved issues! They are eating away at your wife. And, quite frankly, she may not even realize it. As we discussed earlier, she may not recognize the depth of her need to connect until she finds a sympathetic listener in another man.

Spend a few minutes right now thinking about any unresolved issues you have with your wife. Then ask her if she is aware of any. And if she says, "Oh, nothing, dear," don't give a sigh of relief and settle down in front of the television. Do a little probing—and a lot more listening. Let her talk until she reaches to the bottom of her heart and finds the real problem.

Here are some real, practical ways you can listen:

- Give her your undivided attention when she talks to you. Put down the newspaper. Turn off the television. Look her in the eyes.

- Let the answering machine get the call if the phone rings while the two of you are talking.
- Find a shared sport to do together. This will not only give you physical togetherness but also provide plenty of time to talk and listen. Go biking, walking, or golfing.
- Sit down together at the end of each day and talk about all that went on. Refrain from solving problems, and just listen.
- Get ready for bed together, and go to bed at the same time. You have an opportunity to end the day together listening to each other, holding each other.

Show Her an Understanding Heart

Are you judgmental with your wife? You probably quickly answered no to this question. But think about it. Do you, either by your words or your attitude, sometimes make her feel ashamed or silly about the way she feels? Do you tell her she worries too much? When she dreams big, do you offer reasons why it won't work, or do you get defensive?

Is she worried about how busy your family schedule is next month? And have you responded with, "Don't worry about anything. It always works out." How about trying, "Honey, we really do have a lot going on. Let's take a look at our calendar and just walk through some of the plans." I can guarantee you that when you finish talking, your calendar will look exactly the same. But by spending a few minutes talking through it with your wife, you'll give her an incredible sense of relief.

When a woman sees her husband willing to open up and share with her—and beyond this, to show understanding and the desire to help lift *her* burdens—she will in turn honor him and his needs. If her emotional needs aren't fulfilled, however, she'll feel disconnected. And when this happens twenty-three-and-a-half hours a day, you may as well forget trying to connect physically in that final half hour. I can assure you there will be *no* connection. But *beware:* If your motivation to connect emotionally with your wife is just to get her to connect physically, she will see right through you.

She's watching you every day, all week. If you are not consistently tender and appreciative, she will find it difficult to trust you and give herself to you completely. For a woman, intimacy must be genuine and constant, and believe me, she knows if you just turn on the charm when you want her in the bedroom.

God wired women with the desire to experience mutual emotional nurturing. The moment you realize how strong this need is for your wife—and you're willing to go the extra mile in achieving it—your marriage can be transformed!

Want a few tips?

- Write her a letter, and tell her everything that has been burdening you. If you let her into the deepest parts of your heart, it will change both of your lives.
- Pray with her daily. And remember to thank God, in her hearing, that he has given you such a wonderful wife.
- Meet her for lunch, and ask her what you could do to lighten her load.
- Enter the conversation when she is sharing a story or burden by repeating what you heard and cheering her on. She needs you to be her advocate.
- Tune in to your wife the minute you walk through the door at the end of the day.

Give Her Attention and Affection

The Bible encourages husbands to be attentive to their wives. "In the same way, you husbands must give honor to your wives. Treat her with understanding as you live together" (1 Pet. 3:7).

Has your wife ever said, "You are not paying enough attention to our marriage"? If she has, she is really saying, "I feel emotionally distant from you, and you're not paying enough attention to *me!*" How did you win her in the first place? You gave her your undivided attention. You listened to her. You were thoughtful about the small things.

A loving husband cares for and nurtures the real woman inside his wife. Be specific. Point out positive changes she has made in her life. Stop and take a good look at what she's doing in her world. But do more than notice; say it out loud. Your wife also needs your closeness, your nonsexual touch that communicates genuine caring and reminds her that she is loved for more than just her body. Your gentle touch communicates to her: "I'm here. You're not alone. I enjoy you. I'll take care of you."

Attention to the smallest details shows your wife you are thinking of her and that she's the most important person in your world. Romance her:

- Give her a kiss and a hug when you leave and return home.
- Buy tickets to a musical that she loves.
- Give her a long-stemmed rose as a public declaration that you love her.
- Make an effort to spend time alone together: go out to dinner, go for a walk, go out for coffee. Show her (and others) that you enjoy the intimacy of being alone with her.
- Go with her when she runs errands to the mall, grocery store, or bank. Show her that you enjoy being her companion.
- Surprise her with a picnic lunch, including tablecloth and candlesticks. Or build a romantic fire, and snuggle together with a blanket and hot chocolate.

Build Rapport with Her

When men talk to each other, they report. They talk about scores, highlights, events of the weekend, new car performance—the list is endless. In their "report talk" men condense their stories and edit out the details to get to the point quickly.

Women, however, are wired for "rapport talk." Details are important to women. We don't want the abridged version; we want the whole nine yards. As we talk, we discover who we are and why we think the way we do. We process as we discuss. We resolve issues as we converse. We talk it through. Somehow our hearing, speech, and thoughts are all interrelated, and we need to have all three working at once to express ourselves fully.

So if you want to connect emotionally with your wife, you must build rapport with her. Your wife wants to know what you are thinking. She wants to process things with you.

Pay close attention to your wife when she reaches out to you, but don't always try to offer answers. Much of the time she simply wants you to join her as she processes her thoughts. She needs an audience that loves her.

As you try to build rapport with your wife, remember these guidelines:

- Don't see every complaint as an attack. Women think that as long as they feel the marriage is working, they can talk about it. Men feel that the relationship isn't working if they have to talk about it. When your wife brings up a grievance, try to see it as an act of love.
- Resist the urge to solve it—whatever "it" is. Your wife needs you to

acknowledge her feelings; she needs to know that what she is saying is registering with you. Even if you don't agree with her,
your acknowledgment of her emotions lets her know that you aren't dismissing them by overlooking them and rushing to suggest a solution.

- Recognize her strong emotions as exclamation marks. When she is upset, angry, or frustrated, realize that these emotions are her way of letting you know how very much this matters to her.
- Reserve your judgment. Listen to her and empathize. Allow her to feel heard and understood.
- Have a respectful attitude. Don't presume to know her thoughts and understand her feelings.
- Find the treasure in the facts. Gather information from what she is communicating, and validate what she has done right. There's a good saying for this: "Make the most of the best, and the least of the worst." Far too often we reverse it and discourage our spouse.
- Be there emotionally. If she is struggling, the last thing she needs is to be told why she shouldn't be struggling. What she needs is for you to be there *with* her.

Resolve Conflict

In Ephesians 4:31-32, Paul tells us to "get rid of all bitterness, rage, anger, harsh words, and slander, as well as all types of malicious behavior. Instead, be kind to each other, tenderhearted, forgiving one another, just as God through Christ has forgiven you."

You cannot connect emotionally if you are living with, or stirring up, resentment, bitterness, or anger. These emotions are toxic to a relationship. In the spiritual realm, the enemy uses these emotions as doorways to usher in every kind of disorder in a marriage.

Since you are reading this book, I know you have some level of commitment to your wife. Draw on the power of your wedding vows, and allow this commitment to break you loose from the chains of disharmony that can so easily keep you from true emotional intimacy.

Resist any desire to use critical, resentful, or sarcastic words. After a marriage seminar, one wife wrote me this note: "How grateful I am for the impact your talk made on Rick in the men's session at the Five Love Needs of Men and Women Conference. He has heard it a *million* times:

Words hurt women! But your word picture of how it physically hurts us, as if beaten by stones, finally hit home."

Harsh, brash, and critical words bruise your wife's soul and break her spirit. Verbal abuse is every bit as bad as physical abuse. It doesn't leave any physical scars, but the emotional damage is just as devastating and painful. You hold your wife's heart in your hands. It will be forever changed for good or for evil because of the impact of your words.

You've heard the expression, "Don't give it a second thought." Well, you can't afford to give negative thoughts and negative comments a foothold—a second thought—if you want to remain clearheaded and cleanhearted with your spouse. A woman will never connect emotionally, intimately, with a man who tears her down.

Have you ever been around couples like that? Where you cringe emotionally when you hear a husband say cutting things to his wife? Critical words. Demeaning words. "Put her in her place" kinds of words.

I cringed over that very thing recently in an airport. I was in the baggage-claim area waiting for my luggage when I noticed a man and a woman with a pushcart jam-packed with luggage. Suddenly he stopped, spun around, and started yelling at her. I couldn't hear what he was saying, but just the look on his face frightened me. Sometimes the expression on your face, let alone the full impact of your words, can frighten your wife.

Denying honest emotions isn't healthy, but neither is making a habit of "throwing up" the negative ones just so you'll feel better. It's not trite to say that when you're angry or frustrated, talk to God. If you don't learn to manage these toxic emotions in a healthy way, I promise that one of three things will occur: Your wife will respond by fighting, fleeing, or freezing. All three are bad options.

Is there conflict in your relationship? Are you aware of anything for which you need to forgive your wife? Are you harboring any bitterness over anything in your relationship? If so, it's important to resolve your conflict.

Peter has an extremely close-knit extended family, and it was hard for his family to accept Linda into their circle when they got married. And Peter did not help the situation. In theory, he put Linda first, but in action, he had a hard time letting go of Mom and Dad. For example, if Peter and Linda made plans for the weekend but his mother called and invited them for dinner, guess what they did? You guessed it. They dropped their plans and went to his parents' house for dinner. For three years Peter and Linda fought over this issue. Every conflict seemed to arouse that smoldering issue—that Peter couldn't cut the apron strings. It worsened with each conflict until finally Linda had had it! Peter's dependency on his family was ruining a potentially healthy marriage, but she was tired of talking about it. So she reverted to silence.

Linda's withdrawal startled Peter—and scared him. Enough so that for the first time he began to see the truth. He realized the pain he had caused his wife by allowing his relationship with his parents to be more important than his relationship with her. Peter and Linda got down to business and resolved to let go of all the pain that they had caused in each other. They vowed to move on. They haven't had conflict over the issue since.

If you have conflict in your marriage, work through it. Talk to God about it. Then talk to your wife. Forgive if you need to. Confess if you need to. Let go of your resentments. Harboring resentments may offer an immediate sense of gratification or power, but resentments fester and ultimately control you. The way to restore harmony in your marriage is to remove resentments, not relive them. No marriage is capable of recovering from disappointments and moving on to maturity unless both husband and wife let go of bitterness. You can't trust and love your wife while you are either secretly or openly resentful of her.

Letting go of the grudges, the bitterness, the resentment, the anger is something we do for ourselves as well as for our partner. Anger darkens our own hearts. And when we are in darkness, we cannot live in the light. God must be the source of that letting go—that forgiveness—as we draw from the deep well he supplies. God wants us to love as we have been loved, to comfort as we have been comforted, and to forgive as we have been forgiven (1 John 4:11; 2 Cor. 1:4; Eph. 4:32).

Safeguard Your Relationships

To put it bluntly, it is easy for a man to begin capturing another woman's heart without even realizing it. You think you're just having an enjoyable conversation with a coworker, but she may see it as the only attention she's had all week. Before you know it, your conversations move from friendly chatter to intimate subjects. I'm not suggesting you can't have friendships with other women. I'm only warning you that it's easier than you think to capture the heart of another woman outside of your marriage.

Here are some danger signals to look for in other women:

- Flattery
- Intense eye contact
- Inappropriate gushing
- Excessive reference to your importance
- Wanting to talk about intimate topics
- Touching your arm or rubbing your back during conversation
- Talking more about you than about her husband
- Performing as if you're her audience

Think of it this way, if this woman invited you into her house and you were alone, would the topics and conversation stay the same as they do in public and/or with an audience? If she is suggestive in her conversation, confiding about her husband's not meeting her needs, causing you to sympathize with her or pity her, watch out. Does she tell stories that have any suggestive tone or lead you to see her in that light? Does she make references to her body or inferences about her bedroom?

I know this may sound extreme, but it is best if you do not encourage touch with a woman other than your wife. If a woman is touching physically, it's a good indication she is touching emotionally. If you are accessing the emotions of a woman other than your wife, you are entering a major danger zone. It is as intimate for her as preparing for sex. It is that serious. No matter how appealing the attention of another woman is to your manhood, an innocent friendship can quickly take you by surprise and lead you down a path that you'll soon regret.

A word of advice: Trust your wife's instincts in this area. If she suggests that another woman is behaving inappropriately, your wife is probably right. Most women have radar, an innate alertness to nonverbal communication and an ability to translate body language into emotional facts. Your wife probably is able to see these things clearly, so don't criticize or blame her warnings on insecurity. Regard it as a gift from God that will keep you out of danger.

THE REWARDS OF EMOTIONAL INTIMACY

The summer before our younger daughter, Missy, was going off to college, I drove her to her favorite place in the world, Kamp Kanakuk.

For twenty-six days she would be a camper with significant leadership responsibilities with two hundred young girls from across the nation.

While this trip had a very special meaning for our daughter, it also had overwhelming significance for me. I knew this was the beginning of the end of an era. I would soon be facing an empty nest. Our two little girls were all grown up. When Missy returned home, she would immediately leave for college. At the same time we were planning our daughter Sarah's wedding. As a mother, I felt as if a lifetime of support, involvement, and commitment was about to vanish over the horizon, and I would wake up—without our children.

I hung around the camp as long as I could and helped Missy get settled. Then, finally, I knew I had to leave. We were both crying as we hugged each other. Then I pulled myself together momentarily, told her to have a wonderful time, and began my eight-hour drive back home.

I wanted to get home to Gary as soon as I could—I needed to connect with him and feel his support and understanding—so I decided to take a shortcut. By cutting across some two-lane country roads, I could knock an hour off the trip. My mind swirled with thoughts of Missy, our little girl. When did she grow up? I needed her. She brought us such joy. Then I began to weep again when I realized that I was driving alone into *the rest of my life without our daughters at home.* More and more tears gushed, to the point where I couldn't see a thing. I pulled off to the side of the road and buried my face in my arms, crying out my pain.

Just then, Gary called on the car phone, and I let loose. We talked, cried, looked to the future, and talked some more. Gary was so connected to me that I was convinced he was in the car with me. Finally we hung up, and I began driving again. I felt sustained and strengthened for the rest of the journey. I just wanted to get home and collapse into the arms of my husband—my soul mate and best friend.

My confidence had been restored, but Gary's confidence in me was waning. He was concerned about my driving alone over such a great distance. He began calling me, checking on how I was doing. He was concerned about my safety and dealt with it by trying to fix the problem. He pressured me to pull off the road and stay overnight at a motel. *Forget his solution,* I thought. The idea made me furious. I needed his presence, his companionship; I needed *him,* not some motel room. I would gladly have driven to the end of the earth to find him.

Several phone calls later, Gary announced that he had made a hotel reservation in Kansas City, midway between home and the camp. I was pretty angry with him at this point. What he didn't tell me was that he was, even at that moment, driving four hours to meet me in that hotel room. When I arrived, he was there waiting for me! He knew what I needed; I needed his presence. He met me emotionally, and once again I was confident and flourishing.

The next morning as the sun came up, I opened one eye and heard that wonderful voice say, "Baby, baby, baby." I smiled and thought, *Hey, maybe having an empty nest won't be all bad!* And I was more convinced than ever that as a couple we could go through anything—as long as we went through it emotionally intimate and always together.

The way Gary set the tone that day by ushering in our empty nesting with such a strong, emotionally supportive posture is the kind of sacrificial love and intimate connection he has demonstrated over and over in our relationship. It is the kind of emotional intimacy that has built a fortress of protection around our marriage.

I encourage you to build walls of protection around your wife by committing yourself to meet her need for emotional intimacy and communication. If you do, she will blossom and move closer to you, both emotionally and physically. This truly is the key to a woman's heart.

CHAPTER 5

FRIENDSHIP

A HUSBAND'S #3 LOVE NEED

"I need you as my most trusted companion."

Gary talks to wives

B arb, I'm coming home. I need to talk to you right away. I've got some great news that I need to tell you in person!"

I knew that other people would be eager to hear this news, too, but I wanted Barb to hear it first. And I wanted her to hear it straight from me.

When I walked in the back door, Barb was waiting for me. "Barb, it's wonderful," I said, smiling broadly. "My dad just trusted Christ as his Savior!"

To understand the significance of that announcement, you need to have a little history. I did not grow up in a Christian home. Our family went to church, gave money, and respected God, but I never heard about a personal relationship with Jesus Christ until 1973, when I heard a Campus Crusade for Christ presentation in my college fraternity. By the summer of 1973 I had committed my life to Jesus Christ as my Lord and Savior.

When I told my parents about this, my father reacted strongly. He thought I had joined a cult and was afraid I was heading off the deep end. Almost immediately I found myself stuck between the proverbial rock and a hard place. I was thirsty for this new relationship with Christ and incredibly burdened for my dad's salvation, but I also needed his affirmation, which he wasn't about to give.

For the next twenty-one years I prayed for my father and shared my faith with him intermittently to no avail. Then, on the eve of his seventy-fifth birthday, as he was facing serious heart surgery, I wrote him a letter and handed it to him just before I left town. In this letter I recounted dozens of father-son memories we had experienced together. I also assured him that if he didn't survive the surgery, I would take care of Mom, financially and emotionally. Finally, I told him once again about his need for a personal relationship with Jesus Christ. I told him that if he didn't survive the surgery and if I hadn't taken the risk to share my heart and the Good News with him one last time, I would regret it for the rest of my life.

The last words in the letter were these: "Dad . . . I will call you in two days, just before the day of your surgery, and ask you one question: 'Did you pray that prayer [salvation prayer] on page 205 in my book *Guard Your Heart?*'"

When I called two days later, my mom asked, "What did you say to your dad in that letter? He is carrying around your book with his finger in a page, but he won't show me the page. He just keeps reading it, Gary."

"Put him on the phone, Mom."

When my father came on the line, I asked him, "Dad, did you pray that prayer?"

"Son, today I became a Christian," he said.

You can't imagine the joy that thrilled my soul when I heard those words, and the first thing I wanted to do was get home and tell Barb—my wife, my lover, my best friend, the one who had prayed with me all these years for my father's salvation. Other people had prayed too—our daughters, my prayer-group buddies—but Barb had to be the first to hear the news.

I wanted to tell Barb first because, bottom line, best friends tell each other their greatest fears and joys. That is what the friendship part of a marriage is all about.

The look in her eyes when I walked through the door was worth a thousand words. It said to me: "You always believed, Gary, and your greatest desire has just been realized. You have the assurance of eternal life with your dad." When your wife, as your best friend, gets to share in the mountaintop experiences of life after you've endured the pain of the valley together, you truly are on the mountaintop. It really doesn't get any better than this. This really is what marriage is all about: intimacy achieved through the locking together of two hearts, souls, and minds in the midst of both joy and pain.

When the rubber meets the road, there is one person I know I can count on no matter what. Barb. And no matter how much I bond with my brothers in Christ at a men's conference or in our weekly accountability groups, Barb really is my number one friend—my best friend.

Just as Barb had received me in unconditional love the day I came home with the painful news of losing half of our income (as I shared in chapter 1), she received me on this day in celebration. That's what best friends do: They receive you regardless of the story you bring. Whether it's pain, hurt, hope, loss, or celebration. Friends, best friends, connect to you in the midst of any experience. That's what being a soul mate with your spouse is all about.

When I share the story of my dad's salvation, people readily resonate with my celebration of God's faithfulness. It stimulates some to tell me of their own answered prayers and encourages others to tell me of their hope that their prayers about a loved one will someday be answered. One day at a conference, however, a woman asked me, "Just what did Barb say and do that made you feel so connected? I would love to access my husband's heart as his best friend." As I told her, it was really a number of things.

- Barb dropped everything and gave me her undivided attention.
- Barb connected to my soul with a deep expression of joy and celebrated with me.
- Because Barb had prayed with me for so long, her genuine, heartfelt prayers were also answered, so she rejoiced in God's working in both of our lives.

What did I need from her at that moment? Her attention. Access to her soul. Her genuine gratefulness that her best friend was celebrating the answer to his longest ongoing prayer. That's what best friends do: They give as well as seek; they put aside their agendas to search out the heart of the other; they feel *with* you rather than impose their own feelings on you.

My friendship with Barb is what defines much of our marriage. I not only love her with an *agape* (unconditional Christlike) love. I also am in love with her with an *eros* (romantic) love. But my deep *phileo* (friendship) love for my wife is as essential as my *agape* and *eros* love are.

It is no coincidence that our survey research about spouses' love needs indicates that a husband's top three love needs mirror the biblical descriptions of love. *Agape, eros,* and *phileo* love topped husbands' responses to needs in their marriages (and in that order).

Sadly, I have seen a pattern over and over in the counseling room: A man and woman fall in love romantically, commit to each other in marriage, but lack the depth of friendship love in their relationship.

Renee and Patrick are an example. Renee told me in a counseling session, "If I were really honest—and I don't know how to admit this even to myself, let alone tell Patrick—I am the one standing in the way of building a strong friendship in our marriage."

It took courage for Renee to admit this, but that confession was the beginning of their ability to build a great marriage. Patrick wanted a deep friendship with Renee, but she just wouldn't let him in. Renee had been abandoned by her father when she was a teenager. Just when she was at a critical time of adolescent development, her dad left his wife and four children. The day her dad left, Renee promised herself, "I will never trust a man again." Now Patrick was unwittingly paying the price for her father's betrayal. Renee's past experience and lack of trust got in the way, and rather than looking at *phileo* love for her husband as the means of building an intimate relationship with him, she just pretended things were fine. Only when Renee began to tear down her own self-protective walls and deal with the unresolved pain of her past did she begin to step close to Patrick. Today, their relationship is growing as their openness and trust is strengthened day by day.

I know it sounds like a paradox to say that you have to let go in order to build up, but it is true. Walls aren't built in a day, and they can't be torn down quickly. Instead, they need to come down brick by brick. The internal walls that divide a husband and wife need to be replaced with a healthy wall around the marriage. This, then, allows us to take risks and experience vulnerability and transparency within the marriage relationship, and when that happens, two souls connect in *phileo* love.

WHAT DOES YOUR HUSBAND NEED IN A FRIENDSHIP WITH YOU?

On our survey, the love need that ranked third among the greatest percentage of men is companionship, or friendship. This really shouldn't surprise us. Ever since God placed Adam, the first man, on the earth, men have needed to be completed by their wives. I often tell people, "I am not good alone. I need Barb." Adam experienced the same thing as he named the animals. He was alone. He just didn't realize his aloneness until he saw all the pairs he was naming. There he was, working in the Garden of Eden when "the Lord God said, 'It is not good for the man to be alone. I will make a companion who will help him'" (Gen. 2:18). So as Adam was fulfilling God's plan for him by naming the animals, God was fulfilling his plan for Adam: "The Lord God caused Adam to fall into a deep sleep. He took one of Adam's ribs and closed up the place from which he had taken it. Then the Lord God made a woman from the rib and brought her to Adam" (Gen. 2:21-22).

God brought Eve to Adam to complete him. They were the original soul mates. The kind of friendship they experienced has been an important need for men and women ever since. We want that close relationship, just as God wanted a relationship with his creation. We as men need our wives' friendship. Adam needed Eve. I need Barb. Your husband needs you. This may sound like a mystery, so let's dig a little deeper.

We must decipher what a man means when he says, "I need my wife's friendship and companionship." We also need to compare that to what you mean when you think in those terms.

When you hear the word *friendship,* what goes through your mind? Vulnerability? Transparency? Heart-to-heart communication? These are probably a good start in describing a woman's needs. Now, allow me to give you some insight into your husband's heart. He needs the same things, but he probably won't articulate it in the same way or in the same terms. He knows, at least deep down, that he wants to be safe with you to explore what he is churning around in his heart and mind. The truth is, he is probably somewhat insecure inside, but he is unlikely to tell you that straight out. He just knows that if he takes a risk with you, he doesn't want to be judged or rejected. Most guys I know want to reach out; they just don't want to be misunderstood.

Have you ever heard anyone say these kinds of things: "I thought we had plenty of time." Or, "Where have the years gone?" Or, "I never thought we would grow old so quickly."

If you are in your twenties or thirties, you're probably thinking, *Give me a break. That sounds like something my parents or grandparents would say.* Well, you won't believe how quickly the years are going to fly past. When our kids are young, we dream of having time alone with our spouse. (Hey, when they are really young, we dream of just getting four hours of uninterrupted sleep!) But before you know it, you are in your forties and staring into an empty nest. You long for some noise in the house from the kids and their friends.

So here's the scoop: Start building those friendship patterns as early as possible in your marriage relationship. Is it too late to do so later in life? No. But the earlier you start, the better you end. Not only will you be great role models for your children, but you and your husband will benefit from the added dimension that true friendship brings to your relationship.

Friendship doesn't happen overnight, even between marriage partners. Aren't you suspicious of anyone who claims that a recent acquaintance is "my new best friend"? True friendship, which involves trust and vulnerability, honesty and encouragement, shared interests and activities, takes time to develop and mature. And friendship between marriage partners requires the same. I call it "the velveteen rabbit syndrome." By the time our hair is rubbed off and our eyes go bad, we're finally comfortable with each other. We're comfortable enough to say what we need to say and be what we need to be with honor and grace and without condemnation.

Your husband wants to be able to put on his favorite stretched-out sweatshirt and his favorite pair of jeans and be at home with you. You know, the sweatshirt that you keep threatening to use for rags and the jeans that don't look too good but fit just right and are his first choice when the closet door opens. It takes time to get them there. The stiff stage, the "nice pants" stage, has to be worked through to get them comfy. The same is true in a marriage. You have to work through the relationship until you reach the friendship and companionship stage, which makes a great marriage feel "comfortable."

With that in mind, then, let's look at some of the ways your husband may need your friendship.

He Needs You to Have Realistic Expectations

In a play on the title of Wellington Boone's book *Your Wife Is Not Your Momma,* I want to remind you that "your husband is not your girlfriend." Think about that. Wives and husbands approach this need for friendship differently.

Your husband is never going to be just like "one of the girls." That's not the kind of friendship and companionship he needs from you. He isn't one of the girls. And you don't want him to be.

What Barb says she needs from a female friend is a ton of words, a trusting relationship in which she can explore a whole range of emotions, and a whopper of a hug when the conversation ends on a deeper note. What I often need from Barb, as a friend, are fewer words, a short range of emotion so I don't feel out of control, and a whopper of a hug after a heart-to-heart conversation.

A while back I was eavesdropping on Barb while she was on the phone with a friend. They were bouncing from feeling to feeling and topic to topic. When she was done, I said, "How could anyone make any sense of that? I know how to solve your problem. Just do this . . ."

Barb shook her head and profoundly said, "Gary, you just aren't a woman."

To which I responded, "Thank you, Jesus."

She ignored me and continued, "I know you like to 'speak woman' at times, but you weren't designed to be my girlfriend . . . just my best friend."

That was a brilliant statement. When I think of realistic expectations as a friendship component of our marriage, I think of us both realizing who we are and who we aren't. At times of intense pressure I will use a lot of words. At times of exuberant joy I may explode with a lot of words. But in the day-to-day experiences of life, ministry, and family times, I may not express what I am thinking and feeling with as many words. That doesn't mean I don't need Barb. It means I need her to understand that fewer words do not mean less of a need for companionship.

You need to grab on to that realization with your husband as well. We as men don't dip into that whole range of emotions as frequently, expressing them as readily and as freely as you do. When you do experience that with us, you want more of it—and that makes sense. Just realize that most men won't go there as often or perhaps as deeply. Am I saying, "Take what you can get, but don't expect a lot more"? Perhaps. But, more important, I am encouraging you to receive your husband and model deep communication, but be realistic in your expectations of him.

And when he does "go there with you," remember to keep it between the two of you.

He Needs You to Speak the Truth in Love

Being honest means being vulnerable, and vulnerability can be murky water for men. First of all, it's *very* tough for men to open up to other men, primarily because of this pride thing we have going. It's often called "being macho," but what it really is, is being afraid of looking like a jerk. If we get too honest, we figure we're admitting we need someone to help fix a problem. In essence we're saying, "I don't know how to do this. Will you tell me?" (It's like having to stop and ask for directions!) Then we feel inadequate, and when we feel that way, we're afraid we'll end up looking like a jerk. And we hate looking like a jerk to another man. But there is one thing we hate even more: looking like a jerk to you.

But if we husbands are truly going to be best friends with our wives, we have to develop a level of trust that will enable us to feel that we can be honest with them.

Last summer Barb and I were standing in the kitchen one morning, waiting for the coffee to brew, when I asked her what I thought would be a simple question: "Honey, can you think of a time when you saw me full of pride but I didn't recognize it?" Her response caught me off guard because she used my vulnerability to lovingly but honestly point out something we had never even discussed.

A few months earlier I had spoken at a large secular event where there were several TV cameras and bright lights. A little too bright for my own good, as it turned out. The governor of Iowa, who happens to be a dear friend as well as a member of my weekly men's Bible study, preceded me at the podium and made some gracious comments about me. When I spoke, the crowd responded positively to my presentation, and I felt that I had managed the tenuous balance of bringing home a message to a secular audience while not violating the trust the meeting planners had in me to "play it straight" (that is, not preach).

Following the event, Barb and I went out for dinner, and I began talking about the achievement of the evening, with a little too much of *me* in the discussion. Now, Barb reminded me of this and told me how on that evening she felt, for the first time, that I was beginning to believe my own press clippings.

When she said that, a cold chill crept down my spine. One of my greatest concerns is that I never forget that apart from God I can do nothing.

"Honey, I had never seen you like that before," Barb said. "It wasn't evident from the platform, but at dinner it was as if you were bitten by the enemy, and you began to swell up. It was almost as if you had an allergic reaction to a bug bite. I remember praying that God would meet you at that point and would gently do his work in you to bring you back to the place I see you day in and day out." She paused and looked me in the eye to see how I was taking her honesty, then continued. "You have a servant's heart and a humility that demonstrates the anointing that God has blessed you with." (I didn't recognize it at the time, but she was wisely doing some rebuilding to the minor alterations she had given my ego.) "But I have to admit, Gary. I was a little scared that night."

There's no doubt that I took a risk when I made myself vulnerable by asking Barb that question. But Barb also took a risk when she was honest with me about my behavior. At first I felt insecure and wanted to defend myself. Then I realized that this truly was my best friend talking to me.

Barb told me the truth—as a best friend would—and her timing was perfect. In addition, she did it with a tone of comfort, encouragement, and grace. As my loving wife *and* my best friend, she met me at my most vulnerable spot (my pride) and gently gave me a dose of reality. She didn't treat me like an ego-infested idiot but rather like a man in process. And she waited until I was both receptive and teachable. (She didn't nail me at the dinner table that night after the event because she sensed that I wasn't ready to hear it then.)

In all of these ways, she reinforced my trust in her and in our relationship.

He Needs You to Be Forgiving

Kent came to me after I recently spoke to our men's group about a husband's need to be best friends with his wife. "I want to know Nina," he said, "and I want her to know me, but we aren't close. I have this hole in my heart the size of a Mack truck. I can't think of the last time she encouraged or affirmed anything about me. We have four great kids. Our business is flourishing. But when it comes to this marriage . . . well, I just feel empty. She seems to find fault in everything I do."

I knew the whole story, so I was aware that early in their marriage, Kent had messed up by working sixteen- to eighteen-hour days while trying to establish a business. Then Nina drifted away and had an emotional relationship with Kent's best friend. When Kent found out, he did the right thing. Instead of putting all of the blame on her, he sought her forgiveness and did everything he could to close that loop of bitterness.

Unfortunately, while Nina forgave Kent on the outside, her anger simmered for years. She was still resentful that Kent had not met her emotional needs early in the marriage, when she deeply needed him to know her the way she needed to be known: her fears, her passion, her hopes and dreams. Kent continued to try to reach out to her, but her punishing behaviors kept coming to the surface when they would begin to get close.

"I just don't think she will ever let it go," he continued. "I feel that no matter what I do, I'm still paying for my past mistake. The trust is shot. So when I hear you talk about my having an intimate friendship with my wife, it sounds great. But I just can't see getting to that point."

Many couples live with the kind of painful distance that Kent is talking about. The reasons may be different, but the result is the same. Perhaps your husband made some immature mistakes early in your marriage. Maybe he piled up incredible financial debt that you're still trying to recover from. Perhaps your husband was incredibly selfish about his sexual desires, totally disregarding your needs. Perhaps he has given first place to his career, developing workaholic patterns. Perhaps he's been insensitive about your career—or the reverse, your desire to be a full-time homemaker.

All kinds of things can cause problems in a marriage, and they need to be dealt with. But we must not allow past issues, or even current patterns, to get in the way of building a great marriage. We need to work through the problems, and once we have done so, we must not carry the bitterness with us.

He Needs You to Be Honest

One of the things I know about myself is that honesty is a major building block of my relationships. Whether it is with Barb, our daughters, my friends, or my ministry team, I put a high value on honesty. So does your husband, I would guess. Honesty builds trust. Trust builds friendship. Dishonesty breaks down trust. Distrust impairs healthy relationships.

When a husband knows his wife is honest with him, he begins to trust her and becomes increasingly vulnerable with her. When he senses he can't trust her, he pulls back or becomes more controlling. This is manifested in the way we do all sorts of things in our marriages: handling our finances, parenting the kids, communicating with our parents, or deciding how to spend our time. When a husband knows that his wife's yes is yes and her no is no, he begins to trust her.

If she tries to cover up or is dishonest about spending patterns, trust breaks down. If she changes their agreed-upon parental discipline with the children, trust breaks down. If his parents call and ask them to come for the weekend and she fabricates an excuse, trust breaks down.

Please know that each of these examples can go both ways. Some husbands are not trustworthy in their finances or in their fathering. Some husbands may invent obstacles when they want to avoid a weekend with their in-laws. But on either side, such behavior breaks down trust.

Honesty is crucial in building your marriage relationship and meeting each other's needs. Without honesty, ordinary friendships are flimsy or superficial at best. But without honesty in marriage, true companionship between husband and wife is impossible.

He Needs You to Enter His World

Barb was having lunch with some of her female friends one afternoon, and one of the women began complaining that her husband was going golfing too often.

"Why don't you go with him?" Barb asked.

"I can't stand to golf!" her friend proclaimed.

"But you love your husband, Anna. Go out and play with him. Join him. Crawl into his world."

What Barb helped her friend get a handle on was that you don't have to be "good" at everything your husband excels at and you don't have to be as enthusiastic about things as he is. What matters to him is that you validate his interest and join him in some of his activities. Play with him. Recreate with him. Certainly he will have "his things," and you will have "your things." You may never like bagging a pheasant, and he may never get excited over a new mall in town, but you can walk alongside him through a field some beautiful fall day, and he can walk alongside you during a trip to the new department store.

What excites your husband? Playing the stock market? Join an investment club and learn the lingo. Watching a football game? Pop some corn and join him for a quarter of the game. This doesn't mean that the stock market or football has to become your passion; what it does mean is that *your husband* needs to be your passion. Just as you desire your husband to enter your world, enter his. Encourage him. Cheer him on. If you don't, who will? (And we don't even want to go there.)

HOW CAN YOU MEET YOUR HUSBAND'S FRIENDSHIP NEEDS?

To understand the basic components of your husband's need for a best friend and soul mate, let me recap here.

Temper your expectations of your husband by remembering that he is a man. Don't try to treat him as if he's your girlfriend. Enjoy his masculinity. Treasure those precious times of deep and open transparency he shares with you, but realize that he probably won't give you a daily diet of deep and vulnerable communication.

Build and strengthen the trust between you and your husband. When he blows it, as I did that night at dinner, deal with him honorably and graciously. Remember that a few sharp words from you can tear him down quickly. Allow the Holy Spirit to control your tongue and your comments. Build him up, especially when you are commenting on his behavior.

Exercise forgiveness, and then let the offense go. Don't keep harboring it or rehearsing the hurt with harsh behavior. Even when we forgive, we don't forget completely. Only God has the capacity to do that. Sometimes we need to remember so that we can help each other learn what we are hearing from God. But we want to remember with grace.

Take a firm approach to honesty—not in a way that is harsh and condescending, but trustworthy and edifying. Couples who have deep, mature relationships of trust and friendship are committed to that kind of foundational honesty.

Step closer to your husband by stepping into his world and enjoying the passions of his life. While his choice of recreation or relaxation may not be your first choice of the way to spend an afternoon or a vacation, *he* is your first choice. And your stepping into his world will only encourage him to learn to step into yours.

Let Your Husband Know You Want to Be His Best Friend

Ed was awestruck when he heard me tell our weekly men's study group that our wives desire not only to be our friends but also to be our *best* friends.

"I never heard Charlene say that she needed this from me," he told me later. "I'm going home to ask her tonight, and I'll let you know next week what she said. I think you missed the boat on this one, Rosberg."

After our meeting on the following week, Ed told me, "You were right. When I asked her why she hadn't told me this, she said she thought I would think it could never happen, so she didn't even want to take the risk. It really opened up some good discussion."

The best place to start building your friendship with your husband is by informing him that, from your perspective, this is a real need in your relationship. Your husband grew up hanging around the guys and doing "stuff" with them. Playing sports. Driving cars. Hanging out. When men get married, they sometimes need to learn how to do "stuff" with their wives. If your husband knows you want to spend time with him—other than just taking care of the household needs and parenting the kids—he may take the risk to ask you to join him. Where do you start?

- Take inventory of some of your husband's hobbies and interests, and ask him if you can join him in one of them.
- Read up on some of the things he is interested in, and begin to tell him what you are learning.
- Ask him questions about what he is doing at work, at play, in leisure. Not the kinds of questions that feel like an inquisition, but the kind that show real interest.
- Share some of your own experiences with him to draw him closer to you as well.
- Tell him that you need *phileo* (friendship) love from him and that this biblical kind of love is important to you too.
- Remind him that your relationship is a secure and safe place to sort out whatever is going on in his heart. Anytime. Anyplace.

Make Your Relationship a Safe Place for Your Husband to Face His Pain

Many men are working through some painful events or some unresolved issues in their lives. An alcoholic dad. A broken family. Hard knocks as a kid. The list is endless.

The truth is, you may very well be the key to helping him work through these issues. Some people may say, "That sounds as if you're breeding codependent relationships." That's not what I'm saying at all. Your husband is responsible for taking his issues to the Lord just as you are responsible for your own issues before the Lord. Only your husband can deal with the pain in his heart by humbling himself and taking a strong and honest look at life.

As his wife and best friend, however, you can be—and need to be—the safe place for him to go when he's ready to sink below the waterline. Your encouragement, support, and nurture can help create an environment in which he feels able to confront his pain and begin to deal with it.

Tell him he is safe with you. Remind him that you are there for him. Show him in words and deeds that nothing can separate you from him and that nothing can get in the way of God's love for him. Then tell him again. And again. And again.

When Chad learned that his mother was leaving his dad, everything that had made sense seemed to be thrown to the wind. He didn't want to admit to anyone the deep pain he felt, not even to Jan, his wife. But as he got quieter and quieter and pulled further into himself, she lovingly created a safe environment in which he could deal with his pain. Finally, one night everything he had dammed up broke through, and he admitted what he was thinking and feeling. "Jan, I can't believe my mother is leaving my father. After all the years of raising us kids with the message that a Christian home stays together, she walks out on him? I know he can be a pain to live with sometimes, but this is really wrong."

How did Jan create a safe place for Chad when his world was turned upside down?

- She listened and didn't judge.
- She validated his feelings and fears.
- She encouraged him not only to take the time to sort out the issue with his mom but also to seek God's direction in how to communicate with her.
- She reminded him she would never leave him.
- She reminded him that the Cross is the safest place on earth.

Be Willing to Love Sacrificially

Are you holding back things that are important to your husband until you get what's important to you? You're only human. Yet as we build intimate, soul-deep marriages, we need to love our spouses sacrificially. We need to love them in a manner that is welcoming, in a manner that says to each other, "I want to be God with skin on to you." "I want to love you as God loves you—unconditionally, without reserve." "I want you to welcome me into your life just as I want to welcome you into mine."

When you withhold *welcoming love* from your spouse, you are living in a conditional relationship. And for a follower of Jesus Christ, this is unacceptable. The number one example—the most profound example—of sacrificial love is God's provision of his Son as our only means to eternal life. I know I discussed this in the first chapter, but it bears repeating: We need to follow our Savior's lead and love as he loves. If he held back his blessings the way many of us hold back our love from our spouses, if his love for us were conditional the way we make our love conditional, we would be miserable on earth and never find ourselves in heaven.

We bring absolutely nothing that can earn our salvation. So let me ask you a few questions: What if we approached our marriages in the same selfless manner that Christ approaches our salvation? What if we tried to outserve, outlove, outsacrifice our spouses? What if we not only didn't withhold but also gave even when our spouses didn't deserve it?

The principle taught in 1 Peter 3:9 works every time: "Don't repay evil for evil. Don't retaliate when people say unkind things about you. Instead, pay them back with a blessing. That is what God wants you to do, and he will bless you for it." You know why? Because God mandated it. Some pop psychologist didn't dream it up; God ordained it. And here's another gentle admonition, friends: "Encourage each other and build each other up, just as you are already doing" (1 Thess. 5:11). It worked in the first-century church, and it works today.

So if you want an intimate friendship relationship with your husband, if you want the type of friendship that automatically causes him to want to come to you first, in good times and bad, here are some specific places to begin:

First, review the points in this chapter and identify the issues that are getting in the way of a close friendship between you and your spouse. Are you resistant to this need? Is your spouse?

Second, deal with this matter in prayer, asking God to reveal to you where you may be blocking your need for intimate marital friendship. As you ask God for insight into your marriage, confess any of your own hard-heartedness or any desire you have to put up walls of self-protection, keeping your husband at a distance. Ask God to reveal to your husband any areas where he is either neglecting or blocking your friendship.

Third, share these concerns with your husband. You might write him a letter. Begin the letter by reaffirming your commitment and love for him. Remind him that you are a "one-man woman" and that you are finishing the race with him—and that you want to finish strong. Then you can go on to explain why this friendship area of your relationship needs some work. Resist the tendency to lay it all out in the letter, however. Simply use the letter as a springboard to enter into communication with your husband. Then tell him you have written him something and want him to read it in a private moment. Be careful not to use the written word as a tool to blast him. Use it instead as a way to draw him to you. Word pictures can be very helpful in describing your feelings.[1]

Fourth, confess whatever you have done to hurt him, and ask him to help you identify blind spots in your own life. Also, ask him for permission to share with him where he may be blind in some areas (as Barb did with me on my issue of pride).

Fifth, as you have confessed, expressed sorrow, and demonstrated repentance, don't forget to seek his forgiveness. And then, if you're able, gently tell him about any areas where you need him to seek your forgiveness.

Sixth, don't be shy about expressing the kind of friendship you need from your husband. Be specific and positive. "Honey, when you do this [list behavior] with me, it really helps build the friendship part of our marriage." Ask him what you can do to meet his friendship needs. Be as specific as you possibly can with one another. Then begin practicing those things that build that trust foundation.

Finally, find and focus on activities, sports, and recreational pursuits you both can enjoy doing together. Get creative! And when your spouse is reaching out and participating in these friendship activities, be sure to reinforce this with affirmation. "Thank you for doing this for me. It really makes me feel loved and cared for."

If you build this type of friendship from the very beginning of your marriage, you will have a solid foundation before and when you come to hard times and pressure points. But it's never too late to start. Even if you are in the midst of tough times or have come through them, begin to reach out and build this type of friendship with your spouse for both now and the future.

[1]For help in using word pictures, I recommend Gary Smalley and John Trent's book *The Language of Love* (Colorado Springs, Colo.: Focus on the Family, 1992). It is the best book I have read on the subject.

FINDING ONENESS IN THE GROWING SEASONS OF LIFE

During one of the most painful times of our lives a few years ago, Barb and I learned just how important our friendship was in our marriage. At the beginning of this chapter, I told you how I had prayed for twenty-one years for my father to enter into a personal relationship with Jesus Christ. As you might imagine, then, it was one of the happiest days of my life when I heard the words "Son, today I became a Christian." Sixteen months after those words rang through the telephone line, however, I received another call—the call every child fears. It was my mother calling to tell me, "Dad just went into a coma."

Moments later I was on the phone with the neurologist who was treating my father. "He is not likely to survive," I was told. "Come now if you want to see him."

Within two hours, Barb had me on a plane, and I arrived at my dad's bedside in time to have two and a half hours with him before he died.

My dad's death hit me like a ton of bricks, even though I knew that he was with the Lord. Yet two days after the funeral I was back on the road, speaking and ministering to families across America. I never really grieved over my father's death. Oh, I experienced the initial stages of grief, but instead of walking through the grieving process, I stayed busy to numb the deep hurt inside my heart. I stuck my grief in a box and chose not to deal with it. (Remember those compartmentalized boxes we discussed in chapter 3?)

Not surprisingly, a year later my body and spirit eventually gave out, and I went into a depression. That year was truly the longest year of my life. Some days I simply isolated myself from others and shut down. Some afternoons I would sneak out the back door of my office and drive down the highway looking for a place to be alone, to cry. I didn't think I could provide for my family. I didn't think God could use me. I didn't think I would ever come out of this deep hole. During those times I would often walk for hours, hoping the exercise would bring relief. It helped, but the deep feelings of failure and insecurity were more than I could bear.

One day I found myself sitting for hours on a park bench with my Bible and a bottle of water. I cried out to God, "I am not leaving until you reveal yourself and your promises to me in your Word." In the fifth hour I came across Exodus 14:13-14: "Moses answered the people, 'Do not be afraid. Stand firm and you will see the deliverance the Lord will bring you today. . . . The Lord will fight for you; you need only to be still'" (NIV).

After God revealed to me his promise to Moses, I drove home to Barb, my best friend, and told her what had just happened.

"I know there's hope, Barb," I said. "I'm going to come through this."

As we talked, she once again reminded me of some basic truths that are foundational in our marriage.

"Gary, I don't expect you just to get over this. I expect you to walk through it with me by your side. I also want you to remember that God will fight for you, just as he revealed to you on that bench. You need to trust him and be still. Let him carry you in your spirit, and let me carry you as your soul mate."

She reminded me that I could trust her. "I am sticking to you like glue, and nothing can separate me from you. We are one. Those wedding vows are the real thing. That covenant is true. For better or worse means that even at the worst of times, we are a team."

We talked about how some of my behaviors during those months of depression were wounding to her. My silences had hurt her. My withdrawal had frustrated her. My deep sense of fear had, at times, frightened her. We closed some loops during those days. Forgiveness abounded as I recaptured my hope and optimism that God wasn't through with me yet.

Barb was never less than honest with me during those times. She assured me and reassured me that she would never leave me, that she loved me and trusted me, and that she would stand with me through this time, just as she has done during our times of joy. And I trusted her, knowing that we could go through anything together.

We even began to learn to play together more as I came through this time of depression. We took more walks. We laughed more. We had more nights out on dates.

During those difficult months, several male friends were also there for me as mentors, encouragers, and prayer partners. But the one person on earth I needed more than anyone else was my lifelong partner, my best friend, my wife. And she was always there, in my corner. She lived out her marriage vows as I grieved over the death of my father. She loved, honored, and cherished me. She stood with me for better or for worse, for richer or for poorer, in sickness and in health. As a result, the intimacy forged in our marriage is so deep and impenetrable that only God will be able to peel one of us from the other when he is ready to call one of us home.

That is intimate friendship. That is marital oneness. That is what Barb and I have, and that is what we want for you. Why? Because this is God's plan.

For some of you, this means taking a baby step in the right direction and then implementing the principles in this chapter.

For others, you're already there! If so, the next time you see your husband, hug him and remind him of your love and commitment.

When you pray together, remind God of your unfailing love for one another.

When you sit down to talk with each other, go deeper and share another piece of who you are with the husband God has given you.

Then steal an hour together, and go out for a treat. Celebrate a marriage friendship of three: the Lord, your husband, and you!

CHAPTER 6

SPIRITUAL INTIMACY

A WIFE'S #3 LOVE NEED

"There is no greater comfort and security than this."

Barb talks to husbands

D ear Dr. Rosberg,
Many good Christian books for men sit on the end table beside my husband's living-room chair. I've read most of them, and they are terrific, helpful books with all kinds of wonderful advice. My husband never even picks them up. He hasn't read them, so how could he possibly apply any of the good stuff that's in there? I dust them off and put them back in their places each week. They look real good when we have guests, and I'm sure everyone must think he is a super husband. The truth is, he's a lousy husband. He puts on a good show and attends Promise Keepers and brings home more of those great books. We attend church together, and he attends leadership meetings and is active in our church. He considers himself to be a good Christian man.

He seldom talks to me, never gives me a compliment, criticizes me in private and in public, and is quick to point a finger at someone else who is not leading a "good" life. If we are driving down the road, he doesn't miss anything new being built and notices every detail about it, but he doesn't notice when I've had my hair done or when I'm wearing something especially attractive.

On the outside, we look pretty normal. On the inside, I'm hurt, lonely, sad, and disappointed. Our marriage is not at all what I expected it to be. I thought we would have an intimate relationship, emotionally and physically, that we would go places together and laugh a lot and have fun,

*whether we were sitting at home together or having dinner out. I thought
we would have a daily Bible study and pray together because he appeared
to be such a good Christian man. Instead of lifting me up, he puts me
down; instead of a smile, he usually wears a frown. He can always find
something to be negative about. I have always been an optimist, and I
usually have a smile on my face in spite of his constant criticism and his
habit of picking at unimportant things. I treat my husband pretty well,
considering the way he ignores, neglects, and criticizes me.*

*Then after a day of being criticized and ignored, I'm expected to
become a sexy bombshell when he discovers that I'm a warm body next
to him in the bed. Then he gets all huffy when I say "forget it," and he has
the nerve to whine about feeling "rejected." After his entire day of rejecting me in one way or another.*

What's wrong with this picture?

*Frankly, I'm fed up with it. I'm not sure I want to continue in a
marriage like this. I'm a Christian woman, and I believe in the sanctity of
marriage. While I'm not being physically abused, I'm sure not being
treated as Christ treats his church, which is the model that you Promise
Keepers hold up to your men.*

*I just want my husband to love me, and I want it to be obvious to
others and me that he loves me and thinks I'm very special. I want
him to cherish me, as I still cherish him even though it's become harder
and harder for me to remember the reasons that I came to love him
in the first place. All the bad is burying the good. One of these days
none of the good will be visible, and it will be too late to try to dig it out
again.*

This anonymous letter that Gary recently received breaks my heart. I
hurt not only for this woman but also for other women who are getting
the same kind of treatment from their husbands. Sadly, this is not the
only "Christian home" where the husband has, either subtly or deliberately, taken his eyes off Jesus Christ and focused them on himself. The
outcome is always the same: Everyone suffers.

If you truly want to meet your wife's love need for spiritual intimacy,
then you must view your marriage as a cord with three strands: God,
husband, and wife. God is the central strand around which the other two
are woven. And since God must be inextricably woven throughout the
marriage relationship, it is not surprising that the need for spiritual inti-

macy factored high on our needs survey for both men and women. Spiritual intimacy may take several forms, but from a wife's perspective it involves her husband's own spiritual growth, their shared spiritual growth as husband and wife, her communication with her husband about spiritual matters, and her husband's spiritual leadership in the home.

At the heart of spiritual intimacy lies trust. Your wife trusts you not because of your rank or position—or even just because you are her husband. It's true that a measure of trust is built during courtship and in your commitment to the wedding vows, but *complete* trust is established over time and under the pressure of daily life. And from my own experience as well as the experience of countless women I've talked to, when it comes to spiritual matters, a woman needs to trust her husband in

- his own walk with God,
- his support of her spiritual growth,
- his spiritual upbringing of the children,
- his decisions that affect the family, and
- his spiritual leadership in the home.

In 1 Peter we find a clear statement of how crucial your role is not only to your own spiritual life but also to your marriage relationship: "In the same way, you husbands must give honor to your wives. Treat her with understanding as you live together. She may be weaker than you are, but she is your equal partner in God's gift of new life. If you don't treat her as you should, your prayers will not be heard" (1 Pet. 3:7). By the way, the point here about your wife being "weaker" does not mean that she is morally or mentally weaker or inferior to you; rather, it most likely is referring to relative physical strength.

God is asking a lot of you! But because you've chosen to accept this mission (right?), you will have an unbelievable impact on your wife. Your wife longs to experience the fulfillment that comes from knowing you love God and are willing to serve him by being an effective husband and father. So as you strengthen *your* relationship with God and take on your God-given role in the home, you will help her strengthen *her* relationship with God and with you.

Don't take my word for this, though. Ask your wife about her specific needs in this area.

WHAT ARE YOUR WIFE'S NEEDS FOR SPIRITUAL INTIMACY?

A wife's need for spiritual intimacy has several components, all of which encourage her spiritual growth and increase her security in your marriage relationship. She needs to be growing spiritually; she needs to be in fellowship with other Christians, especially you; she needs to express her spiritual gifts; and she needs you to be a spiritual leader in the home.

She Needs to Be Growing Spiritually

Your wife needs to be growing spiritually, and while you are not ultimately responsible for her growth, you can contribute to that growth in significant ways. As you approach her, remember that you are not the source of spiritual strength for your wife. God should be her source of strength; he is the One who truly meets her heart's cry. But as a husband, you *are* fully responsible for modeling Christ's love for her and pointing her to that exclusive One who can meet her deepest needs. And you can encourage her to quench her spiritual thirst by her involvement in Bible studies, prayer groups, women's conferences, or other settings where she can grow in her relationship to Christ.

Terry works forty hours a week as a classroom teacher. Each night she has papers to grade and lesson plans to make for the next day. She is growing increasingly frustrated with her job because it is consuming all her time. Consequently, she is more and more short-tempered and impatient with her husband, John. A job she once loved has now become a source of resentment. She is tired, empty, and burned out; she feels she has nothing left to give to anyone.

Terry and John are both wise enough to know that the solution lies outside of themselves. They both know that Terry needs to take some time to pull away from everyone and go deeper in her faith, cultivating her own heart. John has gone through this himself and knows the impact that soul-care time has been on his own life. As her husband, John is in the key position to help Terry get help. If he does not, he is not fulfilling that supportive leadership role God has given him.

A woman by nature is a responder in her relationship with her husband. She's like a star receiver with a quarterback. Both are good at their job, but both need each other. In this case, Terry needs John to step in and help her with her overwhelming load. John can best do that by encouraging his wife to take time to refresh her own soul and then make it possible for her to do so. Has she taken her workload to God? Can they pray together about the situation? Can she join the women's Bible study that meets on Tuesday nights at the church? And then, very practically, what can he do around the house to make it easier for her to take the time to do this?

God is the source of rest and refreshment, and we need our husbands to help point us to him.

She Needs to Be in Fellowship with Other Christians, Especially You

Spiritual fellowship is a relationship of two or more people who are hungry and thirsty for the same thing and who are mutually satisfied as they jointly experience it together in Christ. Fellowship occurs when we encourage and support each other and pray for each other; it's joining together as a happy, healthy spiritual family, where we can open up, feel connected, and enjoy each other.

One night Carl and Rosie were sitting in their Jacuzzi and talking about everything—the kids, work, the family dog, you name it. Before long, Rosie was telling Carl about how out of touch she felt. With all the children in school, she had gone back to work, which meant she could no longer meet with her Wednesday morning women's Bible study group. And since they had recently changed churches, she felt cut off from her Christian friends there.

Because Carl is her best friend, he listened to her and asked questions so that he could try to understand her needs better. Then he took her hand and prayed for God to meet her need. But shortly after he finished praying, he said, "You know, there's something I've been giving a lot of thought to but hadn't mentioned to you yet. What would you think if we started a couples Bible study in our home? That way we could grow together in studying about the Lord, and we could get to know some new couples from church. From that group you might also make some new friends."

That evening was more than two people relaxing in a Jacuzzi; it was a husband and a wife having spiritual fellowship with the kind of intimacy that makes them one.

She Needs to Express Her Spiritual Gifts

God has given each one of us varied spiritual gifts. As we exercise those different gifts, our faith grows, strengthening our character to sustain us in fighting the battle in other areas of our lives. "By faith these people overthrew kingdoms, ruled with justice, and received what God had promised them. They shut the mouths of lions, quenched the flames of fire, and escaped death by the edge of the sword. Their weakness was turned to strength. They became strong in battle and put whole armies to flight" (Heb. 11:33-34).

Growth in faith is a direct result of activating and using our spiritual gifts. Women grow in their faith as they are stretched to lean on the Holy Spirit to equip them to do his work. They stand back in awe of what God does as he gives them gifts and skills to accomplish his work.

Laura works twenty-five hours a week, has three children, and hosts a neighborhood Bible study for thirty women in her home. Laura sees leading this Bible study as one of the most important things she does. She loves to teach, and watching what God is doing in the other women's lives deepens her own faith. Her husband, Lance, has been totally supportive about her leading this group, and this has also strongly influenced her life. He makes sure that she has the time to study, prepare the lessons, and develop relationships with the women in the group. Although he doesn't participate in this group, he does not view it as competition for his own time with her. Teaching this study has been a life dream for his wife and has been a valuable means of her personal growth with God. Lance has encouraged her to grow outside her relationship with him—which, in turn, has only made her appreciate him more fully.

What are your wife's spiritual gifts? Maybe, like Laura, your wife loves to teach. Maybe her compassionate heart makes her a good counselor for other people. Perhaps she is interested in the needs of the sick or the poor. Maybe she is a detail person and is drawn to groups that need her organizational skills. Your wife may be creative in music, art, or writing. Perhaps she has great gifts of hospitality. Maybe she is an intercessor. What spiritual gifts do you see in her? What spiritual gifts does she see in herself? Is she exercising those gifts? How can you help her exercise them so that she and the people around her will grow spiritually?

She Needs You to Be a Spiritual Leader in the Home

Early in our marriage, Gary was working and going to graduate school full time. Absorbed with his work and his studies, he had very little time or energy left over for me and our two preschool daughters. It's not that he woke up one morning and decided to neglect our family; he was just overworked and overbooked. He was never home.

Since I truly wanted him to succeed, I jumped in and provided the leadership—both emotional and spiritual—our family needed. But I sorely missed his presence in our lives. I longed for spiritual interaction with him, and I longed for him to be the spiritual leader in our home.

Then one day, during the time that Gary was cramming for his doctoral thesis in counseling, our five-year-old daughter, Sarah, burst into his study with a family portrait she had drawn. "Let me see your picture, honey . . . ah, that's nice," he said absently. "I'll hang it on the wall."

Then he did a double take. Sarah had drawn Mommy and Sarah and Missy and the dog, but there was no Daddy in the picture.

"Honey, where's your daddy?" Gary asked.

"You're at the library," she replied nonchalantly.

One picture drawn with a green crayon was worth a thousand words I wanted to say to Gary about his absence.

I didn't learn about this until some weeks later when he finally found the courage to say, "Barb, is it too late for me to come home, to take my place again in this family?"

He said this one night as we both lay in our darkened bedroom. I thought he was sleeping, and he startled me when I heard him whispering, "Can I come home?" Although my eyes were shut, my heart was open and receptive to him. I hurt for him as I heard in his voice a vulnerability that I had never heard there before. The last thing I wanted to do was hurt this wonderful man who was trying to make a change for our family.

"The girls and I love you very much. We want you home," I said. "But you haven't been here. I've felt like a single parent for some time. We crave your spiritual leadership."

To be honest, when Gary finally recognized his self-absorbed focus and began to make a change, it was difficult for me to change gears. I was exhausted, but I had been putting out fires for so long that I had a hard time thinking he was up to handling the job. Deep down, however, I knew our home was out of order, and I didn't like it. I wanted my husband to be a vibrant leader in our family.

How can you be a spiritual leader in your home? What does your wife need from you?

For one thing, *she needs you to be a spiritual sounding board,* to tune in and listen to her. She may have a greater need to talk about spiritual things than you do. Don't be put off by that. Listen. Ask questions. Share your insights with her.

Your wife needs you to focus on her spiritual strengths. When you see her make a hard decision based on her convictions, commend her. When you see in her a depth of character, tell her what you see. When you are drawn to God because of her, let her know.

Your wife needs you to have a vibrant spiritual life. She needs to see that God has first place in your life. When you fill that place with your work, your interests, or your activities, you rob God of his rightful place, and everyone suffers. Things that consume you can weaken you as a person and eventually can tear down a marriage. This reveals itself through chaos and frustration in your home. When you ignore your need of God and stop growing spiritually, you are not only placing yourself at risk but also jeopardizing your marriage and your family. But when you place God first and keep him there, you provide not only a strong model for members of your family but also a sense of security for them.

Your wife looks to you to lead by example. A spiritual leader goes to church with the family. A spiritual leader is consistent, acting the same in public and in private. He demonstrates a desire to grow. A spiritual leader leads the family in studying the Bible; he leads in prayer. These things may be hard for you. If you take even small steps toward this kind of leadership, your wife will love it and be encouraged by it. You don't have to fear the pressure of praying for an hour; just take her hand and pray over a meal. It's that simple. Your willingness means everything to her.

Some men find spiritual leadership a difficult thing because they have had no role models. Many men—and you may be one of them—come from broken homes or from homes in which one or both parents were not Christians or from homes in which lip service was paid to Christianity but the reality inside the four walls was quite another matter. Because these men have lacked adequate role models in their own families, many of them have learned unhealthy patterns and selfish habits. They're expected to be spiritual leaders, but they don't know the rules, and they don't have a coach.

Think about your own life. Did you or do you have a good role model to look to? Many of Gary's and my male friends are the only Christians in their families, and most of them have struggled in knowing what their spiritual responsibilities are to their wives and family. Those who have recognized this have sought out a male mentor in their church or are reading books about the subject.

How are you doing as a spiritual leader? Review the following checklist.

- Do you pray out loud with your wife? (You can't get any more intimate than praying together as a couple.)
- Are you studying the Word of God daily? You might spend some time together reading something like *The One Year Bible*, which divides the Bible into 365 readings, one for each day of the year. Or you each could read the same devotional book or study guide in your individual devotional time and then share insights with each other at another time.
- Have you discovered the fun of a shared ministry? Two unique people may not automatically be drawn to the same interests, but if you can minister as a team, it will initiate a wonderful spiritual harmony.
- Does your wife see you reading the Bible?
- Do you pray with your wife at bedtime?
- Do you pray daily for your wife and then tell her what you have specifically prayed for her?
- Do you read books that will help you build up your confidence by understanding how to lead your wife spiritually?[1]
- Do you lead your family in decision making? Are you teaching your children, by example, the importance of husband-and-wife agreement in making decisions? Do you demonstrate harmony to them? Do you listen to the counsel of your wife?
- Are you open with your children? Are you teaching your children, by example, to depend on the power of God when they are going through adversity? Do you tell them stories of how God helped you through troubled times? Do you help them understand how adversity builds strength and character?
- Do your kids see you reading the Bible?
- Do you pray with your kids at bedtime?
- Do you count your blessings, making a mental list throughout the

[1] I recommend Gary Rosberg's *Guard Your Heart* (Sisters, Oreg.: Questar, 1994); Steve Farrar's *Point Man: How a Man Can Lead His Family* (Sisters, Oreg.: Multnomah, 1992); and Stu Weber's *Tender Warrior* (Sisters, Oreg.: Multnomah 1993).

day of how God answered your prayers and then telling your family in the evening?

• Do you pray daily for your children and then tell how you specifically have prayed for each of them?

HOW YOU CAN MEET YOUR WIFE'S NEED FOR SPIRITUAL INTIMACY

If you want to grow in your ability to meet your wife's need for spiritual intimacy, here are a few things you can do.

Encourage Her Spiritual Growth

When it comes to your wife's relationship with Jesus Christ, what helps her grow? Have you ever discussed this with her? Does your wife ever talk with you about her own prayer life? What makes her tick spiritually? Do you know when she is going through a "spiritual dry spell"? How can you tell? What is your response when this happens?

And what does your wife do as a result of her faith? How does she express her own spiritual commitment? Does she lead or participate in Bible studies? Does she serve in the nursery at church or help with Meals on Wheels? Is she writing letters to missionaries or working with battered wives?

As Yogi Berra once said, "You can observe a lot by watching things." Notice what it takes to help her faith grow, and then encourage her to pursue those activities.

Several years ago Gene was attending a men's Bible Study Fellowship, a vibrant study group where people come together and hear strong Bible teaching and learn how to apply the concepts to life in a way that gives real purpose and meaning. One night he came home and encouraged his wife, Mary Jo, to consider going to the women's study group. "Your life will change dramatically if you spend time studying the Word in depth with other women. I know you study the Bible on your own, Mary Jo, but I also know how much this group study has done for me. I think you will get so much out of it."

Because of her husband's leading and encouragement, Mary Jo began attending Bible Study Fellowship. She was amazed at how her understanding of the Word opened up. She was also able to share her struggles with the other women and work together to find solutions. She was

encouraged and, in turn, gave encouragement to women who were dealing with similar issues. God was working personally in her life.

Today Gene and Mary Jo's conversations revolve around faith and
God's purpose for them. They take even the smallest decisions to God for
guidance. But what she loves most is how connected their faith has
become in their relationship. Gene reads a lot, and she loves to hear him
say, "Oh, Mary Jo, you need to read this. There is such insight in it. And
it will encourage you." It does every time.

I'll never forget the first time Gary opened the door to our walk-in closet
and found me in there in the dark, on my knees. That's how he found out
that I truly do have a prayer closet and how precious that time is to me in
my own spiritual growth. If I neglect prayer or focus on things that worry
me rather than praying about them, my heart can quickly become hard.
So one way I commune with God is by going into a secluded place to
pray. Now that Gary knows how vital this private prayer time is for me,
he does everything he can to make sure nothing interferes with that.

Everyone's spiritual growth rhythms are different. Find out what charges
your wife's batteries, and then do what you can to keep them charged.

Encourage Her Fellowship with You and Others

"Michael is the greatest when it comes to encouraging me to get away
with my accountability group," Cheryl told me. "He clears his own
schedule and takes the kids. And no one could be more enthusiastic.
He just says, 'Go!'"

Seven years ago Cheryl and Michael started a couples' Bible study, and
three of those couples still get together. Cheryl says that she credits the
success of the group to the men; over the years, they kept it going. They
maintained a fellowship among themselves, meeting for breakfast and
prayer once a month. This carried over into the couples' dynamics.
Because of that, the wives get together in an accountability group in
which they can fellowship and share their needs as well.

Sue is a small-group leader in a citywide Bible study, but the leadership team meets each Wednesday at 5:25 A.M. So each Wednesday at
5:00 A.M. Jack gets up to pray with his wife before she leaves for the
group. He is proud that she is growing spiritually and wants her to know
how much he supports her. Sue appreciates that he sacrifices sleep on
her behalf so they can experience the seal of spiritual intimacy together
before she shares with the women in her life.

Pat and Timothy have been married for twelve years, and he has always encouraged her to go to women's conferences and events. He has never complained or made her feel guilty that she was burdening him with household chores. And when she comes home, there are no dirty dishes to wash, no diapers to change, no meal to cook, no baths to give. He calls it "Daddy duty." Timothy knows the value of taking care of his wife's heart.

Encourage Her to Express Her Spiritual Gifts

Think about how you feel when others notice your accomplishments. Doesn't such recognition make you feel more complete inside? Your wife is no different. This doesn't mean she needs to be continually lauded or patted on the back. But she needs to be reminded about what a gift of God she is, both to you and to others.

A close friend of mine isn't an up-front type of woman. She doesn't teach Sunday school or serve on church committees, but she has an unparalleled gift of hospitality. All who enter her home immediately know that the Lord lives there. She welcomes her guests in a way that makes them feel they're among old friends, and she offers the kind of friendly comfort zone in which they can relax in Christian fellowship.

Her husband, for his part, encourages her to express this gift of hospitality. He knows she is most fulfilled when she is serving others in this way, so in any way he can, he gives her the time and resources to do it. He knows that when family and friends and other guests leave, they will have sensed something about the Savior.

Your wife hungers to be treated with dignity and respect; she does not want to be taken for granted. Whether she is using her gifts for service in the church, at work, or in the home, she needs to know you appreciate who she is and how God is using her. Marvel at her unique talents, and search for ways that she can increase her natural gifts.

If your wife is uncertain about her spiritual gifts, help her identify them. Share your observations with her, and encourage her to discuss this with those friends who know her well. Then discuss ways in which she might exercise her gifts. For instance, if she has the gift of mercy, she might be interested in doing hospital or nursing-home visitation. If she is timid or unsure, encourage her to step outside her comfort zone and lean on the power of God, learning dependence on him to fulfill the task.

Once she is involved in a ministry, give her relief on the home front and show continued interest in what she is doing. Affirm her value and contribution.

Encourage Her with Your Prayers

Recently, a friend of ours went in for her yearly mammogram. Several women in her family have had breast cancer, so this history added to the blow when she heard those words every woman dreads: "We've spotted something abnormal in your mammogram."

Some of you have probably gone through this experience with your wives, so you know exactly what I'm talking about. How does a husband react in this situation? Well, let me tell you what Carol's husband did. When she walked in the door and told him the news, he simply held out his arms and gathered her close. They sat together for a few minutes on the couch, talking about her fears. He listened and held her as she cried. After a few minutes, he began praying for her. She later said, "There was nothing that could have comforted or assured me more than what Tom did at that moment."

Does your wife know you pray for her? Does she *hear* you pray for her? If you have not prayed for or with your wife, start slowly—but start today. Your prayers for and with her are some of the greatest gifts you can give her.

HOW YOU LEAD IS IMPORTANT TO YOUR WIFE

The issue of your spiritual leadership is a foundational one for your wife. But *how* you lead is as important to her as *that* you lead.

A passage in Ephesians gives some directives about how husbands are to love and lead their wives: "You husbands must love your wives with the same love Christ showed the church. He gave up his life for her to make her holy and clean, washed by baptism and God's word. He did this to present her to himself as a glorious church without a spot or wrinkle or any other blemish. Instead, she will be holy and without fault. In the same way, husbands ought to love their wives as they love their own bodies. For a man is actually loving himself when he loves his wife" (Eph. 5:25-28).

To be like Christ is to lay down your life for your wife. Scripture is clear that a husband is called to "make her holy and clean, washed by . . .

God's word." A kind of divine transaction occurs when a husband exchanges his superficial love for a deep sacrificial love, as he places his wife's need above his own and makes his wife's holiness his goal. In doing this, he fulfills his role in serving her and modeling Christ Jesus.

Such a demonstration of daily godliness in living with his wife produces godly results both in her and in him. He is able to "present her . . . without a spot or wrinkle or any other blemish." She will be "holy and without fault." Notice that this is the second time in this passage that the word *holy* is used. When you pour your life into your wife's life, she becomes holy. What an incredible transaction!

The leadership model described in these verses is one of servant leadership. That's the biblical ideal. But too often the reality in marriages is that a husband falls prey to two extreme styles: control or passivity. Before we explore more fully the servant-leader style, let's look at these extremes.

The Controlling Leader

Christ's way never includes the threat of a husband's towering over his wife in an attempt to control or intimidate her. No woman wants to be married to a man like that.

In their book *Rocking the Roles,* William Hendricks and Robert Lewis conclude that because of original sin (the sinful nature we all inherit from Adam and Eve since the Fall), husbands have an inclination to dominate their wives. "[Genesis] foretells how fallen men will naturally tend to live with their wives. It prophesies that they would dominate them and subjugate them to positions of lower status. As we know, this has indeed been the case. We have thousands of cultures and thousands of years to document that this is exactly what happened. Women have struggled under the harsh dominance of natural men for centuries. Even today, the mournful wails that proceed from too many homes come as a result of the rule of selfish and insensitive bullies" (p. 64).

Even if you have an extremely confident or strong-willed wife (as Gary does at times), every woman is designed to respond to authentic biblical leadership from her husband. Sadly, as Hendricks and Lewis relate, some men take the easy route to "leadership" by trying to be "the boss." This is domination, not spiritual leadership.

Men who are controlling leaders often have the kinds of personalities that enable them to become the movers and the shakers, the quarterbacks, and the entrepreneurs of the world. They are decisive and determined, and they can readily inspire others to fall in line with their plans and visions. The problem is that this type of man, when governed by his natural inclinations, can easily become overbearing. When this happens in a marriage, it leads to serious trouble.

David is a prime example. At work, he runs a tight ship and has a highly productive department. He's not particularly well liked, but he gets the job done. At home, he operates in a similar fashion: He's the head of the household, and everything is going to be under his control. He thinks he can run his family any way he wishes. To him there are only two outcomes to everything: you either win or you lose. And he hates to lose—especially to a woman, even when that woman is his wife. Anyone who crosses him—which also means anyone who differs with him—is a threat. His wife, Ruth, is a warm, caring, capable woman, but she has been cut down so many times by David's cruel words that you can almost see her cringe when he opens his mouth. Bottom line: David is a selfish and demanding man.

While this may seem like an extreme example of how far a Christian man like David, who is a deacon in his church, can go, it's not as rare as you may think. Please realize that while following your instincts, giving orders, and getting things done is sometimes necessary in the business world, it usually won't work with your wife and kids—and it's certainly not the way the Lord intended marriage to work. The controlling leader creates disharmony and discord, rebellion and unhappiness for all who live under his thumb. The result is often a resentful wife who does not want to be ordered around and kids who will easily rebel. The controlling leader certainly is not modeling the love of Christ to his wife and family, and he is not creating a thirst in them for a close relationship with Jesus.

If you fit this description, ask God not only to show you when you are controlling but also to help you put your leadership style under *his* control. Then admit to your wife that you have been a dominating husband and that you would like to change. Ask her to help you. If you are really serious, give your wife permission to tell you when she feels you are being controlling. Then seek help from other Christian men. This is where a men's accountability group is so useful. Men can openly encourage other men to change from dominating controllers to servant leaders.

The Passive Leader

The other extreme is passivity, or abdication of leadership. Have you ever struggled with deciding who takes charge of the spiritual well-being of your family? Many men feel completely comfortable letting their wives do the work, especially if their wives have a more consistent relationship with God or a deeper knowledge of spiritual issues.

Cut it out! Your wife—even if she is a natural leader herself—doesn't want you to abdicate your role as spiritual leader.

When Gary and I speak at marriage conferences, I meet lots of women who want advice on how to handle their passive husbands. June talked with me about her husband, Paul, who is a great father, husband, and provider. He's a pull-yourself-up-by-your-own-bootstraps kind of guy, proficient and self-reliant. But when it comes to spiritual things, he stays in the background, letting his wife take the lead. June would love to have him initiate spiritual leadership with her and their family, but he doesn't seem to know how to begin—or maybe he's just not interested.

Men like Paul may have the knowledge to direct the spiritual welfare of their family, but they're not using it to encourage and help their wives and children acquire a thirst and a hunger for the loving leadership of Jesus. And because they have chosen to back off, there is no biblical example of a godly male in the home. Countless families are being negatively affected by just such spiritually apathetic or indifferent husbands and fathers.

Interestingly enough, the man who is a passive leader at home could be the same man who leads very well in his business all day long. He just doesn't transfer those skills to his roles as father and husband. When he walks through the front door each night, he turns from Mr. Dragon Slayer into Mr. Milquetoast. That is an exaggeration, of course, because there are degrees of passivity, but you get the picture.

If you are a passive leader, this does not mean that you should suddenly become a tyrant. In fact, you should *not* be a tyrant. What it does mean is that you need to acquire—through daily obedience to Jesus Christ—a spiritual stature that draws your wife to you as you take the initiative God intends you to take in the home. When a man does this, his marriage and family will be transformed.[2]

[2]If you want further insights on the subject, I recommend James Walker's *Husbands Who Won't Lead and Wives Who Won't Follow* (Minneapolis: Bethany House, 1989).

The Servant Leader

Balanced leadership involves service to your wife. Here's how Steve Farrar describes this role in his excellent book *Point Man:* "It means, gentlemen, that you take the lead in your submission to Christ to such an extent that you become a model for your wife. A man's willingness to serve his wife and meet her needs will provide an environment and a stimulus for her to respond in submission to his leadership. If she sees that kind of attitude in you, and senses that you are diligently seeking to follow hard after Christ, it will be much easier for her to relax in your leadership in the home. I have yet to meet a Christian woman whose husband provides this kind of leadership who has difficulty with the idea of biblical submission. When a husband loves his wife as the Scriptures commands, it's a win-win situation for everyone" (p. 182).

The Bible clearly indicates that a believing husband should accept his God-given responsibilities to love, lead, and honor his family. This kind of leadership is a balance between leading and serving. When a man steps into this role, he protects and provides for each member of the family.

Al is the picture of servanthood in many areas of his life, but particularly with his wife, Vickie. When his job requires extra hours, he always discusses it with Vickie, making sure that his extra work hours will not interfere with his family commitments. Al always treats Vickie courteously. If she is carrying groceries in from the car, he rushes to take them. When they eat out, they decide together where they will go. From giving the children baths to praying with his family, Al lives out his servanthood.

Biblical leadership is a responsibility that God has given to you. It's an opportunity for you to serve your family. Jesus' words in Mark 10:45 beautifully illustrate biblical leadership: "For even I, the Son of Man, came here not to be served but to serve others, and to give my life as a ransom for many." Jesus left his place of honor at the right hand of God and came to earth in humility to save the world and show what God was really like. Your role is to learn from him and demonstrate the same humility to your wife. Serving your wife at her deepest needs and sacrificing so that she might see more of Jesus will bring a comfort and security that she has never known.

Since you are given the responsibility to be the spiritual leader, you must cultivate your spirit to be sensitive to the gentle leading and guiding of the Holy Spirit. But the challenge doesn't end there. Before you are fully able to minister to your wife, you must be sensitive to her spirit. It takes real discernment—and patience—on your part to be able to read the complex emotional needs of your lifetime wife. But that's why God gives you a lifetime to do it! It takes humility for a man to become sensitive to the Spirit of God, as well as to his wife. As he learns this humility, however, he'll enjoy his marriage more than he ever thought possible.

Servant leadership leads to spiritual intimacy, and this attainable goal can transform you from a husband and wife struggling with egos and battling for control to a loving couple that experiences marriage teamwork at its best!

One sunny December morning many years ago, with five inches of new snow blanketing the ground, Gary baited the girls and me with the offer of a special treat after church. We begged and pleaded with him to reveal the big secret, but he wouldn't tell us. When we arrived home, he told us to dress warmly, and then he marched us out to the front yard.

"Okay, this is it," he said.

"This is *what?*" was my reaction.

"This is our spot for our first-ever snowman."

"That's what we're going to do? We thought we were going somewhere."

"We don't need to go anywhere to have the fun we're going to have," he said. "Watch this." He then bent over and started rolling a snowball that would become the base of the snowman.

The girls and I followed suit, and before long we were giggling and laughing. Soon our Frosty had charcoal eyes, a carrot nose, a smile made of rocks, and a red-and-white-striped hat. It was a great afternoon; none of us needed Disneyland to make a memory as a family. Missy was in and out of the house all day, hugging Frosty and praying that he would "stay with our family forever."

That evening before we left the house to look at Christmas lights, Missy voiced her fear that Scott, a mischievous teenage boy across the street, might knock down the snowman. And when we returned from our drive, our worst fears were realized. Frosty lay in pieces all over the yard.

Missy wept, and Gary and I headed across the street to Scott's house for a little chat. He denied the act. "I've been in the house all night working on a paper."

Recognizing that he wasn't going to confess, we went home and started putting Frosty back together. Soon we heard footsteps coming across the snow. We turned around and saw Scott in tow behind his father, Nick.

"Gary, if you have something to say to my son, I would appreciate it if you would start with me. Scott has been in the house with me all day, working on a paper for school. There's no way he could have done this. Now you and I have a problem." Then Nick and Scott turned on their heels and walked away.

Gary turned to Missy. "Did Scott tell you he would tear down the snowman, or did you just think he might?" We had just assumed that Scott had talked to Missy on one of her trips outside to hug her Frosty.

"Well, he didn't actually say he would."

"Missy, let me get this straight. Scott didn't say he was going to tear Frosty down, but you thought he might do it. Why?"

"Because he's always doing stuff to us, but I don't think he did this one."

Gary took all of us back into the house so we could talk about this family crisis called, "How to alienate the neighbors in thirty seconds." The decision that resulted was that we needed to go across the street and apologize. "I'm not going over there," said one. "Dad, you go. You're the father," said another. "Can I stay home? I feel sick." (I'm not telling which one I was.)

"No," said Gary. "We're all going to go. I'll call Scott and his dad and ask them to meet with us. But before I do, I think we need to talk about what we're learning from this." His leadership caused us to recognize that we had falsely accused Scott. We all felt terrible about what we had done. Then, although we were afraid to face the neighbors, Gary led us to put into practice some sorely needed humility. Gary called Nick and asked if we could come over and talk with him and Scott.

"There is nothing I want to talk with you about," said Nick.

"Please, just come to the front door and give me a couple of minutes," said Gary. "It's important that my whole family talk with you and your son."

"Okay," said Nick and slammed down the receiver.

As we bundled up for that walk across the street, we prayed! Oh how we prayed!

The first words out of Gary's mouth were, "Nick and Scott, my family and I have offended you, and we're very sorry. Will you please forgive us?"

Nick, obviously surprised, was the next to speak. "And I'm sorry for getting so mad, Gary. I was pretty hot. Scott had been inside all day, so I know he hadn't torn down your snowman, Missy. It's okay. Let's forget it."

Soon a repentant Missy was weeping and hugging her teenage neighbor as Scott said, "Missy, it's okay. I know how you feel."

When we returned home, Gary led a second family meeting. We sat in a circle on the floor and talked about what we had learned from this experience: that we need to pray much before any accusations leave our lips; that angry words need to be checked before being blurted out; that when you humble yourself, people's hearts are softened; that when you wrong your neighbor, it's worth the risk to ask forgiveness. Gary's spiritual leadership had helped us to do the right thing, to grow as a family, and to sow unity instead of discord.

THE REWARDS OF SPIRITUAL INTIMACY

The Ephesians 5 passage that we explored earlier in this chapter exhorts a husband to give up his life for his wife "to make her holy and clean, washed by . . . God's word." Have you ever washed your wife in the Word?

Gary often opens his Bible and says to me, "Listen to this, Barb . . ." Then he reads to me what the living, breathing Word of God is doing in his own heart and how it's changing his life. What a witness and testimony that is, then, for my own life.

Sometimes, truthfully, I don't feel comfortable with what he's reading because it challenges my selfish nature. Yet I can't deny that my thoughts are altered, and I learn to become more like Christ because of it.

I recall one powerful example of this in our lives. Gary and I were speaking at a FamilyLife conference in Jacksonville, Florida. Our plane landed late the night before the conference was to begin, and we were both exhausted. As we sat in our hotel room with every intention of looking over our notes in preparation for the following day, we were suddenly both overwhelmed.

Gary, who at that time was still dealing with the grief over his dad's death, was emotionally spent. And that week I had received a harsh letter from someone I greatly admired and respected, and I was devastated.

But as we sat in that hotel room, Gary picked up his Bible and began reading to me. Initially, I resisted. My own wound felt too fresh, the pain too deep. But he insisted and kept reading. We were both in tears as he continued to pour the Word of God into our hearts and minds. Gently, God's words pried open my guarded heart and began to heal my wounded spirit. God's Word strengthened both of us, and by the time Gary finished reading, we both felt brand-new. Clean and refreshed. Yes, even holy and clean.

The following week we got a call from the FamilyLife conference manager. His first words were, "What happened in Jacksonville last week? Your evaluations were unbelievable. You hit it out of the ballpark!"

What happened was that God met us as broken people and restored our souls through his Word in a time of true spiritual intimacy.

When Gary takes the lead in this way, he reflects God's character. As a result of seeing this kind of godliness in his life, I am encouraged to trust God more and follow Jesus more closely. This brings a level of trust and security into our relationship that can be found nowhere else.

Now please understand—we struggle with family issues just like everyone else. For example, we struggle with finances. We face a pile of bills: college tuition for our daughter, charges for our daughter's wedding, income taxes, and retirement contributions. The list is endless. But when Gary leans over in church and says, "Let's give more this week," I sit in awe of what God is doing in my husband. His generosity and obedience to God melt my heart.

Do I still have some insecurity about giving more money? Sure I do, but I trust Gary's judgment *and* his leadership in this matter because he's a man who follows God.

When you independently tune in to God, then turn and tune in to your wife, you create an openness that is the ultimate intimacy between a husband and wife.

A husband and wife who build their marriage on the foundational commitment to pursue God above all are able to share fears, anxieties, joys, and dreams. They are able to open themselves up and share thoughts and feelings, even when they hurt. They are free to experience transparent honesty, knowing that they love each other unconditionally and that neither will ever walk away or point fingers.

BUILDING THE FUTURE

Do you realize that you are grooming the next generation of husbands? There's an old adage that says: "If you want to know what kind of a husband a man will be, watch how he treats his mother." And a man treats his mother, by and large, the way he has seen his father treat her as his wife. So the way you love, lead, and protect your wife and children speaks loudly to your children. It models to your son the type of man he should become; it models to your daughter the kind of man she should look for in a husband. One of the most valuable lessons you can teach your children is how a godly man should relate to his wife and how he should lovingly lead his family.

Gary took Scott, our son-in-law, aside before he married our daughter Sarah. "Scott, you have the opportunity to start right out of the chute with prayer and spiritual intimacy with Sarah. Start your relationship by spiritually leading in your home. Every morning when you wake up, or at night right before you go to bed, take Sarah's hands and pray out loud together. How many men do you think can say at the end of their lives that they prayed daily with their wives? I'm not legalistic. If you miss, you miss. But how about being the only guy in America that commits to pray daily with his wife? If you do, it will be easier for her to trust you and place her confidence in your leadership. It will motivate her to desire to be one in mind and spirit with you as well. If you want a biblical family, then you need to pray with your wife. God has promised to bless that kind of spiritual legacy."

Do you pray every night with your wife? As much as Gary and I pray together, we don't have that kind of record. But take it from me, praying with your wife will draw the two of you together in security, encouragement, and spiritual intimacy. Nothing makes a woman feel more safe, secure, and protected.

But I can't close this chapter until I tell you about my friend Emma. She and her husband are both believers, but his distance and failure to meet her need for spiritual intimacy are a source of great pain for her. Recently she shared some of this with me, choking back tears. "It's just that I vividly remember my mom and dad after church on Sundays, the drive home, a closed bedroom door as they changed their clothes, their laughter together." Her voice wavered. "I saw spiritual intimacy lived out. When we went to church, we were one. On Sunday afternoons we were truly together as a family, whether we were taking a drive or visiting a museum or sitting around reading. That intimacy has carried them through fifty-five years of marriage. Now Mom has Alzheimer's. Recently she came home from the hospital. Dad was exhausted, but he sat down on the bed and reached out to hold her. 'I'm so glad to have you home,' he said. As she relaxed in those familiar arms, she said, 'I'm so glad to be home.'" Secure in her memories but washed over with pain, Emma closed her eyes. "I felt their intimacy. I heard their intimacy. I don't have it with Jordan." Her voice faltered. "Maybe someday."

Don't leave your wife hurting and yearning to experience spiritual intimacy, longing for what could have been. Today's a new day. Begin it by committing yourself to developing a spiritual closeness with your wife—your very best friend.

CHAPTER 7

ENCOURAGEMENT

A HUSBAND'S #4 LOVE NEED

"Cheer me on, and believe in me."

Gary talks to wives

I hate to break this to you, but men are really boys trapped in oversized bodies. I know, I know, you're totally flabbergasted.

Believe it or not, this not-so-well-kept secret isn't easy for me, or any man, to admit. I think women have gotten a bad rap about their sensitivity to aging, as if somehow the male ego is impervious to the passing years. But let me tell you, on behalf of all us guys, it's tough to see skin on the top of our head instead of hair. And when we begin adding inches to our waistline, it can be pretty demoralizing. After all, that waist expansion means we have to go out and shop for new pants, and you know how much we love to shop.

Remember the old Bob Dylan song, "The Times, They Are A Changin'"? Well, our theme song as men could be, "The Old Body, It Is A Changin'." Most men, however, don't let go without a fight. So we comb our hair more strategically, work out, attempt to stay in shape, and try to keep off the "see food" diet. And then every once in a while, we pull on our sneakers and head for the court, field, or diamond to attempt to prove we've still "got it." Until the ankles or knees betray us, that is. I'm not exaggerating here. Recently, within one week, three different guys came to me on crutches, with canes, and in casts, singing their song of athletic woe. One blew out his knee in an over-forty basketball league at the YMCA. Another tore ligaments at his church softball league (but he made the catch!). The third broke his arm while wrestling with one of his teenagers.

You, wise woman that you are, are probably sitting back saying, "What is it with you guys? Why can't you get it through your thick skulls that you can't act as if you're twenty-four when you are thirty-four or forty-four or fifty-four or sixty-four?"

On the surface, that makes a lot of sense . . . until your daughter tosses you a basketball. Then you're immediately transported back to your adolescent days, and nothing can stop you from taking her on in the driveway—in your business suit. Or maybe your son throws a block on you as you're helping your wife clear the table after dinner. Your only choice is to give him that look that says, "Come on. I can still take you." Or one of the guys from church calls and challenges you with, "Are you too old to make it down to the court for a little basketball? You aren't in that bad a shape, are you?"

As you hang up, all you can say is, "Honey! Where are my ankle braces and high-tops?"

Men encounter challenges like this almost daily: "Go for it!" "Suck it up!" "Just do it!" And even though I'm wise enough to know better, I'm no different from your husband. I can't help but jump in with both feet (and usually end up with one of them in a cast). Just ask my kids.

When our oldest daughter, Sarah, was ten years old, I signed up to be the assistant coach for her basketball team. I thought it would give us some good bonding time. Nobody told me that during the last weekend of the series, the coaches suit up and take on their kids in front of a hundred screaming fans. It was the first basketball game I had played in twenty years, and I looked pretty good . . . the first three times down the court. Then the heavy-leggedness and the light-headedness appeared out of nowhere. Let me tell you, it wasn't pretty. My kids still laugh when they reminisce about that day. So do I . . . now.

Why did I do it? Because like most of us men, I can't get enough of competition. We love the thrill of victory. But even more than that, we want someone cheering us on to that victory. Ask kids who compete in a sport, play a musical instrument, or participate in a school activity, and they can tell you every instance when their parents were there. Why? Because all of us want and need a fan cheering us on; we need to know we are special, that our family is proud of us.

And believe me, no matter how old your husband is, that's still true for him. He needs to know that he is special, that someone is rooting for him—and that that someone is *you*, his wife.

YOUR HUSBAND'S NEED FOR ENCOURAGEMENT

The nature of the game may change from youth to adulthood, but our need for affirmation and encouragement doesn't. Men still need to know they have a few fans left. It's the way we're wired. That's why the more than seven hundred men surveyed for this book said that their number four love need in marriage is for encouragement and affirmation.

While it's true that as men get older the need for high fives from their male friends subsides a bit, they still need the strong support of other Christian men. But the voice of affirmation they long to hear most is that of their wife.

I can't tell you how many times I've heard a husband say, "She devotes all her time and attention to the kids. Now don't get me wrong, I love my kids. But what about me?" This is not just the poor-me tune of a self-centered whiner. This is a man who feels neglected and in need of his wife's attention, affirmation, and encouragement.

So what happens when a man doesn't hear his wife cheering him on? Two things: He'll continually feel discouraged and defeated. Or, like Tim, he'll seek the applause somewhere else.

Tim and Grace enjoyed most of the trappings of material success. As a young dual-income, childless couple, they devoted most of their time and attention to their careers . . . to the detriment of their marriage. But even as Tim became more and more successful in his business, the person he longed to impress—Grace—seemed totally involved in her own world. Neither of them guarded the boundaries of their relationship, and Tim eventually found himself opening his heart to a coworker at the office. Rita was always there, friendly, helpful, praising his accomplishments and listening sympathetically to his needs. Months later, in my counseling office, Tim confessed to Grace that his heart was being drawn to another woman.

When asked how and why this happened, Tim said, "Grace was never there for me. She was so caught up in her own things that I got tired of trying to get her attention. Rita seemed interested in what I did. She would ask me how my projects were going. She affirmed me a lot. She seemed to value who I am. Rita encouraged me when I was struggling."

Grace sat there stunned at first, the pain written on her face. Then the questions came fast and furiously. "Tim, did it get physical? Did she kiss you? Did you touch her?"

"Grace, nothing physical ever happened. We just talked. Remember how we used to do that? I just needed affirmation from someone. I am sorry I have hurt you this way. I let down my guard and let her in. I know it isn't right. And I want you, not Rita. But I really need you to support me. To encourage me. To let me know that you think I'm a good guy."

Both Tim and Grace heard this clear wake-up call, and, thankfully, they made it safely through the depths of betrayal and pain. Over the course of several months of counseling, they both sought to understand how to recapture the joy of a safe and encouraging marriage. As they began to put into practice what they were learning, the wall around their marriage got stronger, and the walls between them began to come down. They began to listen to each other. To encourage each other. To share what they were thinking and feeling. To respond to each other.

That's what Tim had been looking for in his relationship with Grace: acceptance, access (a listening ear), attention, and affirmation. Or, to wrap it up in one word: encouragement.

Let me begin by telling you what encouragement from a wife looks like to a husband:

- Encouragement is stepping away from the distractions of the kids, the house, your job, the bills, and tuning in to him. During those moments he knows that he is the only one in your world. You have reserved the energy and the time to focus totally on him.
- Encouragement is listening—active listening—when he is talking about work, his hopes and dreams, his insecurities and stresses.
- Encouragement is reminding him that you believe in him. As he opens his world to you, remind him that you love him, that he can make it through the stresses that seem overwhelming to him.
- Encouragement is cheering him on when he tells you how younger guys at work seem to be pushing for his job or threatening stiff competition. Remind him that God has brought him this far and is going to continue to strengthen and use him.
- Encouragement is reminding him that you would marry him all over again. Remind him that he isn't getting older, he's getting better. Be his cheerleader.

Some women may not respond positively to the image of the cheerleader. Perhaps it smacks too much of being on the sidelines while others are in the game. Don't think of it that way. Remember, the cheering section isn't just the cheerleaders; it's the pep team, it's the fans, it's the whole marching

band. You're all of those things and more for your husband. When the two of you come together at the end of a long day and he's exhausted, beaten down by the stress of the job, you're the one person he knows he can confide in, be honest with about his feelings, share what he's dealing with. You are the one person he can rely on to reassure and encourage him.

If you look up the word *encouragement* in several dictionaries, you will find synonyms such as these: to cheer, comfort, hearten, inspire, buoy up, boost, invigorate, put one on top of the world, rejoice the heart, do the heart good. Do you realize what it would do for your marriage relationship if you did all those things for your husband?

Your husband needs to be encouraged and affirmed during the good days as well as the tough ones. Specifying the greatest commandment, Jesus said, "You must love the Lord your God with all your heart, all your soul, and all your mind" (Matt. 22:37). You must love your spouse the same way.

During a recent church service I noticed Todd with his wife, Jody, and their kids. I had heard that Todd had a serious problem at work and that his career was on the line. I wondered how he was doing. After the service, Barb and I went over to them to offer support. As we began to talk, Jody started to cry. Barb pulled her close and said, "I love you. And I want you to know that in the painful times, Gary and I have yet to see God fail to pull us through."

I grabbed Todd and did the same thing, reminding him that God has not abandoned him, that we love him, and that what matters most is how he responds to the pain he's in. We all stood there in a group hug until finally Todd said, through his tears, "Gary, all I know how to do is work. With that gone, I don't know what my future holds."

"I don't either, Todd. But the absolute truth is: God does."

Later, as we were leaving church, Jody had her arm through Todd's and she said, "I'm going to hang on to Todd through whatever God has planned for us. I love him. I just want to help carry the pain."

As we've kept in contact with this couple, we have seen Jody responding just the way she needs to:

- She is reminding her husband of God's grace.
- She is drawing the kids close to Todd in the midst of this struggle.
- She is calling Todd's buddies to tell them that they need to be present in Todd's life.

- She is on her knees praying.
- She is right beside him, as close as she can be, encouraging him.

That is what an encouraging wife does, in the tough times and the good times. This is what those wedding vows are all about—to love, honor, and cherish.

HOW TO ENCOURAGE YOUR HUSBAND

If you want to grow in your ability to encourage your husband, practice several of these suggestions.

Encourage Him to Hear the Applause

For the Christian man, the applause from heaven—God's approval—is essential. But like every other guy, I've discovered that heavenly applause is sometimes tough to hear.

Why? Well, for one thing, some men don't know it exists. They love the salvation part of the Christian message, but when it comes to actually *knowing* God, they either don't get it, or they feel they don't really need it.

Other men have turned the volume down—way down. They aren't spending enough time with God, especially enough quiet time apart from this noisy world, to clearly hear his voice. Their ears are so filled with the sounds of this world that they are constantly missing that still small voice.

That's where you can provide real spiritual encouragement.

Perhaps your husband's priorities are messed up. He may be ambitious in the marketplace but not always ambitious to hear God's voice. He may believe he is too busy to pray, read the Bible, and fellowship with other believers.

That kind of man is in danger of listening to the wrong voices, and he needs to tune in to this truth: The enemy of God, Satan, doesn't want men to listen to God's voice. He wants them to be overwhelmed and distracted by other voices. God wants your husband to win the race, but he's well aware that Satan wants your husband to get picked off before he reaches the finish line. That is why Paul said in Galatians 5:7, "You were running a good race. Who cut in on you and kept you from obeying the truth?" (NIV). We know the answer. It's the enemy who gets in the way.

What a man really needs is to have as his highest ambition the "well done, my good and faithful servant" echo ringing in his ear (Matt.

25:21). He should want the approving voice of Jesus so much that he blocks out all other distracting voices. But to do so means he must be humble enough to put aside *his* pride and tune in. It means he must train his ear to hear the Lord's voice.

Those of you who are mothers know that you can hear your child's cry above all others on a busy playground. That's because you've trained your ear to hear that voice. And we need to train our ears to hear the voice of Jesus. You can encourage your husband to do that. God has strategically placed you in your husband's life to be his live-in encourager.

Remind him of two things: God and you are there for him twenty-four hours a day, seven days a week. He can go to God—and to you—with anything. Just like the Father, you want to be a loud voice of encouragement when he struggles. Make no mistake, he depends on hearing applause from you. Check out these encouraging reminder statements I've heard wives tell their husbands in my office:

- "I believe in you, Bill."
- "Honey, I know you are deeply disappointed about work, but we'll get through this valley time. Remember, I'm here for you, and I'm sticking to you like superglue."
- "No matter what, Randy, I know God is going to help you through this tough time. And so am I."
- "I know it's hard to work through this. Justin is rebelling and breaking your heart, but we need to keep on trusting that all the years we put into him will bring him around. I am with you."

These women are encouraging their husbands by speaking the truth in love and cheering them on. They have become their husbands' number one cheerleader, even in the midst of their own needs and life struggles.

Help your husband to hear God's voice. Remind your husband that the Father speaks to him too. If God were speaking to your husband, he might say things such as:

- "I love you. I sent my Son to die for you."
- "I have given you the power of the Holy Spirit to fuel your passion and pursuit of holiness."
- "Son, stay on course. Guard your heart. Finish strong. I am with you."

Encourage Him by Reminding Him of God's Work in His Life

Ross doesn't have a clue about how to get his life in order. His business is shaky, he's not connecting with his wife, and his kids . . . well, he just doesn't know where they are. Ross rarely goes to church anymore, and when he's not at work, he's totally involved in his own "wide world of sports." He coaches three different sports because he loves the immediate feedback and adulation he gets from the kids and fans. It's his whole life. Well, almost his whole life. In a time of vulnerability, he admitted to a mutual friend that some other things are beginning to turn his head. The woman who just transferred into his department. The dream of big bucks. The lure of toys that will validate his importance. Ross is a midlife crisis waiting to happen.

His wife, Vicky, loves Christ and she loves Ross. But she is discouraged. She has tried to reach him, but he can't seem to hear her amid the sea of competing voices. What can she do? The most important thing she can do, for a start, is to help Ross see how God is working in his life. You know how I know? That is what Barb does for me.

Barb has discovered how to cheer me on as she consistently and appropriately reminds me of what God is doing in our lives. We'll be driving down the street, having a conversation about something overwhelming in our lives, and she brings up what she has read that day in her *One Year Bible*. At other times, because she knows me and my moods so well, she'll realize that I'm struggling with insecurity about the ministry or a relationship, and she'll offer to pray—for me and with me. More than once when I was discouraged she has encouraged me by pointing out a biblical example of how God worked through flawed men in spite of their shortcomings.

She is able to do this because she has planted "good seed" in her own life, and her root system now runs deep, grounded in the Word of God. This has enabled her to weather countless storms. And while she freely admits that she loves me and the girls more than her own life, she shows by her actions that she loves Jesus Christ even more. Her skill at being an encourager is top-notch because she goes to the Source to obtain her own refreshment—God's wisdom in the Bible and the person of Jesus Christ.

In case you're wondering if everything is perfect in our relationship, well, no, of course not. We're two human beings, just like you. But we do have a great marriage, and a great deal of credit for that goes to Barb, who has mastered the skills necessary to become the consummate cheerleader and encourager. When I'm up against tough stuff, I go to God . . . and to Barb. And if I go to Barb first, she will hear me out, encourage me, and then push me to the Lord.

Not only are these the two voices I know I need to seek, but because of my wife, these are the two major voices I *want* to seek.

How are you seeking to encourage your husband to see God's work in his life? Here are a few suggestions:

- When you see your husband take a stand for what is right, affirm him by telling him you see God's character in him.
- Bless your husband with encouragement from God's Word when he is discouraged. Send a carefully worded greeting card with an affirming message to surprise him at his workplace. Remind him of God's faithfulness to him in the past.
- Tell your husband how you see God working in other people through his activities or relationships.
- Affirm your husband's expression of the gifts of the Spirit (love, joy, peace, patience, kindness, goodness, faithfulness, gentleness, and self-control) when you see him act in any of these ways.

Encourage Him to Be Accountable

God has given me five solid, strong friends to walk through life with me and to hold me accountable. Rather than resent the time I spend with these men, Barb understands how important this interaction is in my life.

Since the late 1970s, I have met weekly with Jerry, Tim, and Mike. They are my accountability group. Another man who has the freedom to ask me the tough questions is my friend Steve Farrar. Even though he lives in Texas and I live in Iowa, we usually talk two to three times a week and share each other's burdens. Then there is my son-in-law, Scott, whom I mentor, talk to, and see almost daily. This mentoring process is really a two-way street, though. He gives as much as he receives.

Perhaps your husband has gone to Promise Keepers, and you have seen the work of a holy God in his heart when he came home: He is more tender, more spiritually focused, and more interested in strengthening your family. Or some other working of the Holy Spirit has prompted him to begin to grow spiritually. You, as his wife, must be his main encourager in making God-focused changes, but godly men can also be a strong support for him in this process.

Strong Christian friends will encourage your husband to be accountable. They will ask the hard questions and push on his chest a little because they care about him and want to help him guard his heart. They will ask him things such as

- How is your thought life?
- Are you struggling with any secret sin?
- Are you in the Word and prayer on a regular basis?
- Are your business practices ethical and above reproach?
- Are you giving your employer an honest day's work?
- Are you dealing with any sexual temptation or pornography?
- Are you tending to the needs of your family?

Some men balk at this kind of accountability because they think it means they are giving up control of their lives. It doesn't, of course. But all of us need Christian brothers to walk through life with us. That's why wise old Solomon said, "But pity the man who falls and has no one to help him up!" (Eccles. 4:10, NIV). Your husband needs godly men who will walk with him, lift him up, encourage him, and hold him accountable. "Though one may be overpowered, two can defend themselves," Solomon says a few verses later (Eccles. 4:12, NIV).

Encourage your husband to step close to other godly guys. He needs this kind of connection in his life.

Encourage Him to Connect with His Children

Standing in line at a ticket counter is not a new experience for me. Receiving wisdom from someone in line ahead of me is. A few months ago I was standing behind a mother and her daughter, who looked to be about three years old. I couldn't take my eyes off this little girl, who was holding her mom's hand, smiling, and playing with her stuffed bear. The woman must have sensed my staring because she looked at me. "You have a beautiful little girl there," I said as she caught my eye. "See those three gorgeous women over there? Those are my daughters and my wife. My girls used to be your age, honey," I said to the little girl. "Now they're all grown up."

Without skipping a beat, the woman ahead of me said, "Dad, you blinked."

Yes, I sure did. I blinked. And at that moment I was reminded of how quickly time goes by. Yesterday Sarah and Missy were two little angels hugging their teddy bears; today one is a young wife and the other a college student. I blinked. But I have no regrets because Barb was always there to encourage me to stay connected to my children.

A father needs his children as much as they need him. When I would get preoccupied, Barb was always there to encourage me to spend time with the girls. She would remind me to make the most of my time (Ps. 90:12) because our girls would not be under our roof forever. Barb is an expert at seeing the subtle areas of life. For instance, if my heart gets a little hard or distant, she will pick up on that and suggest that I take a night out with one of our daughters. Or she will encourage me to leave the office early and take the girls to the mall, or to a movie, or for an ice-cream cone. Anything that will get me connected one-on-one with my family.

An encouraging wife senses when there is a little too much distance between her husband and the kids—and she gently steers him closer. Barb has always done that for me, and it always pays off. As a result, I have the kind of relationship with our daughters that is truly a love affair of the heart. I am theirs. They are mine. We just fit.

Encourage Him to Reach Out and Grow

Barb is also tuned in to my need to continue to develop as a man. She gently encourages me to participate in events that will stretch me or help me grow. Like jumping on a bus with the guys and going to a Promise Keepers event. Even though I often speak at the stadium events, this past summer she urged me to attend a Promise Keepers event with a group of guys from our men's group, CrossTrainers. This is a group of six hundred men whom I have taught weekly since 1979. We are walking through life together, and as a result, we are seeing God strengthen homes all across Iowa.

"You need that time just to be one of the men in the stands, not on the platform," she said. "Allow God and those other guys to fill your own spiritual tank. Go for it!"

Encouraging your husband may be doing something as simple as suggesting that he play Christian music on the stereo, reminding him of a new devotional book that you think he would enjoy, or pointing out an article in a Christian magazine. It's true that you can't force, whine, or nag your husband to be spiritually and relationally thirsty (and you shouldn't try). But you must make a conscious, daily choice to root for your man. He is thirsty for your encouragement.

Like all human beings, your husband is a complex creature. But in another sense, he is also pretty basic: He needs God; he needs you; he needs your kids, if you have children; he needs his buddies. Your husband is a relational being just like you. He probably isn't the best at verbalizing his need for these relationships, but make no mistake—he does need them. Why? Because God created him that way.

Help him grow as a man, intrapersonally and interpersonally.

THE POWER OF ENCOURAGEMENT

Most guys I know have a favorite movie. You know the ones I'm talking about—the ones your husband watches over and over until he can recite the dialogue verbatim. Like *The Dirty Dozen* or *Jaws* or *The Godfather*. Well, mine is *Rocky*. Okay, the next question is "Which one?" Right? There have only been about seventeen of them. Right now I'm thinking about a scene at the end of *Rocky II*.

Rocky had just knocked out Apollo Creed and was in the ring with the microphone. "I just want to say one thing . . . Apollo, you're the greatest." (This is the guy he just knocked out.) "I want to thank Mickey, my trainer." (Mickey snarls.) Then you hear the fans yelling, "Rocky, we love you." To which Rocky belts out, "I love you" (to the cheers of the crowd). "But most of all, I want to thank God. . . . Next to my kid being born, this is the greatest day of my life." (Not bad, Rock.)

And then came the punch line, "Yo, Adrian [his wife, who is watching on TV at home] . . . I love you!" To which she mouths the return, "I love you too, Rock."

Whenever I hear that triumphant *Rocky* theme music, I get chills down my spine. And I bet your husband does too. Why, you wonder? Because many guys think they are Rocky Balboa. And when they see Rocky yell out in front of the entire world, "Yo, Adrian, I love you," and see her respond, "I love you too, Rock," he wants just one thing: for his Adrian—you—to cheer him on! To encourage him! To believe in him!

But don't take my word for it—ask your husband. Find out what encourages him. It may be that twinkle in your eye, that nod of approval, that gentle smile that sends the message "I am proud of you." You can say it in a store-bought card or on a sticky note you put on his calendar or his mirror. But say it frequently, positively, and authentically.

If you have not developed the habit of doing this, start today. It's never too late. Here are a few ideas to get you started:

- Write him a note telling him how proud you are of him.
- Find out where his heart is with the Lord. What is he learning?
- Tell him in front of the kids that you are thankful for the way he provides for your family's needs.
- Call his parents and brag about him a little, if possible when he can overhear you.
- Affirm him for the way he loves you.

Your husband also needs your prayers. Get into the habit of praying in very specific ways for him every day.

- Pray for him to hear the applause from heaven.
- Pray for his prayer life and for his faithfulness to study the Word of God.
- Pray about ways that you might stimulate him to talk about his own faith.
- Pray that he will establish a few close friendships with godly men who will encourage him and hold him accountable, men with whom he can be honest about his heart and his needs, men who will stand with him during good times and bad.
- Pray that God will continue to keep the communication open between your husband and your children, if you have them. Pray that he will be a loving and gentle father. Pray for your own sensitivity in seeing ways that you can encourage this.

Men are really struggling today. I see this all the time in my counseling office and in my ministry with other men. Just this week in CrossTrainers, I had men approach me with the following needs: One man is facing the one-year anniversary of his son's death. Another just lost his job. One man, who lost his father a few years ago, just learned that his mother has cancer. One of our men has been diagnosed with depression. One of the newer, younger guys has just had to tell his wife that they are in real financial trouble; he has been secretly spending excessive amounts of money she didn't know about.

When we men are in the midst of such trials, pushing our limits, we need to hear the voice of God leading and sustaining us, and we need to hear our wives encouraging and believing in us.

Continually work to be a strong presence in your husband's world. Remind him of his worth in God's eyes, as well as to you and your children. Build him up. Cheer him on. Encourage him to continue to fight the good fight, to finish the race, to remain faithful (2 Tim. 4:7). And help him fight the good fight and finish the race *with you*. Encourage him to be the best he can be so that one day, when one of you must place the other in the arms of the Savior, you can hear the words that Jesus wants each of us to hear, "Well done, my good and faithful servant."

Finishing together is the best encouragement of all: A man and a woman finishing well, loving their families and friends, proclaiming boldly their love for their Lord and for one another.

When you finish reading this chapter, I want you to do one of the following things. If your husband is at work, give him an encouraging call. If he is lying in bed next to you while you're reading this, give him a big, wet, sloppy kiss. If he is in the other room, go on in and sit by him and tell him how much you love him. If he is unavailable at the moment, write him a note telling him you are proud of him, crazy about him, and wanting to finish life with him. And if something is blocking you from freely reaching out to your husband in this way, I want you to put aside your feelings and do it anyway.

Life is short.

And when all is said and done, our relationships with Jesus Christ and each other are the only things that will matter.

CHAPTER 8

ENCOURAGEMENT

A WIFE'S #4 LOVE NEED

"Remind me that I'm your one and only."

Barb talks to husbands

A few months ago Gary stuck his head into my office and asked if I would join him for the final few minutes of a counseling session. Since I don't typically do this, I was surprised, but I knew he had a good reason for wanting me there.

"Amy is facing major issues with her husband," Gary said. "I think she could use some encouragement from you."

Amy's husband had grown callous toward her over the past couple years, and his spirit had gradually hardened. Initially, she thought they had grown apart because of his increasingly long workdays and frequent weekend business trips. What brought her to Gary's office for counseling, however, was the shock of learning that her husband was having an affair—with her best friend! Amy's life was spinning out of control. The two people she loved most were breaking her heart.

Gary was doing his best to give Amy hope and counsel in her darkest hour. But at this moment she also needed something that he, as a man who was not her husband, could not provide: She needed to be held and comforted. She needed someone to hug her, cry with her, and genuinely encourage her. She needed "God with skin on." That was why Gary brought me into the picture.

When people are hurting, they need more than a diagnosis, more than professional advice. They need to sense that someone genuinely cares about them—and not simply because it's their job. Or, as the apostle Paul wrote, "As apostles of Christ we could have been a burden to you, but we were gentle among you, like a mother caring for her little children. We loved you so much that we were delighted to share with you not only the gospel of God but our lives as well, because you had become so dear to us" (1 Thess. 2:6-8, NIV).

Two days later we received the following letter:

> *Dear Gary and Barb,*
>
> *Thank you, thank you, thank you! From the bottom of my heart, I want to thank you for your prayers that were spoken in your office. I feel so humbled and in awe of God. You two don't know how many times I debated calling to see if there was any way Barb could sit in on my counseling session with Gary. I dismissed the thought each time, thinking it was too much to ask. But despite my hesitation and doubting, Barb, God had you there. He knew you needed to be there, and he made it happen. This was the first time in two months that you were in the office when I have been there for an appointment. Wow! What a great God! An immediate need was met when you gave me the picture of God saying, "Come sit on my lap, and I will be as a husband to you." You knew I wasn't getting this from my earthly husband. I now picture Christ holding me, loving me unconditionally, and giving me all the tenderness that I could ever ask for.*
>
> *Thanks to both of you for pointing me to Christ for the answers, for getting on your knees and praying with such fervent hearts for my husband, our marriage, and our family. I now have real hope that my husband's heart is going to break and that he will become a changed man! I have renewed faith that he will again live for Christ!*

What Gary and I offered Amy that day was encouragement, in several forms. As you can see, it is powerful stuff.

I hope that your wife has never faced the kind of devastating betrayal that Amy faced. But I know that she has times when she is discouraged, misunderstood, or afraid. We all do. Who does she turn to when the proverbial rug has been pulled out from under her? Where does she go when she is feeling alone or out of control? Who does she turn to when she is overwhelmed by circumstances?

That's when she needs the encouraging presence of

- someone who will offer hope and support,
- someone who will listen,

- someone who is trustworthy,
- someone who will understand,
- someone who will crawl into the foxhole with her when the battle is fierce.

Encouragement literally means "to give courage; to inspire with courage, spirit, or hope; to hearten." It's a word that immediately came to mind when I recently saw some World War II footage on the History Channel. The photographer had captured events from the night before D day, when General Eisenhower was in England, walking among the paratroopers before they took off across the English Channel. Eisenhower must have known that most of these young men would never return. But his presence reminded them that what they were doing was important for the cause of freedom and that they were valuable in the eyes of their commanding general. Throughout history this kind of encouragement has inspired ordinary men and women to behave gallantly in perilous situations.

What does all this have to do with your wife? Well, your wife fights battles every day. And do you know what keeps her pressing ahead? Your encouragement.

Both men and women need encouragement. So much so that *both* men and women rated encouragement as their number four need on our marriage survey. But because men and women are different, that encouragement can take different forms. Check out these two lists of needs:

Husbands need	*Wives need*
1. a card once or twice a year to tell them that they are loved	1. daily doses of "I love you" (cards and flowers work well too!)
2. an evening out every so often	2. one evening every week with just the two of you
3. a golfing (or sailing, or bowling) buddy	3. a female friend in whom she can confide
4. a new challenge every five years to keep life interesting	4. frequent time-outs from her routine to recharge her battery
5. a slap on the back from the guys on the basketball court	5. supportive hugs from her female friends

Do you get the picture? Women need *a lot* of encouragement! It's the way God wired us. Not better or worse, just different.

YOUR WIFE'S NEED FOR ENCOURAGEMENT

Watch a game of golf on TV, or walk the course during a professional tournament, and you would think the only three words some guys know are, "You the man!" It's their way of encouraging a favorite golfer. And even though the pros must hear this phrase a gazillion times, when they smack a three-hundred-yard drive dead center down the fairway and then hear a chorus of "You the man," the bounce in their step is noticeable.

Though your wife never needs to hear you say, "You the man!" (trust me on this), she does need to hear your appropriate version of affirmation to keep a bounce in her step. Phrases like . . .

- "You're the best wife a husband could ever have."
- "Have I told you lately you're my hero?"
- "I love growing old with you."
- "You're my best friend."

A woman has a larger-than-life need for her husband to whisper, declare, and shout to the world that she is the most important person in his life!

I'm not afraid to admit that Gary holds an incredible position of power in my life. Why? Because he knows me best. And because he cares enough to understand that I think differently from how he thinks, he also understands what I need when it comes to encouragement. A good example is a typical situation in the Rosberg household.

It's the end of a busy day, and I'm rushing around the house feeling exhausted, going from making dinner, to laundry, to dinner, to tidying up, to dinner, to answering the phone, to dinner . . . you get the idea. Then Gary walks in the room and says, "You're the most wonderful woman in the universe!"

He knows how to energize a worn-out female, and his edifying words add several more hours of energy to me. His vote of confidence strengthens my spirit, rekindles my energy, and reassures me that I'm not alone in the world. That's the power of encouragement.

It's not enough just to appreciate your wife; you have to *tell* her how much. And let me warn you: If you don't appreciate and encourage your wife, she will turn elsewhere to get her needs met. More than a few marriages have ended up on the rocks for this very reason. If encouragement from you isn't a steady part of your wife's diet, she's starving for it.

Many women turn to their careers to find encouragement. I am not suggesting that a woman should not derive satisfaction and affirmation from her work. But she needs to hear the loudest, most passionate cheers from her husband.

When Gary and I were first married, I taught art in the elementary schools. I loved it! I loved the kids—the 350 budding young artists under my wing. And I treasured the affirmation I got from their notes. Then I got pregnant with our first child and began to devote my gifts and energies to homemaking and child rearing.

The birth of a child, especially the first baby, is a life-changing miracle for a woman. It also can be the beginning of a lonely journey. I loved being at home with Sarah. I cherished my time with her. But I also missed those daily notes from my students, those constant reinforcements that I was doing a good job. I longed for that same kind of encouragement in my role as a mother and a homemaker for my family. Gary met that foundational need in my life by offering daily doses of encouragement.

There are countless ways that a husband can encourage his wife in the daily routine of life:

- Tell her how valuable and important she is as a wife.
- Have a smile on your face when you walk in the door at night.
- Listen when she expresses her frustration about her own workday. Remember that her pressures and stresses are just as real as your own.
- Be patient when she is tired and grouchy.
- Give her some space when she needs it.
- Let her talk your ear off when she needs to do that.
- Lift her spirits by reminding her of all the things she is doing right.
- Leave her thank-you love notes on the bathroom mirror.
- Take home a bouquet of flowers for no particular reason.
- Tell your wife how valuable and important she is as a mother if you have children.
- Let her know that you understand that being at home with young children can be hard and lonely work. Steady her emotions by recognizing that babies and preschoolers require a lot of energy.

- Step in to help during those endless bouts of chicken pox, flu, earaches, and sore throats.
- Give your wife extra help with errands, laundry, and grocery shopping, especially if she is housebound with sick children.

Women spend so much time supporting, helping, and nurturing the people in their lives, but they don't always get the support, help, and nurture they need in return. Because each woman is unique, you need to be a student of your own wife (sound familiar?). Understanding her personality and character will allow you to tailor your encouragement specifically for her.

Let's look at three basic types of women and see how you can be the best encourager to the woman you married.

THE INDEPENDENT WOMAN

She is sometimes known as superwoman. She's able to leap tall buildings—or at least she thinks she can. She has a strong work ethic and often has a career outside the home. Early in your relationship, this woman's confidence, strength, and independent spirit attracted you to her. But sometimes the very thing that drew you together in the first place can keep you from growing closer.

Sheila is a strong, confident woman. She is the top saleswoman for an international line of women's clothing and is well respected in the fashion industry. She exudes self-assurance, and her desire to succeed consumes her. She talks about work all the time and has the attitude "I love my husband, but I don't need him."

Don't get me wrong. Confidence is not a bad thing. But it can be when it's hiding a larger problem. In Sheila's case, she gains her sense of self-worth from her job instead of from her heart. Her drive to achieve success in her career is a way to prove to her husband and those around her that she is worthwhile.

If this sounds like your wife, then you need to show her how proud you are of her regardless of how she chooses to use her talents. Remind her that she doesn't need to achieve anything to be a success in your eyes. Encourage her to slow down, spend time with you, and love herself unconditionally.

Sometimes the independent woman is hiding a fairly significant prob-

lem. Her detached attitude toward her husband could be fear of getting too close to him—a sort of whistling in the dark. Women like this often fear abandonment, so they hunker down in the bunker of "I don't need anyone, not even my husband."

A childhood experience may lie behind this attitude—something that has caused her to think it is not safe to confide in or depend on another person. If she has been humiliated or rejected in the past, she may be guarding herself by keeping her distance, under the guise of not needing anyone.

Control can also be an issue with the independent woman. Life is safe only if she is in control. She sees bonding as bondage, and she worries about losing her freedom.

With this woman, you must prove yourself trustworthy in both large and small ways. You must help her see that she is missing out on the fulfillment that comes from true closeness in marriage. Encourage her to step close, and continue to step close yourself—really close—and start pushing through those walls. Let her know you adore her. Show her that she doesn't need to earn your love and that you will never, ever leave.

THE INSECURE WOMAN

Betty has many wonderful qualities, but she wards off any and all compliments (either verbally or mentally). If you say, "What a great meal," she says, "Oh, you were just hungry." If you say, "The house looks beautiful," she says, "You should see the closets." If you say, "You're looking really sharp," she says, "Oh, I'm too fat." If you say, "Your kids are so well behaved," she says, "They're always better around other people." If you say, "Good job," she says, "I got lucky this time."

Betty rejects the truth about herself. You can see it in her eyes. The minute you compliment her, she breaks eye contact and glances away. She seems ill at ease, a bit anxious. She can't understand how you could say those kind, positive things about her. Internally she is arguing with you.

This woman does not know how to accept your affirmation. What's worse, she often challenges that affirmation—at least to herself! She sees it as exaggeration, flattery, fawning—blarney!

Chances are she has lived with self-doubt for a long time, perhaps since she was a little girl. Maybe she spent too much time alone. Maybe her parents were always working or so distracted and busy that they didn't take the time to pour words of encouragement into a thirsty little girl. Whatever the specifics of her experience, something in her past pounded messages of self-doubt into her.

This woman refuses to believe that she is "fearfully and wonderfully made" (Ps. 139:14, NIV). If you are married to an insecure woman, encourage her by challenging her negative thinking. As the one who loves and cares about her most, encourage her to break free from these underlying attitudes of self-depreciation.

- Speak the truth to her often. Tell her what is going well in your life. Remind her of what she is doing right. Point out her giftedness and praise her strengths. Ignore any protestations on her part, and speak the truth in love!
- Encourage her to focus on the message of Philippians 4:8, "Fix your thoughts on what is true and honorable and right. Think about things that are pure and lovely and admirable. Think about things that are excellent and worthy of praise." Gently encourage her to recognize how her attitude is affecting her life and your relationship. She may not even be aware of what she is doing. A huge first step is getting her to see and/or admit what she is doing.
- Work out a plan of action *with* her. Ask her permission to help by lovingly challenging her negative thinking with declarations of positive truth.
- Teach her to receive. Remember when your dad taught you to catch a baseball—with both hands opened up, reaching into the ball? At first it bounced off your head or hit your chest, but eventually you caught it! Encourage your wife to be open, to lean in and catch your affirmation. If she can begin by simply responding with two little words, "Thank you," she'll be on her way.

THE BALANCED WOMAN

The independent woman and the insecure woman are extreme examples. Most women fit somewhere in the middle of this spectrum. And all women are a complex combination of these and many other traits, personalities, backgrounds, talents, and temperaments.

Ultimately, you want to encourage your wife to achieve a healthy balance in her life. To do this, you must understand the unique person that she is.

- Can you tell when you've struck a sensitive nerve with your wife? Find out what makes her touchy or defensive. Why is she feeling stressed?
- Does she have any underlying insecurity? If she does, often it will be related to self-esteem, performance, or a drive for perfectionism.
- Is she driven by self-imposed performance-based demands?

Much of a woman's healthy self-esteem is based in her realization of her value before God and her understanding of his wealth of love for her. Even the most confident woman will, at times, forget this. At that point she needs to have her husband come alongside with the appropriate affirmation.

In his insightful book *The Five Love Languages,* Dr. Gary Chapman says that we communicate love and encouragement to our spouses in the way that we ourselves need to receive love and encouragement. How does your wife encourage you? Is it by doing thoughtful things for you? Is it offering you words of praise and affirmation? Is it through touch, rubbing your back, snuggling close? Does she give you extra doses of time and attention? Does she buy you little gifts when you need perking up or for no reason at all? All of these are different languages of love that demonstrate encouragement. Return your love and encouragement in the same language, and she will get the message.

HOW TO ENCOURAGE YOUR WIFE

In the early days of the Ford Motor Company in Detroit, the manufacturing plant suddenly lost all its electricity. Henry Ford tried everything he could think of to fix the problem, but to no avail. Finally, he called in an electrician. The man walked over to the electrical box, fooled around with a couple of wires, and the power was restored. He then handed Ford a bill for ten thousand dollars.

Ford was astonished. "Why should this thirty-second job fixing the wiring cost so much?"

"There's no charge for fixing the wiring," said the electrician. "The ten thousand dollars is for knowing which wires to jiggle."

So here's the ten-thousand-dollar question, men: Do you know your wife's wiring well enough to know what wires to jiggle to encourage her? One of the best ways to learn is by observation, by being, as we have said before, a student of your wife.

Understand Her Wiring

The next time you see two women talking, watch them. Notice how intense they are. Listen to them. Even if you can't hear the words, listen to the tone of their voices. Notice how connected they sound. Notice how the conversation moves back and forth, sort of like a tennis ball. Sometimes they even finish each other's sentences! Sometimes the flow is serious and fluid; sometimes it is light and peppery. For a woman, this form of connected conversation acts as a stress reliever and even a kind of therapeutic release.

While your wife's friends are certainly important to her, it is absolutely vital that your wife get this kind of support from you . . . her husband, her best friend. At the end of a long day she wants to be able to share her feelings with you, without fear of judgment. She's not looking for solutions. She wants to share her intimate thoughts so that her burdens can be lifted and her emotional ties to you strengthened.

When you listen to her share her feelings and thoughts, she feels cherished and valued. She feels validated when you remind her of what she did right. She is refueled and energized, no matter how many responsibilities are facing her.

When it comes to processing an issue, women tend to talk through it aloud. After we monologue—and sometimes dialogue—it through, we're ready to take on the world. Depending on the situation, our emotions can also come into play here. It all has to do with that internal "wiring." Let me analyze it for you.

You and your wife are having a discussion about your mother, who wants to come and spend a week with your family. "Hey, no big deal," you say. "Just change the sheets. Right?" It's not that simple for your wife. She loves her mother-in-law, but a week-long visit is going to require preparation. Your wife has been really busy lately, so the cleaning has been hit or miss. She'll need to clean out a few kitchen drawers, the front-hall closet, and the guest-room closet. She wants you to pick up that mess in the basement. Then there is the meal preparation. She needs to plan out the menus, do the grocery shopping, fix some premade dishes for freezing. And what will she do with your mother for a week? She can't just leave her sitting in the house. And what about the baby shower she is hosting that week for a friend at the office? She can't change that. On and on she goes, talking this through and beginning to sound a little emotional.

What's happening here is that her internal wiring is overloading, and the circuit is about to break! A word of caution: Just as you would never mess with live wiring, so you don't want to argue with her emotions.

Learn how to ease the tension. If she's ready to cry, then encourage her to cry. (Yes, cry.) When her tear ducts release, that's a good sign the overload is lessening. Encourage her by letting her *drain the pain.* Then she's able to listen. If your advice or solution is good, you'll sound like the best counselor in the world. When she's in the midst of processing her feelings about the situation, your logic or desire to fix it will be unwelcome, sometimes even offensive. Later, however, she'll probably invite you to help her solve it! But remember: As you begin your fixing, start by validating her point of view. The smallest of validations can make you soar from Clark Kent to Superman in your wife's eyes!

Give Her First Place

Whether men are participating in the game or coaching from a recliner, most of them love a good sporting event. And we women want you to enjoy your sports, to bond with the guys, or to scream "You the man!" to your favorite player. Involvement in sports can be a great stress reducer, and we're all for reducing stress in your life. It extends your life and makes you a much more enjoyable companion. Besides, we want you to relax and have fun. You deserve it!

But the tension begins to mount inside us when shooting hoops, hitting golf balls, or watching game after game on the tube takes precedence over time with us. We begin to feel neglected. How would you feel coming in second to a rubber ball? And what if the tables were turned and your wife was off with her friends on weekends and/or several nights a week? When we aren't first place in your life, it really doesn't matter if we're second, third, or fourth. It's all the same. We feel completely overlooked and unimportant.

Sometimes what you give first place to may seem so important that you don't even recognize what you are doing.

Let's imagine that you are a man who owns his own business. You have two or three (or more) people who work for you, but ultimately you're the one responsible for the success of your company. Then sales begin slipping, and unhappy customers start calling. You're overwhelmed. You spend your time putting out one fire after another instead of getting ahead. You have to find a way to salvage all of this so you don't lose your customers to the competition.

What do you do to solve this problem? You work sixty, seventy, eighty-plus hours a week. You pour your heart and soul into your company. After all, it's your family's future, right?

All men want to succeed in their careers. There's nothing wrong with that. And working long hours from time to time may be necessary. But if you find your job continually pulling you away from your wife and family, something is wrong. You think to yourself, *It's just temporary. If I work really hard for a while, things will get better.* But the in box is always full, the phone is always ringing, and the weeks turn into years. Day and night you're drained, with no energy left for your wife. It may start with a few missed dinners, but it soon turns into late-night meals by yourself and a full family calendar without you in the picture. What's worse is that when you are home, today's regrets and tomorrow's plans steal into your every thought. You're emotionally distant and disengaged. Your work has become a thief that steals time away from the most important people in your life.

If you can identify with any of this, you have to stop this behavior. Not tomorrow or next week, but right now. It doesn't matter how you justify it, no career is more important than your wife (or your family, if you have been blessed with children). Whether or not your wife shows it, she is lonely, unappreciated, and unloved. Would you ever think of starving your wife of the food she needs to sustain her physical body? No, I can't imagine that you would. Yet you are starving her of the very encouragement she needs to survive.

If she tells you that you are spending too much time at work, don't feel threatened. She is telling you that no one can replace you in her life and that she needs your companionship and encouragement to complete her the way no one else can. The core message is "I love you and need you."

Point Out Her Potential

Years ago I was taking a night class in painting and portraiture to continue my growth and education as an artist. The instructor was well respected, but his manner of criticism left something to be desired. One night, after I had spent the entire evening working on a painting, the instructor stopped beside me, took my canvas from the easel, and verbally ripped it apart. I was devastated and went home in tears, determined never to paint again.

The next day, Gary came home from work and handed me two packages. Inside were an easel and a wooden box full of Rembrandt pastels. "Enough of your wallowing!" he said. "God gave you a talent, and you're going to paint. Get moving—now!" None of this was said harshly. But it was said firmly, with love, as he affirmed the truth about my abilities.

It reminds me of the story of Jesus and his dealings with the paralytic man who was let down through the roof to be healed. The Savior was strong, direct, and clear. He told the man to stand up, take his mat, and go home (Luke 5:24). And he did. Gary told me to take my palette and paint. And I did.

Or I think of how Jesus saw potential in a man named Simon. Jesus even changed Simon's name to Peter, which means *rock* in Greek, at a time when Simon appeared anything but rocklike. He didn't seem like a rock of strength when he lost his temper or when he took his eyes off Christ as he was walking on water or when he denied knowing Christ on the eve of the Crucifixion. But Jesus recognized the potential Simon had to be a great man of God, and when we read about Peter in Acts or in his epistles, we realize how right God was.

We still see with human eyes, of course, but all of us can remind each other of our God-given potential. Do this for your wife. Focus on her strengths, not her weaknesses. Try to see her the way Jesus would see her.

Appreciate Her Contribution

Not long ago Gary and I were interviewing the former governor of Iowa, Terry Branstad, on our radio show. He and his wife, Chris, had recently celebrated their twenty-fifth wedding anniversary by taking a cruise to Alaska. Being a romantic, I asked the governor on the air, "What was the best part of your cruise?" I fully expected to hear him say "being with Chris" or something to that effect, because I know how much this man loves his wife and values his marriage. Instead, the governor looked at the men in our radio studio and said, "Catching a fifty-two-pound salmon!"

The men in the room went nuts! "Yessss!" Male bonding skyrocketed! I think I even heard someone say, "You the man!"

But after the laughter died down, the governor's eyes took on a serious look, and he said, "The best part of my cruise was Chris. I love my wife more than my life. She's always there for me." Then he continued to talk about what her support has meant to him and their family, and about his deep love and appreciation for her.

His initial response for the radio audience was humorous, and I'm sure he instantly connected with the male listeners, as he had with the guys in the studio. But he used that connection to immediately go on and underscore how much he values his wife. This is a man who knows his wife deserves to be appreciated. He also knows that he needs to take advantage of moments to brag about his wife in public.

You need to do the same. In both private and public ways, you need to let your wife know how much she is appreciated. Here are a couple of suggestions:

- Praise her three different times during a day. Since this is her soul food, nourish her! When Gary says to me, "I love to be in your company," or, "You take such great care of all of us!" I walk on air for days! Try this for a month, and I guarantee you will change the quality of your marriage.
- Brag about her to your friends. Let her catch you at it! She may act as if she's embarrassed, but deep down it will convince her that you really mean it.

If you're a very talented man, a high-powered personality, or a highly successful person, you need to take extra care. Your wife could, even unintentionally, fall into your shadow. Many women give up a great deal of themselves for their family—and they do it willingly and lovingly. But when they receive no appreciation, they sooner or later feel hurt and resentful.

Nothing will encourage your wife more than for you to recognize her sacrifices and affirm her love and devotion to your family. Think about it: She would do anything to strengthen and support you and your kids, right? She often does this so you can get ahead in your career. Encouragement from you will serve as a continual reminder to her that it's all worth it.

A brief warning here: Some women hear a word of praise only when they have performed well or done something nice. But when words of praise and value are linked solely to a woman's performance, she'll soon ask herself, *Am I loved for who I am, or for what I do?* Praise her for who she is.

Finally, be aware that your silence sounds like rejection to your wife. Don't assume she automatically knows how you feel about her. She needs to be continually reminded. Worry, stress, the kids, your mother— anything can knock the wind out of her, causing her to forget what you told her last week. She is on the front lines of battle and needs constant reinforcement.

WHAT IT MEANS TO BE AN ENCOURAGER

For a woman, a simple act or word of encouragement at the right moment can be the turning point during a struggle.

Emily is afraid. She just received a call from the doctor's office. The results of her latest physical are in, and the doctor wants to see her now, this afternoon, for a biopsy. She calls her husband, and his immediate response is "I'll be home within the hour." He will take her to the doctor. He doesn't want her to go alone. He'll be right there with her, whatever happens.

Jackie is a bookkeeper in the accounting department of a large banking corporation. She has caught a sizable accounting error that someone in her office has been making on each quarterly tax-payment deposit. The financial penalty will be severe and could place the corporation in financial jeopardy. If she remains silent, her integrity is at risk; if she reports the error, her job will be on the line. Her husband, Robert, listens as Jackie explains her dilemma. He encourages her to hold on to her convictions; she is right to abide by the law. If she loses her job, so be it. Together they work out a plan for her to talk to her department manager with the proper documentation in hand. Robert encourages her honesty and prays with her for strength and wisdom to handle the situation properly without losing her job.

Because of their husbands' encouragement, neither Emily nor Jackie has to go into battle alone.

A major element of encouragement is communication. In light of that, I suggest that you watch the way your life relates to other women. Often, we wives get some of our greatest encouragement from other women— whether from a mother or a sister or a female friend. No matter what we're stressed about, these women come through for us. This is true of my friend Pat Holmertz. I can be totally honest with her about how I am feeling or what I am dealing with, and she listens. Then, like a bugle call in battle, she offers words that give me the courage to step back into the ranks and move forward.

Analyze what goes on between your wife and her best friend or the other supportive women in her life. Is there any way that you can duplicate some of that encouraging body language, eye contact, active listening, and unconditional acceptance in your own interaction with your wife?

If you need a few ideas on getting started, try these:

- Open up to her. Talk. Let her see what is going on in your heart. Women are drawn to and encouraged by communicative men!
- One-up her. When she tells you she loves you, make sure you tell her two more times! See it like a tennis game: When she hits the ball to you, volley it right back. The same goes in affirmation. When she compliments you, make sure you express appreciation right back to her. Remind her throughout the day of what she does well.
- Reflect her love language to her. How does she communicate her love and appreciation of you? Through words of affirmation? Through thoughtful gifts? Through preparing your favorite meal? Chances are that's what she would love in return!
- Have a love affair with her! Get to know her all over again. Treat her as if you've known her for only a few days. Take her back to those early days when you were really trying to impress her.
- Set aside a night for the two of you every week. Tune in to what's important to her. Obviously it's important for you to do things you both enjoy together. But be willing to sacrifice your own preferences for something you know she would really love to do.
- Give her that Rhett Butler look. A wink and a smile when she least expects them will sweep her off her feet.
- Say it with flowers. Whether it is one or a dozen, they will send the right message.
- Vacuum out the inside of her car and clean the windows. Leave a note that reads, "Simply because I love you!"
- Accept her sensitivity. What appears at times to be oversensitivity to you is the very dimension of womanhood that makes her alert and sensitive to your needs. Resist the urge of trying to change her.

Be a Barnabas

Without thinking for more than ten seconds, I'm certain you can recall someone's words of criticism that still hurt today. That's how powerful words are. Researchers tell us that we need eight to ten positive comments to neutralize every negative one. Yet that kind of neutralization rarely happens for any of us.

What we all need are people in the midst of our life yelling words of encouragement: "Go for it!" "I know you can do it!" "I'm with you all the way." "I'm committed to you!" "I believe in you!"

Throughout the Scriptures we find evidence of the power and importance of the spoken word. In the book of Genesis alone, the phrase "God said" appears more than twenty times. Later, God's own Son is described as the Word who "became human and lived here on earth among us" (John 1:14). God has always communicated his love for us through spoken words. And words are the way we speak love and encouragement to others.

In the days of the early church, Barnabas was a man known for his generous encouragement. In fact, his given name was John, but the apostles called him Barnabas, which means "son of encouragement" or, literally, "son of refreshment." Acts 11:23 tells us that "he encouraged the believers to stay true to the Lord."

Gary is my Barnabas.

He knows my strengths and weaknesses; he knows all of me! He is both wise and tender with me. Because he knows that the forgiveness Christ gives is fresh each new day, he's quick to remind me of the grace of God when I'm down and discouraged. And he doesn't allow me to turn inward. He will admonish me to reach out and be forgiving to those who offend me. Sometimes, his encouragement is something as simple as reminding me over and over what God has done for us.

Most important, though, Gary dares me to become more of what God has called me to be, and my husband doesn't back down when I resist. There are times that I would prefer to run and hide, but Gary dares me to open up and be transparent, to let him see my hurts as well as my hopes.

Actress Celeste Holm once said, "We live by encouragement and die without it. Slowly, sadly, and angrily." What saddens me is that authentic encouragement is rare in many homes today. Too many homes are full of discouraged people desperately waiting for a kind word.

THE POWER OF ENCOURAGEMENT

Several years ago *Reader's Digest* printed the story of a remarkable junior high math teacher at St. Mary's School in Morris, Minnesota. One Friday afternoon this teacher asked her students to make a list of the names of all the other students in the class. Then she told them to write down, beside each name, the nicest thing they could say about each of their classmates. At the end of the period she collected the sheets. Then, over the weekend she made a separate sheet for each student, and on that sheet she listed all the things that had been said about each person by his or her classmates. On Monday she gave each student his or her list.

As the kids began reading, they started whispering to each other. "I never knew you thought that about me." "I didn't know others liked me so much." The papers were never discussed in the class, but the teacher knew the exercise was a success because she could see the difference this positive feedback made in the students' attitudes about themselves.

Several years later one of the students, Mark Ekland, was killed in Vietnam. After his body was returned to Minnesota, most of his classmates, as well as the math teacher, attended the funeral. At the luncheon after the service Mark's father approached the teacher and said, "They found this on Mark when he was killed. We thought you might recognize it." He handed her two worn sheets of notebook paper that had been taped, folded, and refolded many times. It was the list of good things Mark's classmates had written about him.

"Thank you so much for doing that," Mark's father told the teacher. "As you can see, our son treasured it." Several of Mark's classmates had been standing nearby and overheard this conversation. One by one they began to reveal that each of them still carried his or her sheet of comments and read it often. Some carried it in a billfold; one had even put it in his wedding album. One young man said, "I think we all saved our list."

That's the power of affirming, encouraging words.

Do you think your wife has a list like that tucked away somewhere in her mind? Are you noticing, appreciating, and verbalizing the nicest things you can say about your wife?

"You the man," right? Then show your wife, in word and in deed, some encouragement each and every day, and I guarantee you'll not only hear that phrase from her often (in her own way, of course), but she'll do all she can to make you feel that you *are* the man!

CHAPTER 9

SPIRITUAL CONNECTION

A HUSBAND'S #5 LOVE NEED

"I need you to help me grow spiritually."

Gary talks to wives

Your husband, like every Christian husband, needs to be growing spiritually. He needs spiritual connection—with God, with you, and with other believers. If husbands are going to take the Bible seriously, then they know that one of the key dimensions of their spiritual life is the spiritual leadership they must provide.

"I hate that verse that tells husbands that we must be the head of our wives as Christ is the head of the church," said Joseph.

"Why do you say that?" I asked him.

"Because it means that I have to be 'on' spiritually all the time. I'm supposed to be the leader in the home, so I have to lead whether I feel weak or strong. If I fall down, I'm not only letting myself down, I'm also letting my wife and my children down." Joseph paused and looked me straight in the eye. "Gary, be honest with me. Do you ever feel that way?"

Before I tell you what I told Joseph, let me assure you that he is not alone in his frustration. If you could read the hearts and minds of most Christian men, you would find that leadership—real servant leadership—is the biggest challenge they face on a daily basis.

In his Word, God commands men to be servant leaders in their marriages and in their homes. But servant leadership is a two-sided coin. On one side is the great honor and opportunity that kind of leadership offers: honor in being entrusted with such a high call and opportunity to help meet our family's deepest needs. However, the other side of the coin is that servant leadership is a very tough job!

This spiritual responsibility weighs heavily on your husband when he recognizes that you and your children are relying on him to take the lead. Add to that the fact that he knows that God is going to hold him accountable for the way he carries out that mandate.

> And you husbands must love your wives with the same love Christ showed the church. He gave up his life for her to make her holy and clean, washed by baptism and God's word. He did this to present her to himself as a glorious church without a spot or wrinkle or any other blemish. Instead, she will be holy and without fault. In the same way, husbands ought to love their wives as they love their own bodies. For a man is actually loving himself when he loves his wife. No one hates his own body but lovingly cares for it, just as Christ cares for his body, which is the church. And we are his body. As the Scriptures say, "A man leaves his father and mother and is joined to his wife, and the two are united into one." (Eph. 5:25-31)

That isn't a suggestion or an option; it's a straightforward command.

So how did I answer Joseph? Well, I was honest.

"Yes, Joseph, sometimes I do feel that way," I told him. "But whenever I do, the Holy Spirit tends to yank me back to the reality that the Christian life isn't about my feelings. It's about the truth. I *am* inadequate. But God isn't. That's the good news. Whether I always feel like being the leader really isn't the issue. The issue is that I *am* the leader. And because of this fact, I find myself getting humbled all over again. I fall to my knees and ask God to give me the wisdom, humility, and courage to do what he wants me to do."

I then told Joseph about Richard, hoping it would give him more insight on the subject.

THE IMPORTANCE OF SPIRITUAL CONNECTION

Richard loved his wife and kids. He worked hard to provide for them, and he tried to keep all the plates up in the air and spinning. But several years ago, things got out of balance. His job became unbearably demanding. The stress involved went beyond the periodic times of pressure that most guys experience. He was working long hours, taking on too many responsibilities, and beginning to burn out.

On top of the job stress, his father became ill. Then Richard's wife, Lynn, had a car accident and had to undergo physical therapy for several months. The only stable part of his life seemed to be his church. That's where he had courted Lynn, where he had grown as a new Christian, and where he and Lynn had dedicated their children to God. Richard had matured spiritually, relationally, and emotionally in his church. Friendships there ran deep. Bible studies were rich, and his gifts were being used. When he walked in the door of that sanctuary, he knew that God would minister to him and that the church family would surround him with their support of loving fellowship.

Then came the devastating news: Division was ripping through the congregation, leaving families and hearts torn apart. As families chose sides, Richard felt himself torn right down the middle. Suddenly, along with all the other stresses in his life, his place of refuge, his sanctuary, was gone. His church home was now just another source of stress and hurt. Some Sundays he even rationalized and stayed home. *Why go and feel more pain?* he said to himself.

Richard began to get spiritually dry, and both he and his family suffered. The kids were losing their spiritual edge. His wife was crying out for a stable church home. Richard soon felt as if he wasn't pleasing anyone. He couldn't lead his family well or follow his Lord well. This servant leadership thing was more like a noose around his neck than a position given to him by a loving God.

In the midst of all this, Richard and his family took a vacation to southern California. While there, they went to Sunday morning worship at the church where Chuck Swindoll was then the pastor. For years Richard and his family had listened to Chuck Swindoll's daily radio program. They appreciated his teaching and couldn't pass up the opportunity to worship at his church and hear him preach.

Richard entered that huge sanctuary feeling a bit defensive and plenty hurt, but deep inside he was praying that God would revive his barren heart. Ten minutes into the worship service, tears began to well up in Richard's eyes. It had been months since he had felt any spiritual movement in his heart. Suddenly he was beginning to feel alive again. The worship. The teaching. The fellowship. The study of the Word. The prayer time. Richard had allowed the storms of life to loosen these spiritual connections, these spiritual disciplines. Now he was connecting again. He was being reminded that God was still alive and well—that God had been there all the time. It was he, Richard, who had broken the connection.

Richard knew that he had to take the lead in their home as he and Lynn made a tough decision: Their family needed to find a new church home, a place where they could worship, drink from the Word, and get their spiritual equilibrium back. Richard was honest with his pastor about why they wanted to be released and blessed as they looked for a new church home. The pastor was gracious and understanding.

The next Sunday Richard and his family walked into a gymnasium where a small church of about sixty people held its services. From the beginning, Richard and Lynn knew this was going to be their church home.

As the weeks and months passed, Richard's joy in the Lord returned. His quiet times became more vibrant, and his study of the Word regained the richness he had experienced earlier in his Christian walk. Richard and his wife got involved in a couples Bible study, and the kids made good friends in their youth group. Richard began to lead again, yet in a different way. His confidence was tempered with a good kind of brokenness as his desire to make things happen through his own human strength was replaced with a spirit of servanthood grounded in God's love.

When I finished the story, Joseph nodded his head in understanding. "I can really relate to Richard," he said. "He's been there. He has gone through the desert of spiritual dryness and has experienced the fire of refinement. He knows what brokenness is all about. Whatever happened to him?"

I smiled and said, "You're looking at him, Joseph. Richard is my middle name. It's Gary Richard Rosberg. Lynn is really my wife, Barbara Lynn."

"Rosberg, I don't know whether to slap you or give you a high five," he said with a grin.

"Joseph, all of us men go through these times. Days when we feel as if we're lousy leaders. Weeks when we think we don't deserve to lead, or don't know how. And times when we need God to do work in our own hearts, reminding us of who he is. That's why we need that spiritual connection."

UNDERSTANDING YOUR HUSBAND'S HEART

Being the spiritual leader of your family is the toughest job your husband will ever take on. Why? Because in order to do it, he must reject everything the culture teaches him about his masculinity. Let me explain.

If we as men are going to lead our families, we must humble ourselves and follow God. There are two challenges in that statement: to lead and to follow. Both are tough. Many men don't lead very well, and a lot of men don't know how to follow.

When we're leading our family and following God, we have to reject our know-it-all attitude. We have to recognize that our world is out of our control. We have to decrease and allow Jesus Christ to increase. The Bible is real clear on this: The Father calls us to die to self and, through our rebirth, to grow in him. He commands us to lay down our life, magnify him, and serve others so that the world—including our family—will see him through us. It's through this kind of servant leadership that our family will thrive and experience God's grace, even as we do.

You are a major part of the equation in keeping your marriage spiritually on track. As we've said frequently throughout this book, a marriage is really a relationship of three: God, your husband, and you. When your husband's spiritual connection isn't in place, your entire relationship suffers.

UNDERSTANDING THE STRUGGLE

If servant leadership is so clear in God's Word, why do men continually struggle? In short, because we're human. We're also sinful and self-centered. "Yes, I am the vine; you are the branches," Jesus said, "Those who remain in me, and I in them, will produce much fruit. For apart from me you can do nothing" (John 15:5).

Apart from him, we can do nothing. Zero. Zip. Apart from his grace we are lost. Only through our relationship with Jesus Christ can we experience the hope God gives us. We can read books and go to great conferences and attend any number of seminars, but the only real hope we have is in the power of the Holy Spirit to help us overcome the world that is working overtime to pull our marriages and families apart.

Just think about some of the destructive behaviors that shatter marriages and destroy homes:

- Adultery
- Hard-heartedness
- Men who won't lead
- Women who won't follow
- Kids who rebel against their parents and against God

I don't like putting people into categories, but I've worked with enough men to know that guys basically fall into three groups when it comes to a failure to connect spiritually with their wives and children: those who don't get it, those who get it but are inconsistent, and those who just plain rebel.

Let's start with the guys who don't get it—those who are ignorant of their spiritual role in the marriage relationship. Usually this can be attributed to one of the following:

- He did not grow up in a family that taught biblical roles.
- His dad wasn't a servant leader—probably because his dad's dad wasn't.
- He's a first-generation Christian.

The man in this category may sense that he's lacking something, but he doesn't know what it is. He has no experience to tell him how to get there from here.

Some Christian men have spiritual understanding, but they are inconsistent; they get what I call the "spiritual hiccups." They go through times, as I did, when they drift away from their spiritual moorings. They lose their edge. They put their spiritual life on automatic pilot for a while. All of a sudden, a month has gone by, and they haven't been reading or studying God's Word. Another month passes, and they realize that they are neglecting the spiritual disciplines that are so essential to the Christian life: Bible study, prayer, meditation, fellowship, and worship. They are going in the wrong direction and taking their family with them. When they recognize this, they usually get on track again.

Some men, however, are offtrack intentionally. This kind of man purposely fails to connect spiritually because something is going on in his own heart. His wife knows it and he knows it. And God certainly knows it. It may be a secret sin. A guilty conscience. An overwhelming sense of fear or anxiety. You show me a man who is rebelling spiritually, and I will show you a man who is struggling deep in his heart and spirit. When this happens, a man will invariably do one of two things: run away from God or run to him.

We may run away because of our shame and guilt. We believe the lie that Satan is telling us, "God doesn't want anything to do with you because of what you've done." (How is it that we so easily forget that it was that very sin—our sin—that sent Christ to the cross?) Well, you can run, but you can't hide. God is the hound of heaven; he pursues his children as far as they try to run.

If your husband is running, remember that when he comes to his senses, as the Prodigal Son did, he will run back to God. And the Father is waiting at the door. He's waiting for any of his children, as long as they are willing to humble themselves before him.

The only problem with humility is that, in our culture, it is so "unmasculine." Men aren't raised to be humble. We are conditioned to be proud and not let anyone get in our way. That is why the Christian walk is so countercultural. And that is why you, as his wife and a woman of faith, need to be there for him.

YOUR HUSBAND NEEDS YOUR HELP

If your husband is going to stand strong in his faith and fulfill God's plan for his life in his role as husband and father, he needs you. He wasn't designed to do this alone.

Many women are ignorant of the role they play in the spiritual connection between husband and wife. They haven't seen it modeled by their own parents, or they haven't learned it in their churches.

Other women try to play Junior Holy Spirit. They so desperately want their husbands to be the spiritual leaders in the home that they try to shame them into action. Invariably, this leads to one of three results: disappointment, short-term gains, or rejection.

If this description sounds painfully familiar, take off the Junior Holy Spirit badge. It's not comfortable—for you or for your husband. Does this mean you won't feel some pain? No, you will. It's a lonely feeling to pray for your husband for months—or years—and not seem to make any progress. It's entirely understandable that you would be frustrated, hurt, disappointed, and even angry when you're trying to get someone to do something he doesn't want to do or doesn't think he needs to do. But don't give in to your feelings. Instead, try this:

1. Confess your loneliness or frustration or hurt or disappointment or anger to God.
2. Then get out of the way, and let God do the work in your husband. If your husband is a believer, God is going to be right there, pursuing him. If your husband is not a believer, then remind yourself that God doesn't want anyone to perish (2 Pet. 3:9). Let God be God.

3. Meanwhile, you are responsible to continue to grow spiritually in your own life and live out your faith with your husband and children.

Still other women struggle because they aren't doing so well in their own spiritual lives. For these women, husbands who are spiritually on fire are more like a guilt-producing reminder than an inspiration. The dilemma of these women is that they really don't mind that the spiritual influence in the home doesn't go beyond saying prayers at mealtime. It's safer.

If this description fits you, not only are you rebelling against your own role and your husband's role, but you are also rebelling against God. Hard hearts aren't packaged only in male bodies. Women have them too. And the same God who wants your husband to confess his pride in order to get beyond it wants you to do the same. If you come to God daily—or even hourly, when the pressure increases—he is capable of calming your restless heart. The Christian walk isn't about self-protection. It's about submitting our wills to God.

Alex and Karla recently visited my office for some counseling. He had broken her heart. Again. He had caved into temptations, distanced from her and the kids, worked too many hours, and disconnected from her and the Lord. Karla had responded with a bitterness that was demoralizing Alex and exacerbating the problem. Trust had broken down. Neither of them was seeking the Lord. Their relationship was at risk.

Karla pleaded, "Gary, I don't know how to get through to him. I want our marriage to be rich in Christ. I miss the quiet times with him, the prayers we used to experience. They just seem to be distant memories now. Help!"

I saw them five or six times and tried to break through some of the pain, but nothing seemed to click until one day during their most recent appointment. They walked in and something had really changed. Alex was more responsive. Karla was more gentle. I looked at them and said, "What happened? You two look like completely different people!" They unraveled their story.

"Gary," Alex started, "last week at work I was so angry with my wife, I decided to write *you* a letter. It was five pages long. I pointed out everything *she* had done to hurt me recently. I was just plain hot. I pointed out the way she cared for the house. I blasted her for her lack of sexual responsiveness to me. I hammered her on her flagrant money misman-agement. I went on and on.

"I felt a little better after I had gotten all that off my chest, so I decided I would write *her* a letter. I had the pen in my hand, and I started to pour out all the poison I had written in my letter to you when a lightning bolt hit me. I just thought, *What am I doing? Here I am trying to force her to follow me, and I am not leading her with love, just anger. I want so much for my wife to connect to me. I want so much to experience God the way I used to. I want so much for our two kids to grow up in a healthy Christian home, and here I am just messing it up.*"

As I listened to Alex pour out his heart, Karla was captivated by his words. She was looking at him as if he had just won a major battle. He had. Listen to the rest of their story.

"Instead of lambasting her, Gary, I started to pour out the hurt. I confessed to her that I wasn't the man I knew she needed me to be. I asked her to forgive me. On the way home I prayed for another chance from God and from her. That he would connect me to my wife and kids and give me another shot. That she would really listen to me. When I got home, I read Karla the letter. Gary, it was unbelievable. She started to cry and open her heart to me. We just sat on our sofa holding each other, and our two-year-old son came up to us and patted us both on the backs. It was as if I had my family back. And I don't ever want to lose my wife again."

What happened to this little family? Alex and Karla connected. But not before Alex connected to God again, experiencing his grace and mercy. As the Lord convicted him in his heart and he broke vertically with God, it opened up the horizontal relationship with his wife. As Karla saw the work God was doing in her husband's life, it allowed her to trust God and the work he was doing in Alex. She still had a lot of trust to rebuild in Alex. But her trust in God allowed her to take the risk to reconnect to her husband.

What did Karla do right? She was willing to take a risk. She opened up by the prompting of the Holy Spirit. Karla let down the walls and allowed her husband to move close. She experienced not only God's work in her marriage but also a resurgence of hope in her own spiritual journey. Karla relied on God's timing instead of her own.

Let me ask you a pretty tough question: If Karla had resisted the Holy Spirit's work in Alex's life as well as her own and if she had refused to be open that night, where would they be today? Alex's brokenness set the pace for their rebuilding. Karla's willingness to be willing allowed the healing to begin. Bottom line? Alex and Karla connected: spiritually, emotionally, and relationally.

They still have some distance to travel to rebuild their marriage, but Alex and Karla are on the right path. Two hard hearts, broken before Christ and healing through his power. It doesn't get any better than that. That is the same hope you have if you are struggling in your marriage.

No matter how much you've messed up, it isn't too much of a mess for God. And that's not theory talking. It's experience. Every time we fall prey to our sense that the answers to our problems are found in us, God reminds us that the answers are in him alone.

Earlier in this chapter, I told you how discouraged Barb and I were when our church experienced a split. Everything inside me tried to fix that painful situation. My emotions ran the gamut: hurt, anger, frustration, discouragement. Humanly, I thought, *Hey, I'm a counselor. Let me step in and help facilitate the healing.* At every turn those attempts were met with resistance. But it soon became obvious that God had a plan even in the midst of those painful days. He was taking a situation beyond my control and using it to remind me that he was in control.

God always proves himself faithful. He answers all our questions in his timing. We just need to trust and obey.

That's how I know that no matter how far adrift I go, God is always a safe harbor of protection. And he invariably uses Barb as a lighthouse to bring me home. Home from my "spiritual hiccups." Home from my passivity. Home from my hard-heartedness. Home from anything I throw at him in my own stubborn way.

Barb isn't the Junior Holy Spirit, but God does use her consistently to help me when I struggle. But that's because I trust her, and she does it with honor and respect for my role in our relationship, and without a critical spirit.

MEETING YOUR HUSBAND'S NEED FOR SPIRITUAL CONNECTION

If your husband is going to experience spiritual intimacy and connection with God, which in turn will produce spiritual intimacy and connection with you, he must be grounded in four basic areas. If any of these areas is missing or inadequate, it will be reflected in both relationships.

Personal Time in the Word

Since the Word of God is a believer's spiritual food and drink, your husband needs to be reading the Word of God daily. Many husbands are on solid ground in their personal Bible reading. If your husband is, re-inforce him. Let him know through notes and comments (both privately and in front of the kids and your friends) that you love his thirst for the Word. If your husband is not reading the Word, realize that you don't want to irritate the situation by crabbing at him. I have met hundreds of discouraged women who want their husbands to be strong biblical lead-ers. Often, in their frustration these women resort to nagging. I urge you to resist nagging. What you can do is pray for your husband to have a thirst for the Scriptures. You can model your own thirst and share with him what you are learning. You can also expose him to some resources that can aid him in his study of the Word. Two that my family and I have found invaluable are *Experiencing God* by Henry Blackaby and Claude King, and *The One Year Bible.*

Experiencing God has had a tremendous impact on my own spiritual growth. Blackaby essentially says that God wants a relationship with us, but he wants us to go where he is at work. If we really go where he is working, we will find ourselves facing major adjustments in our lives. However, it's only through these adjustments that we will truly begin to experience God. God used Blackaby's study to lead me into full-time ministry. Talk about a major adjustment! As radical as that has been for us, we have never looked back.

I want to get practical here. If your husband likes to study and is spiritually thirsty, he will go after this study with zest. If he isn't, then encourage him to just take a day at a time in this study. Some guys get overwhelmed thinking they need to do the whole thing perfectly and quickly. Read along with him, and share with him what you are learning. However, an adjunctive study like *Experiencing God* needs to be just that: a supplement to reading the Bible.

Barb and I use *The One Year Bible* consistently in our own study. As we use these aids to understanding God's Word, the two of us talk about what we're learning. Not only do we connect spiritually in this way, but we prompt each other to study more. It is "iron sharpening iron" (see Proverbs 27:17). Sometimes she initiates. I like that. Other times I share something. Invariably when I do, she responds enthusiastically. During some seasons we study together; at others we develop separate patterns.

The key here is to encourage each other in our study, not try to control the other.

If you and your husband do not read the Bible together, talk with him about starting that habit. Some husbands will take the suggestion and run with it. Others may be hesitant. If that is the case, suggest that you start by including a Scripture reading as a part of your mealtime. Or you could suggest that you read a passage together before going to bed. Do whatever seems like a natural first step for you.

If your husband is completely resistant, you must not let his resistance keep you from your own Scripture study. Spend time every day in personal Bible study and then become part of a women's Bible study in which you will experience spiritual growth and support.

Here are a few other suggestions for helping your husband connect with the Word:

- Share with your husband what God is teaching you. Growth encourages growth.
- Write love notes to your husband, including statements of uplifting truth from God's Word.
- Participate in or lead a couples Bible study together. As you become involved in the journey of others, you learn what roads to take and which ones to avoid.
- Begin to journal what you're learning from God in your times of meditation and study of God's Word. As appropriate, share this with your husband.
- Commit with your husband to begin memorizing Scripture . . . one verse at a time.

Prayer

Consistent prayer is one of the most elusive spiritual disciplines for men. I don't know many men who don't pray, but many do admit that their prayer life is either shallow or undisciplined.

My friend John Yates wrote a great book titled *How a Man Prays for His Family*. If you have not read it, I urge you to do so. His practical insights of helping men get past what he calls the "start and stall" of prayer to establish life-changing habits are alone worth the price of the book. He also reminds us that developing a consistent prayer life connects us to God and builds our faith.

Let me offer you a good hands-on way to approach prayer. This will help you in your own prayer life, but it will also be helpful to your husband. I have often found that men really respond to this style of prayer because it gives them a way to tackle this sometimes elusive spiritual discipline. Men like to develop patterns in approaching a problem. I don't want to cheapen the discipline of prayer by suggesting some quick formula. There is nothing quick about going deep in prayer with God. But I have found that when a man's prayer life is stuck on "Dear God, thanks for this food" or "God, get me out of this one, and I will be in church this Sunday," he needs a tune-up. One thing that helps is the acronym ACTA.

A is for adoration. Pour your adoration and worship on God for what he is doing in your life.

C is for confession. Lay open your heart for the surgery God needs to do in your life. He is always faithful to forgive.

T is for thanksgiving. It is honoring to God when you come to him with a thankful heart for all the blessings he has given to you and your family.

A is for asking. Make your petitions known to God. He already knows them, but he wants you to tell him your needs.

How do you enrich your husband's prayer life? From my own experience, I can say that Barb fuels my prayer life when I see her in prayer. She models it. Her spiritual connectedness encourages mine.

Some other suggestions include the following:

- Pray daily for your husband.
- Spend time alone together discussing and praying about important things happening in your marriage and family.
- Tell your husband about one area in your life where God is working, and ask for prayer for God's perfect will.
- Ask your husband what one area of spiritual growth he needs prayer for, and commit to praying daily for thirty days for that need to be met.

Fellowship and Worship

Earlier in this chapter I referred to our family's visit to Chuck Swindoll's church. When I tell this story, people often ask me, "What did you experience that had such an incredible impact on you?" I believe the major thing was the richness of fellowship and worship we experienced that day with other believers. The need for spiritual connection extends to the entire family of God.

We need each other, and your family needs to worship God and grow in relationship to others in the family of God. This is best done in the local church. Does that mean you should never miss a Sunday service or a Wednesday-night prayer group? No. That would border on legalism. Some of the most meaningful times of worship and fellowship have occurred when our family of four has come before God together, when for one reason or another we weren't in church. But if we are not worshipping and fellowshipping on a regular basis with the people of God, our spiritual growth will diminish.

You and your husband need to be in a strong Bible-teaching church that is presenting the Word of God week in and week out. You need it. Your husband needs it. Your kids need it.

In addition to involvement in a local church, consider these options:

- Join a small group, either in your church or with other Christian friends. Allow this group to be a support and a source of account-ability for you.[1]
- Play worship tapes in your home and as you drive in the car together. Sing along if you're comfortable doing that, or just let the words of the worship songs help you focus on God's character.
- Attend a conference or seminar together. A marriage conference will put you in touch with other couples who can strengthen and encourage you. Get away from the kids and focus on just the two of you and your relationship.
- Spend time with other Christian couples who model spiritual maturity for you. This is especially important if your childhood families have not been adequate models for you.

Spiritual Intimacy in Marriage and Family

When a husband and a wife are both studying God's Word, praying, and in fellowship, then spiritual connection in the family is the natural out-growth. When a husband and a wife are sharing what God is teaching

[1] If you want a study that will enhance your marriage relationship, I recommend a study Barb and I wrote, *Improving Communication in Your Marriage*, part of the HomeBuilders Couples Series.

them in the Word, the family will benefit. When a husband reaches out and takes his wife's hand and prays with her, whether in crisis or in calm, then spiritual intimacy in the marriage is the natural outgrowth. When a husband assumes his God-ordained role of servant leadership in the home with his wife and his children, the family will flourish.

All of this is a process, of course, not an instantaneous event. But you know you are far along in that process when your husband turns to you in the midst of worship with a tear in his eye or when he shares with you some meaningful insight in his experience with God. You know you are well on your way when you and your husband kneel together in prayer, asking the Father to carry you through whatever you are dealing with at the moment.

When Barb helps me study, pray, and worship, when she encourages me to share my heart, she is doing what God calls her to do: be my helper.

If you have just bristled at the word *helper,* thinking that it connotes a second-class job description, think again. The word translated as "helper" is the Hebrew word *ezer.* In Genesis 2:18 we read that "it is not good for the man to be alone. I will make a helper suitable for him" (NIV). God is referring of course to Eve, Adam's helper. The same Hebrew word, *ezer,* is also used in Psalm 70:5, "You are my helper and my savior; O Lord, do not delay!" There is nothing second class about the Lord being our helper. God has designed you in a glorious position as helper to your husband, just as the Lord is our helper.

Here are some suggestions for being a helper to your husband:

- Remind your husband: "I need you. You need me. Let's work on this together. How can I help? How can I encourage you spiritually? How can I encourage you as the leader in our home?"
- Pray for your husband every day for the next thirty days. Ask God to continue to encourage your husband in his spiritual life.
- Ask God to reveal to you where you need to step back and allow your husband to fulfill God's plan for him to be the leader in your home. Then take some steps in that direction to experience God's desires for you.
- Share with your husband on a regular basis something that God is revealing to you in your own study of the Word. Ask for his perspective on your insights.

THE RESULTS OF SPIRITUAL CONNECTION

God did a remarkable work in our family a few years ago. It all began when we were visiting my parents in Door County, Wisconsin. We hadn't been there long when our daughter Missy began to complain of pain in the roof of her mouth. A trip to a nearby clinic resulted in medication for "a minor infection." By the next night we were in an emergency room where we got a new diagnosis: a strep infection. The new medication did not help, and we cut our vacation short so we could get Missy home.

At our local hospital the ER doctor took one look and hospitalized her, commenting on his way out the door, "This is beyond me." The specialist gave us a new diagnosis: a cancerous tumor in the roof of Missy's mouth. Surgery would be necessary.

After the procedure, the surgeon came to Barb and me with a look that a parent never wants to see. He asked us to sit down.

"There was more there than I thought," he said. "We need to send this tissue to the university hospital lab. It may be malignant. It will be a few days before we get the results. I'll call as soon as I find out. Meanwhile, take Missy home. Get some rest."

After a week of living on the edge, I was physically and emotionally exhausted. But given the tense drama that was playing out in our lives, I was afraid to let down or let any of my family know how scared I was. After all, I was the leader.

Barb was an incredible encouragement to me during this time of stress. She not only came alongside in the big areas of prayer and reassurance, but she also knew just when to give me space and when to move closer in comfort. We searched the Psalms together for soothing passages. I remember times of just looking at each other without saying a word, connecting to her soul. She let me lead with the doctors, yet was right next to me day and night. Once again in the face of the hard times of life, we drew closer and our love grew deeper.

The day after Missy's surgery I was sitting with her on the couch in our family room, stroking her hair, silently praying that God would spare my little one's life. That's when she looked up at me, tears spilling out of her eyes, and asked, "Daddy, what is a malignancy?"

"Where did you hear that word, honey?"

"I heard the doctor use it. Does that mean I'm going to die?"

After choking back my own tears, I said, "Missy, I believe with all my heart you are going to be okay. Mom, Sarah, and I are praying for you.

You are praying. Our church and friends are praying. Even the doctor is praying. God is in charge, my little one. He will never abandon us. He will carry us through. We're just waiting for the report."

Later, when Missy was asleep, I went into the privacy of my study, and the days of stress came bursting out of me like an explosion. I had tried to be the rock-solid foundation my family needed, assuring them that Missy would be okay. Now, my own fears finally got the best of me. "Not my little Missy, God," I pleaded. "Please take me, but not her. Please God, heal my daughter."

The next night the doctor called and choked out the words, "It's benign. Gary, it is benign! She's going to be okay. Thank God, Missy is going to be okay."

At that point, I could finally release my emotions, and I began to cry— tears of joy. I could hear the doctor crying too.

We had just witnessed a miracle.

One thing and one thing only got Barb and me through that difficult time: our reliance and dependence upon God and his people. Were we anxious or afraid? Sure we were. We're human. But God met us at every turn. And because our relationship with him was rooted deep—individually, as a couple, and as a family—we all witnessed a deepening of our faith. We didn't run away or turn from God. We ran *to* him. And in the midst of this our girls saw their father and mother on their knees together, petitioning for God's mercy. The spiritual connection between a couple and within a family doesn't get much better than that.

God used that time of trial to refine our family's faith. He also showed our daughters how vital spiritual intimacy is in a Christian marriage—in joy and in sorrow, in sickness and in health.

THE ONLY PERSON YOU CAN CHANGE IS YOU

Where are you and your husband on the spiritual connection scale? I hope that you can say, "My husband loves God. He is our spiritual leader. I trust him. Our children trust him. Our relationship and our family aren't perfect, but we're growing and we're on the right track." If so, don't be bashful about telling your husband right now how much you love him and how proud you are of him.

Or perhaps your situation sounds more like this: "My husband isn't leading the way God intends for him to do. What can I do?"

The truth is, the only person you can change is you. So let God do his work in you. Open your heart to him and continue to pursue a faithful, obedient relationship with the Lord with all your heart, soul, and mind.

At the same time, pray faithfully for your husband. You may even want to ask some of your trusted friends and prayer partners to pray with you that God will work in your husband's life. Then be patient. Don't give up. Ever.

A husband and a wife together with God is an unbeatable team. No matter what the world throws at you, no matter how the enemy tries to thwart you, no matter what kinds of mistakes one or both of you make— with God you can weather it and go deeper.

Spiritual intimacy and connection in a marriage is the greatest kind of connection of all. If you are living it, rejoice. If you are seeking it, never give up. Keep at it. If you are just getting started, welcome to the journey. God is at work in you.

CHAPTER 10

FRIENDSHIP

A WIFE'S #5 LOVE NEED

"I want to grow old with you!"

Barb talks to husbands

Not far from our home lies the setting for a best-selling fictional book and movie, *The Bridges of Madison County*. Richard, a hard-working man, loves his wife, Francesca, yet struggles to express it. Rarely does he talk to her, touch her, spend time with her, or praise her. The story is simple; he doesn't meet the love needs of his wife. As vulnerable prey, Francesca fell to the attention and praise of another man. She didn't mean to have an affair; of course people rarely do. Robert Kincaid simply talked to her. He listened to her and paid close attention to her. He asked about her. He laughed at her jokes. He picked flowers for her. He even picked up his dishes after a meal. He openly shared about his world and asked about hers. He offered her a drink with respect and courtesy. Within a matter of days, Francesca's emotions were heightened as she fought the awful battle within her, yet she lost as she longed for tenderness and love.

Just the mention of *The Bridges of Madison County* brings a dreamy, faraway look to some women's eyes. Believe me it's not an affair with a stranger they long for—it's the affair of her heart with you. Within the framework of friendship, she'd give anything to feel emotionally connected with you, her husband. Hollywood has capitalized on the real need for women to have an intimate male friendship, yet the script was written with the wrong man fulfilling the need! Why not begin today and write your own story of friendship with you as her hero?

Friendship is truly a foundation to any great marriage. That almost goes without saying. And it is significant that both husbands and wives rated companionship in their top five love needs. Husbands rated it as their number three love need; wives rated it as their number five love need. At first I was curious about the fact that husbands seem to need companionship, or friendship, more than their wives do. But I wonder if the difference is explained in the fact that wives' number two need is intimacy—emotional intimacy, that is—and for them, emotional intimacy is one of the core ingredients of friendship.

That brings up an important point: You and your wife may see friendship in marriage a bit differently. When you hear the word *friendship,* what picture goes through your mind? Golfing with your wife? Watching television together? Going to a football game? Refinishing antiques? When your wife hears the same word, she thinks of heart-to-heart communication, special time away with you, growing old together.

Gary and I sometimes have different perspectives about friendship. I look forward to a Saturday-evening walk as the sun goes down; Gary looks forward to reading the Saturday sports page, with me in the adjacent recliner. I can't wait until we can slow down our frenzied life, move to the country, and take long walks in the woods; Gary loves intense involvement in ministry. I like to dream about faraway places, a room with lots of windows, and romantic trips to Europe (and walks, of course); Gary dreams about getting his to-do list done so we can wash the car together.

Maybe you and your wife see friendship a bit differently too, but all of us can agree on one thing: Friendship involves togetherness.

God knew we needed togetherness, companionship. Genesis 2 tells us, "The Lord God said, 'It is not good for the man to be alone. I will make a companion who will help him'" (Gen. 2:18). God's solution to Adam's aloneness was the togetherness, the oneness of having a spouse.

"Living life together with Jeremy is one of the great joys of our marriage," says Lydia, his wife of twenty-two years. "We have been through so much together—infertility, the adoption of our two children, a devastating illness, some tremendous professional opportunities for both of us. But that is what has made our friendship grow. Going through it all *together.* I don't know what I would have done without him. Jeremy has been a support, a helper, an encourager, a problem solver, a protector. He has made me laugh when things looked bleak. He has held me up when I thought I would not make it. He has been by my side. And that has made it worth it. We are very close. God has given us a oneness that at times can take our breath away. Sometimes I don't know where I leave off and Jeremy begins. There is no one I would rather live my life with than my husband."

WHAT DOES FRIENDSHIP IN MARRIAGE LOOK LIKE?

What is it that makes some married couples stand out above the rest of the crowd and enjoy one another's company more than other couples do? The more chemistry they display, the greater my curiosity about their formula. I love to watch for older couples who seem to have an unmistakable connection with each other. They're noticeably appealing to people around them, and they catch my eye. Most often they show a heightened degree of rapport toward each other. They're sympathetic to each other's needs, close and comfortably affectionate. They display a natural ease in their conversations, genuine warmth in their laughter.

Once, I became intrigued by some friends of ours who were talking to each other across the room from us at a restaurant. Steve leaned forward straining to hear the thoughts of his wife, Jen. Without even hearing a word of their discussion, I could see a deep bond of friendship between the two through their body language. They were freely giving each other undivided attention as they shared thoughts and ideas. It was as if they were the only two people on the planet. I remember watching his eyes stay glued on her, never diverting his attention. I was impressed. She looked relaxed and comfortable as she opened up. I could tell she was safe in trusting him with a part of herself, sharing something that may have been weighing heavily on her heart. I will never forget how I had a bird's-eye view of Steve's demonstrating the basic gestures of genuine friendship and devotion to Jen. He was tuned in to what she was saying, obviously caring and attending to her thoughts. Later I looked over at them, and they looked happy and satisfied. Both were relaxed with their heads tipped back, and they were joined in laughter.

Friendship with your wife isn't really that hard. When a husband is emotionally joined to his wife, as Steve is to Jen, he wants to listen. Friendship with your wife is an enjoyable process and a threshold to discovering new aspects of her. It reinforces what is already there and strengthens the marriage bond. A good friendship with your spouse lays the foundation to support other areas of your marriage relationship. Other areas of marriage may fluctuate over the years, but the friendship factor is lasting.

Marriage counselor Ed Wheat writes in his book *Love Life for Every Married Couple,* "The camaraderie of best friends who are lovers seems twice as exciting and doubly precious." Unfortunately, today far too many men and women are living lonely lives. Friendship doesn't exist in their marriages. It's the missing link that's strangely absent from many marriages. Couples dine together in silence, emotionally detached and indifferent. They are bored by the stranger across the table from them.

Contrast this to couples like Jeremy and Lydia or Steve and Jen, who know firsthand how powerful the bond of friendship is. Their relationship declares both in public and in private that "my spouse is my best friend." After many years of marriage, they still have the twinkle in their eyes from spending time with each other.

FULL PARTNERSHIP

The couples who have a vibrant friendship base it on a commitment to a full partnership. Business associates can have limited partnerships, but for your friendship to soar with your wife, it has to be a full, 100 percent partnership. When a husband and wife view each other as equal and valuable partners in friendship, both bringing important qualities to the friendship mix, their friendship becomes grounded on the bedrock of respect and honor. That makes it a cut above the rest. Couples who display a strong willingness to work hard at their marriage maintain the ability to laugh together, play together, stay the course together, and work through the inevitable differences between men and women.

When you think about your prized friendships, you can discern some basic ground rules that are built on respect. You are careful in what you say; you watch your words. You keep quiet when you want to say something that could destroy what you have going. You work to bring out the best in your friends' lives. You tell the truth but never at others' expense.

This is what your wife needs from you. She needs you to want what's best for her. She needs you to work at staying in harmony with her. She needs you to apologize when you have hurt her. She needs you to spend time with her. And she needs you to take your friendship seriously.

A wife isn't supposed to replace your guy friends. You need both of them, but a wife is different from your male buddies. A woman's need for companionship usually differs from a man's need. A man may be content for his need of companionship to be met by simply working alongside another person. That's not a home run for a woman. Our need for your friendship and companionship is deeply intertwined with fulfilling the need for security and trust. When your wife opens up to you and shares confidential parts of herself and you respond as a close, caring friend, she is deeply satisfied. This happens when she feels the safety of disclosing the "real" person to you.

When we genuinely enjoy our spouses, our marriages take on additional intensity, strengthening the foundational friendship. When we genuinely enjoy our spouse's companionship, our mutual admiration for each other skyrockets!

PARK BENCH, SAN FRANCISCO BAY

Imagine two young honeymooners gazing together for the first time at San Francisco's Golden Gate Bridge. It was the summer of 1975, and the skyline was breathtakingly beautiful and romantic for Gary and me. High on a hill we found a park bench that overlooked the San Francisco Bay. We sat on that bench and dreamed about our future, excited about what lay ahead.

When we first found that bench, we did not know that we would return someday and sit in the same place, looking at the same bay, discussing more dreams. But that has been the case. In fact, we have been back to that bench many times, and each time we go there, we sit and talk, hold hands, and listen to the sound of the ocean waves.

We have "staked" that bench and claimed it as "ours." It's our special place, where we talk about our memories together and the miles we've traveled since the last time we sat there. We talk about life: the storms, the sunshine, the sheltering presence of God and each other through all of them.

On this weatherworn wooden bench, where we've carved our initials into the seat, we've celebrated life by both laughing and crying. Each time we've walked away with a renewed love and devotion for each other, reestablishing our relationship as best friends.

Sitting on that bench helps us gauge how we've changed from year to year. It has become a benchmark time for us. That picturesque bay hasn't changed much over the years, but the couple sitting on the bench has.

Do you have a "park bench" in your marriage? Do you have a place where you and your wife have taken the time to reflect on, celebrate, reevaluate, and adjust your friendship?

Sometimes our park benches are not physical. At times life experiences have forced us to reevaluate and adjust. Maybe you have gone through a challenging experience, like having a child or starting a new job, and that challenge has forced some changes in your friendship. Or maybe you have gone through difficult experiences such as illness or a death in the family, and that suffering has brought you to a park bench where you have looked at the past and made new plans for the future of your friendship.

Occasionally when Gary and I sit on our park bench, we look back and see setbacks or situations in which we have failed each other. Maybe you have too. But when we see our failures, we can talk about them, ask for forgiveness if that is necessary, and ask for God's grace to move us into the future. These benchmark times can make us stronger, equipping us to avoid making the same mistakes in the future.

WHAT ARE YOUR WIFE'S FRIENDSHIP NEEDS?

Let's take a look at what some of your wife's specific friendship needs may be. How would you finish these sentences?

- My wife needs me to be the kind of friend who . . .
- My wife's needs for friendship include . . .
- For my wife, the most important ingredient of friendship in our marriage is . . .

How did you do? Could you complete those sentences relatively easily? Or did you get stuck, not quite sure of what your wife needs? The best way to find out what she needs, of course, is to ask her. In addition to talking with her about your friendship, read the next few paragraphs to get a better understanding of what most wives' friendship needs are.

She Needs You to Be Her Best Friend

Your wife probably has several close female friends. She might even consider one or two of them to be her best friends. Those friends meet some of your wife's deep friendship needs. They understand her as a woman, with all of the joys, insecurities, and problems that are unique to women. They nurture her and encourage her. If you think about it, you probably are the beneficiary of those friendships because they strengthen your wife and make her a better spouse. Your wife needs these friendships, and you are a wise husband if you encourage her to maintain them.

But your wife's friendship with you is different. You are her *best* best friend. You are her lifelong companion, the one who will be with her to the end. Her female friends may move away or move into a different phase of life that may diminish their friendship, but you are there for the long haul. Sure, life circumstances will change for you and your wife, and you will face difficulties, but you have committed yourselves to traveling through it together. That makes a difference to her. She feels secure in your commitment to stick with it no matter what.

You alone are the one to see your wife in all life circumstances—her moods, her accomplishments, her failures. Her female friends may see some of this, but you see everything—the good and the bad, the beautiful and the ugly. And you are in the unique, God-ordained position to love and encourage her through it all.

What your wife needs from you as her best friend is your assurance that you will always be her companion no matter what. She needs to know that you will do things together throughout your marriage. Remind her that you will be partners as you develop your careers, raise a family, attend a church, and invite people into your home.

Let your wife know that you enjoy being with her, that she is special to you. Do what you can to make your friendship a comfortable one in which you are both free to be yourselves.

But a *best* best friend outclasses all the others, and she looks to you to meet her needs in ways that surpass her other friends' capabilities to do that. Your wife needs someone with whom she can share absolutely everything: her ups and downs, her struggles and joys. She looks to you as the best friend who will celebrate her joys and victories without competition or jealousy.

Because Gary and I are *best* best friends, our relationship has strengthened us, both as individuals and as a couple. Because of the power of his friendship, I am certain of his love, I am confident he hears me, and I trust that he has my best interests in mind. When your wife can count on you as her *best* best friend, she can achieve far more in life because you are at her side, believing in her.

She Needs a Safe Place to Be Herself

As I mentioned in the previous few paragraphs, your wife needs your friendship to be a safe place, a relationship in which she can completely be herself. I have always treasured the way nineteenth-century English novelist George Eliot describes this kind of friendship: "Oh the comfort, the inexpressible comfort of feeling safe with a person; having neither to weigh thoughts nor measure words but to pour them all out, just as it is, chaff and grain together, knowing that a faithful hand will take them and sift them, keeping what is worth keeping, and then, with the breath of kindness blow the rest away." How valuable is the husband who can be that kind of friend for his wife.

Each day that Gary and I spend time together in friendship, our marriage becomes more comfortable. Because we have shared so many of our thoughts and feelings with each other over the years, we can almost sense what the other is thinking. What Lydia said about her friendship with Jeremy is true: Sometimes Gary and I can't tell where one of us leaves off and the other begins. When I feel troubled, Gary often knows exactly what's disturbing me. One night we were lying in bed, and for some strange reason I felt afraid. I hadn't said a word to Gary about my fear. But as he lay next to me in the dark room, he said, "Barb, do you want to come over to your place?" ("My place" is right under his arm and next to his heart.) I moved closer, and he held me with both arms securely wrapped around me and said, "You are safe here. There is no need to fear." He is my friend not only in his words but also in his presence.

What did Gary communicate that night? He reminded me that I am always safe. I remember sensing his reassurance and quiet reminder that nothing could come between us. I felt once again the quiet, still voice that brought peace to my troubled mind and heart. That's part of what best friends do for one another: They comfort each other and show up during the dark times.

She Needs Your Integrity

My dad always said, "Barb, your word is as precious as gold." That's strong teaching from a strong man. It also was a consistent reminder of my dad's integrity. The same holds true for you and your wife. She wants to know that your yes is yes and your no is no. In other words, she wants to trust you. And it is your integrity that will help build her ability to trust you.

I listen to women all over the country, and what they often tell me is that they just want to know that their husbands are on the up and up. Your wife needs to know that when you say you will be home, you either will be home or will call to inform her of a change of plans. She needs to trust that when you get on the Internet, you are not giving in to the temptation of pornography but are honoring the Lord and your family. She needs to know that your public and private selves are one and the same as you mature and grow in the Lord. These are all issues of integrity.

Let me encourage you to stand tall and continue to be the real thing both in public and private. It will draw your wife to you as she sees the congruence in your life.

She Needs You to Honor Her

One of the most valuable gifts Gary gives to me is honor. Most mornings, if you were to eavesdrop on our conversation, you would hear him affirming me for the littlest of things. He expresses his appreciation for me with an attitude of honor from the time he rises each morning. Once he gets focused for work, he quiets down. The work mode has a way of changing the whole focus of a man. Hours later we can be seated in a serious team meeting at our ministry, and Gary will begin talking about his wonderful wife and something she said that was strong, wise, and relevant. Sometimes when he does this, he catches me so off guard that I lean forward on the boardroom table thinking, *I wish I could meet this woman.* Gary makes me sound far better than I am. But you know the amazing thing that happens when I hear him bragging about me publicly? I learn about what pleases my husband, and I am motivated to become a better wife.

Your wife needs you to honor her. That means you speak to her kindly and respectfully, not berating or belittling her if she does something that frustrates you. Honoring her means that you put her needs before your own. It means that you speak positively about her to others. It means that you tell her whenever you see in her a virtue or quality that speaks of God's character.

As a result of your honor and respect, your wife will blossom with confidence and poise. She will also be very eager to repay you with the same respect and honor.

WHAT CAN YOU DO TO MEET YOUR WIFE'S FRIENDSHIP NEEDS?

Now that you have a better understanding of some of your wife's friendship needs, what will you do to meet them? Remember that you build your friendship in the everydayness of life, in how you treat each other, in how you handle the ups and downs of daily life.

Ask yourself this question: How do I want our friendship to look ten years from now, twenty years from now? Your friendship with your wife will be one of the enduring parts of your marriage. Every day you have an opportunity to build on your friendship, to make an investment for the long haul.

Here are a few ideas. Just consider them some coaching tips on your wife's heart needs.

Do Things Together

Relaxation, kicking back, and laughter are ingredients that add to the emotional environment in which you develop closeness. Unless couples are comfortable with each other, they will rarely feel safe enough to open up. Start out with easy activities that you both enjoy doing together. Don't make it complicated. Women love the simple things as well as the big things, but what rings the bell for her is doing them alongside you. Whatever you do, make sure that it is a meaningful activity for both of you. When activities, interests, goals, and fun are shared as a couple, they can double the pleasure factor in your marriage. You'll find yourself wanting to be with your *best* best friend a lot! Here are some surefire ways to get you started:

- Go on dates, and take turns picking out where you'll go. It celebrates your differences! Over time you'll find that both of you are picking out places to please the other.
- Call her and ask her to stop by the office or go to lunch with you. Tell her, "My day just isn't the same without you right smack in the middle of it."
- Run errands together. Don't drop your wife off at the mall to do some errands and then go to the hardware store to do others. Put aside the "saving time" excuse, and spend the time together. She will feel prized when you do it.
- Similarly, do tasks around the house together. If your wife is doing yard work, step to her side and do it with her.
- Skip your usual baseball game and replace it by spending those

hours with your wife. Make her feel that she is more important to you than sports.

- Turn down a night with the guys and tell them loudly over the phone, "I want to be with my wife." You will be a hero not only to your wife but also to wives of the other guys.
- Take her in your arms and dance with her whether or not there's music.
- Serve together in some ministry capacity: visit sick people, counsel young married couples, have a meal with college students who are away from home, go on a missions trip, or host a Bible study in your home.[1]
- Spend lots of time playing. After all, if she's going to live with you the rest of her life, why not make it *fun?*
- Go to the grocery store and shop together. Sneak over to the floral aisle, and pick up a rose or some daisies. She will love it—and you—for thinking of her!
- Skip cleaning the garage next Saturday, and cuddle under the blankets and watch movies all day instead.
- Go to bed twenty minutes early, turn off the TV, and hold each other while you talk.
- Find companionship through recreation. Pick an activity that you would enjoy doing together: hiking, boating, skiing, attending sports events, restoring antique furniture, traveling.

Create a Secure Place

Women love security. Wives want to know that their financial needs will be met. They want to be reassured about issues of commitment. But a wife's need for security is always met when she senses that her husband is *with her* and *committed to her*. *With her* means that you are connected to your wife and that you are looking out for her. *Committed to her* means that you will not leave her—emotionally, spiritually, or physically.

When your wife feels secure, she is free to express her needs and grow with you. When she feels insecure, she will either put up a wall and protect herself, or she will snap at you. Husbands who develop security in their marriages contribute significantly to healthy families.

Here are a few coaching tips for beefing up the security level of your marriage:

[1]We recommend the HomeBuilders Couples Series *Improving Communication in Your Marriage,* which Gary and I wrote, and which is available from Group Publishing.

- Hide "I'll never leave you" notes in odd places to remind her how secure she can feel.
- Encourage your wife to talk to you about anything that's on her mind. Then listen attentively.
- Make sure your wife never feels as if she needs to hide ideas or thoughts from you.
- Take a walk in the moonlight, hold her hand, and tell her how much she means to you.
- Make a practice of saying to your wife when you come home from work, "It's so good to be back home with you. This is my favorite part of my day."
- Say to your wife, "I'm so glad you are my best friend."
- Apologize to your wife when you are wrong. It will draw her closer, and she will be more tender with you. She will long for your companionship.

Step into Her World

Most men have a fairly clear idea of what their career goals are, and men often fulfill these goals and dreams in the workplace, using their God-given talents and developed skills. In other words, the workplace is where you feel significant, where you find encouragement.

But let me ask you a question. Do you know what makes your wife feel significant? What are her goals and dreams? Have you taken the time to ask your wife about them? Just because she hasn't told you doesn't mean she doesn't have them. Take interest in your wife's world, helping her not only express her dreams but also make them come true.

If your wife does have clear goals, have you stepped into her world and joined in some of her dreams? Are you by her side when she leads a function at your children's school? Do you encourage her in a business she may be running? Do you pick up the slack if she is pursuing further education?

Entering your wife's world is another way to deepen your friendship and show her that you are her best cheerleader. If you are unsure of how to enter her world, ask her what would be meaningful to her. Or try some of these ideas:

- Do you encourage your wife to tell you her dreams? When you know what they are step in and help make those dreams come true.

- Has your wife always wanted to start a business? What can you do to make it a reality?
- Has she always wanted to explore a creative gift—music, art, writing, crafts, decorating? On her next birthday, surprise her with a gift that will communicate that you not only think she can do it but also that you think her creativity is valuable.
- Does your wife read a lot? Ask her about what she is reading.
- Have you ever volunteered for a service group with your wife? Offer to join her in a project.
- Do you listen for the little things? As your wife talks, make mental notes about the things she likes and follow through to please her with some of them.
- Do you discuss everything with her? Start by telling her about your day. It shows that you value her opinion.

Create Benchmark Times

Earlier in this chapter I talked about park benches and benchmarks. Husbands and wives need to establish time to reflect on their relationships and create benchmarks to mark progress in their marriage. Here are a few ideas to consider. If these don't fit your style, find some that will.

- Find a regular time to get away from your home and jobs so that you and your wife can be together to reflect on and celebrate your friendship.
- Take a road trip together.
- Go to a bed-and-breakfast inn.
- Set aside an evening once a month for just the two of you to discuss your dreams and goals.
- Use an anniversary celebration to look back on God's work in your lives. Plan for the future.
- Go back to visit a place that is meaningful in the development of your friendship: the town where you met, a restaurant that creates a memory, the church where you were married. When you visit that spot, take time to give your past to God, and ask for his help and guidance for the future. Recommit yourselves to each other for the coming year.

A SECURE FRIENDSHIP

Gary and I have been friends now for more than twenty-eight years. In some ways we take our friendship for granted because it is so comfortable. But when we hit the tough times, we know that our friendship is one of the rock-solid foundations of our marriage.

I remember the day I discovered a mole that was changing in appearance. I made an appointment to see the dermatologist, and Gary insisted on going with me to see the doctor. After examining the mole, the doctor gruffly said, "Melanoma."

He stood very erect and announced that my mole had all the characteristics of a fatal, fast-growing cancer. He wasted no time in removing it and sent it out to the lab for a battery of tests. He then got up and left the room.

I was shocked. Gary was so tied up in knots that he couldn't talk. When we got home, I went directly to the kitchen, where I busied myself with any routine that would numb the confusion. As I was tending to our young daughters, I heard Gary in the next room. He was weeping. I walked over to him and watched as he grieved over what could be coming. I'll never forget the look on his tearstained face as he turned and said, "Don't worry, honey, I'm always going to be here with you." His look melted all my fears.

For days I clung to his love and devotion as we waited for the report. In desperation we finally called the doctor's office and asked a nurse if the test results were back. She announced that the tests revealed no cancer!

I genuinely felt like Lazarus when Jesus called him from the tomb. I got my life back. Gary held me that day, and we rejoiced in God's mercy.

Five years later we were faced with another near tragedy. The sky was a beautiful September blue, and I was driving to meet Gary for lunch. Both Missy and Sarah were with me, strapped in with their seat belts. Out of nowhere, a car pulled out in front of me, crashed into our minivan, spun it out of control, then crashed into it again. My mind was racing. Then I felt a break in my chest. I couldn't breathe. *The girls, the girls!* was all I could think.

While gasping, I turned to check each of the girls. Sarah was fine, but Missy had been thrown forward and had two swollen eyes that were turning black. Once I knew they were safe, I fell out of the car into the street. I still couldn't breathe. My chest was pulsating with excruciating pain, and I was numb from my neck down to my fingertips. At the point of impact the seat belt had broken my sternum.

The ambulance arrived, and as I was loaded into the back, I heard six-year-old Missy screaming over and over, "My mommy is going to die!" Sarah, however, knew that her daddy would fix this, so she ran to a house and called Gary.

"Daddy, we need you. It's Mommy. She's going to die!" He arrived within minutes and ran to my side. How good it was to see my very best friend, my lifelong companion! I was so relieved just to know he was with me. In the bustle of the moment, we didn't have time to talk, but Gary gave me a look that said, "I love you. We will get through this together." Because our friendship was so solid, his look was all I needed.

As the weeks went by, our friendship carried me through sleepless nights and hours of painful physical therapy. It supported me when I just wanted to be a "real mom," not a bed-bound one. It helped ease my fears as I regained motion in my arms and gradually felt the sternum heal.

I encourage you to give your wife a sense of deep security in your friendship. Build your friendship with such stability that when you face the tough times, you will find comfort and peace in your relationship with each other.

I look forward to the years getting better and better for Gary and me as we continue to grow more deeply as friends and lovers. It's a quiet safety that he's there for me and that I'm there for him. He's the right hand, and I'm the left. Together we complete each other.

My husband is incredible. Gary has brought me indescribable joy by being the kind of man who is centered on Christ, and I see his godliness as a gift from God. I rest on this fact and continually pray that the Lord will allow us to complete our years in each other's arms, committed to the end of our journey together on earth as *best* best friends.

My prayer for you is that your wife also will rise up and shout that you are her *best* best friend as you understand her needs and lovingly meet them with a whole heart. May God bless you and your wife as you together pursue a great marriage!

Part 2

Enjoying the Great Marriage
God Intends

Part 2

Enjoying the Great Marriage

God Intends

CHAPTER 11

GARY'S FINAL WORD TO MEN

As I read Barb's five chapters of comments and suggestions for husbands, I can't help but think, *Boy, she said a lot of good things. I just wish she had told me fifteen or twenty years ago what she has told you!* I also wish I had always had the ears to listen. Of course, back then neither of us had a handle on anything besides making mistakes so we could learn from them. It's been only in the last few years that this marriage thing has hit the sweet spot. We're squarely in midlife and have come to the best bottom line of all: A good marriage isn't enough for the Rosbergs; we want a *great marriage!* And so do you, or you wouldn't have gotten this far in this book. But seeking a great marriage has demanded that I know how to meet Barb's love needs.

Now that you've received some insights from Barb and what she learned from hundreds of women from around America, what are you going to do with all of this great information? Here are a few options:

1. Incorporate all the changes tomorrow.
2. Think it's too much work and not do anything. (After all, you're better than most guys you know.)
3. Pick two or three things to work on in the next few months.

If you picked #1, call my office for an appointment. You're going to need counseling to deal with the overwhelming sense of anxiety you just bit off. If you picked #2, then you are more hard-hearted and hardheaded than I could imagine. As you can probably tell, I recommend #3.

When I attend a conference, read a book, or try to assimilate some change in my life, the first thing I do is step back and try to get a clear perspective. Second, I pray and ask God what he wants me to learn from what I have just studied. Perspective and God. Those are the two things I love to seek out. Sounds like a good place to start, doesn't it?

Here are a few questions to put before God as you move from the learning stage to the application stage of meeting your wife's love needs and pursuing a great marriage:

- God, out of everything I just read, what two or three things do you most want me to begin to implement in my life right now?
- Do you want me to show my unconditional love by serving my wife more fully?
- Do you want me to step outside of my own selfishness and learn how to listen—really listen—to my wife's heart as she expresses her emotions and needs?
- Do you want me to put down my golf clubs, fishing rod, bowling ball, or remote control and step into her world, ministering to her as her friend as well as husband, lover, and partner?
- How about encouragement? Do I need to face the reality that my negative and neutral comments outweigh the affirming ones I give my wife each day?
- Father, how shall I minister to my wife's spirit? Maybe taking her hand in bed tonight to pray together would be a place to start. How about if I initiate reading your Word with her and perhaps taking a walk together to share what we are learning from you?

Finding direction is the best first move. But remember, you can't do it all at once. You have to start somewhere. Let me help you get your arms around the building of a great marriage by taking each of your wife's love needs one by one. When this chapter is over, you'll know where to start.

LOVING UNCONDITIONALLY

Since men and women alike rated unconditional love as their number one love need in order to build a great marriage, this is an important place to begin. If there is one thing I know about Barb, it's that she needs to know she is number one in my life, number two, and, come to think of it, number ninety-nine. In other words, Barb experiences unconditional love from me when she knows that I am completely devoted to her and that our relationship is safe. She needs to know that no matter what happens, we are glued together and are going to finish strong together. That's what *agape* love—selfless love—is all about. It is a Christlike love that isn't based on what we do but on Whose we are. We belong to Jesus Christ and to each other.

While that truth is the bedrock foundation to a great marriage, it needs more. How do you express unconditional love? It's all about servant leadership, friend. Barb talked about expressing our uncondi- tional love in words, actions, and commitment. A clean sweep if you ask me.

Rather than getting overwhelmed about what this actually looks like, let me share an e-mail I received from a friend. As you'll notice, the guy this story is talking about has learned how to model unconditional love.

> *While waiting to pick up a friend at the Portland airport, I had one of those life-changing experiences that you hear other people talk about— the kind that sneaks up on you unexpectedly. This one occurred merely two feet from me.*
>
> *Straining to locate my friend coming off the jetway, I noticed a man coming toward me. He stopped right next to me to greet his family. First, he motioned to his younger son (about six years old) as he laid down his bags. They gave each other a long, loving hug. As they separated enough to look into each other's face, I heard the father say, "It's so good to see you, Son. I missed you so much!" His son smiled somewhat shyly, averted his eyes, and replied softly, "Me too, Dad!"*
>
> *Then the man stood up, gazed into the eyes of his older son (about nine), and while cupping his son's face in his hands, he said, "You're already quite the young man. I love you very much, Zach!" They too hugged a most loving, tender hug.*
>
> *While this was happening, a baby girl (about two years old) was squirming in her mom's arms, never once taking her eyes off her dad. The man said, "Hi, baby girl!" as he gently took the child from her mother. He quickly kissed her face all over and then held her close to his chest while rocking her from side to side. The little girl instantly relaxed and simply laid her head on his shoulder, motionless in pure content- ment.*
>
> *After several moments he handed his daughter to his older son and*

declared, "I've saved the best for last," and proceeded to give his wife the longest, most passionate kiss I ever remember seeing. He gazed into her eyes for several seconds and then silently mouthed, "I love you so much!" They stared at each other's eyes, beaming big smiles at one another, while holding both hands. For an instant they reminded me of newlyweds, but I knew by the age of their kids that they couldn't possibly be.

I puzzled about it for a moment then realized how totally engrossed I was in the wonderful display of unconditional love not more than an arm's length away from me. I suddenly felt uncomfortable, as if I were invading something sacred, and was amazed to hear my own voice nervously ask, "Wow! How long have you two been married?"

"Been together fourteen years total, married twelve of those," he replied without breaking the gaze from his wife's face.

"Well, then, how long have you been away?" I asked. The man finally turned and looked at me, still beaming his joyous smile. "Two whole days!"

Two days? I was stunned. By the intensity of the greeting, I had assumed he had been gone for at least several weeks, if not months.

Wanting to end my intrusion, I said, "I hope my marriage is still that passionate after twelve years!" The man suddenly stopped smiling. He looked me straight in the eye and with forcefulness that burned right into my soul, he told me something that left me a different person. He simply said, "Don't hope, friend. Decide!"

Then he flashed me his wonderful smile again, shook my hand, and said, "God bless!" With that, he and his family turned and strolled away together. I was still watching that exceptional man and his family walk out of sight when my friend came up to me and asked, "What are you looking at?" Without hesitating, and with a curious sense of certainty, I replied, "My future!"

Wow! This man in Portland hit a grand slam. By the way, if Zach's dad is reading this book, give me a call; I want to meet you. From the looks of things, you have a great marriage. You also understand that meeting your wife's love needs pays off.

You can have that kind of closeness, too, and it begins with unconditional love. No matter what comes your way—hurts, disappointments, challenges—commit yourself to love your wife no matter what.

FINDING EMOTIONAL INTIMACY

Getting emotionally close is where we as men short-circuit, isn't it? Barb offered many insights and suggestions in chapter 4. Let me add a few things here.

I remember one weekend a few years ago when Missy was a high-school senior. It was homecoming weekend, and she was on homecoming court. To put it mildly, the three women in our house—Missy, Sarah, and Barb—were making our house "emotionally rich." Insecurity and anxiety led to tears (that was Barb), and Missy and her big sister were experiencing their fill of emotional swings too. It was classic.

What did I do?

I reminded myself, *Okay, Gary, Barb writes that both short-term and long-term marital success is dependent on a husband being able to meet more and more of his wife's emotional needs.* I knew that with a word, look, or discouraging attitude, I could either tune in to or turn off these women who are important to me. My wife and daughters needed my soft side, not my logical, hard side. Whether or not you have daughters in your home, you've been there with your wife.

Barb reminded us men that we need to have compassion in the midst of a woman's emotional stirrings. Remember, it's a "heavenly wiring" issue, not a character flaw. When the wiring trips a breaker, your temptation will be to fix it, to tell her what to do. The only problem is she often doesn't care what she needs to do. She just needs to experience the emotion for a while and know that you will travel with her through the range of feelings she is experiencing. It means you amplify the affirmation side of your character and turn down the reasoning, at least until your wife has had the chance to express her heart.

Have you ever just held your wife when she was struggling? I tried it recently. I resisted every logical bone in my body and looked at Barb and said, "May I just hold you?" She melted in my arms. I couldn't believe it. My mind was racing with thoughts like, *Is this what she keeps telling me she needs? Just to hold her?*

After several minutes and a few tissues she looked at me and said, "Thanks, Gary, for supporting me." I was truly stunned. After Barb moved beyond her emotional distress, I gave her an idea on how to respond to the issue, and she said, "I think I'll try that." I walked into the other room and gave myself a high five! I realized in that moment it wasn't that she was rejecting my logic, just the timing of it. I gave her the comfort and attention she needed, listening for more of the heart issues than the head issues. Our wives need our soft side: It speaks her language.

One more thing I need to mention: When you think of a woman other than your wife, remember Smokey the Bear. Say to yourself, *Only YOU can prevent forest fires.* Translation: Only *you* can prevent an affair of the heart or body. Listen to your wife's God-given discernment and instincts regarding women who are putting your life and family at risk. Listen also to her strong warnings about guarding your own heart and what you may consciously or unconsciously be doing to stir another woman's fire. It just may save your family.

I have learned that Barb's instincts are right on target, and because she's my lifetime partner, I trust her. I have counseled scores of men who were having needs met by women other than their wives. Sometimes the man starts it; other times the woman initiates it. In the end it doesn't matter because both get burned. Bottom line? Guard your heart. For as Solomon said in Proverbs 4:23, "Above all else, guard your heart, for it is the wellspring of life" (NIV).[1]

If you are building or stoking a fire in some other guy's campsite, go home to your own tent. An Old Testament passage says it so well: "Drink water from your own well—share your love only with your wife. Why spill the water of your springs in public, having sex with just anyone? You should reserve it for yourselves. Don't share it with strangers. . . . Why be captivated, my son, with an immoral woman, or embrace the breasts of an adulterous woman?" (Prov. 5:15-20). The chapter closes with the reality of what happens when we step outside of God's protective boundary: "The Lord sees clearly what a man does, examining every path he takes. An evil man is held captive by his own sins; they are ropes that catch and hold him. He will die for lack of self-control; he will be lost because of his incredible folly" (Prov. 5:21-23).

A wife's emotional needs are very real. When you step into your wife's emotional world and seek to understand, empathize, and show love to her, your marriage will grow. When you don't, she will wither on the vine and die. Twenty-five years of working with families has taught me there isn't much of a middle ground. In a nutshell, two pieces of advice

---

[1]For further encouragement and help in identifying the eight areas of risk for a man, I suggest that you read my book *Guard Your Heart* (Sisters, Oreg.: Multnomah, 1994).

keep husbands on track to meeting their wife's love needs and to experiencing a great marriage:

1. Stoke your wife's emotional fire.
2. Stay away from campsites that aren't your own.

SHARING SPIRITUAL GROWTH

A great marriage really is a marriage of three: you, your wife, and the Lord Jesus Christ. No truth in this book is more foundational. Barb talked about the Bible's mandate for you to accept your God-given responsibilities to love, lead, and honor your wife and family.

We are called as husbands to love our wives as Christ loved the church. It's a principle, a word picture that bears repeating. Paul's admonition in Ephesians 5 goes way beyond a mere job description. It's a mission statement. How do I know? Because the principle involved here was the mission of Jesus. "He [Christ] gave up his life for her [his church] to make her holy and clean, washed by baptism and God's word. He did this to present her to himself as a glorious church without a spot or wrinkle or any other blemish. Instead, she will be holy and without fault" (Eph. 5:25-27).

You will have a great marriage when you honor your wife. When you pray with and for your wife, when you read the Word of God with and to her, and when you set the pace for the spiritual growth of your family, you honor God and your wife. Nothing seems more elusive, but nothing brings a richness to the marriage like pursuing spiritual oneness with your wife.

Barb and I have had times of spiritual dryness, and we have had times of spiritual richness. We have stood in stadiums with seventy thousand men singing "Amazing Grace" and "How Great Thou Art," with tears streaming down our faces, and we have gone to bed back-to-back with unresolved pain. Whether we are at the mountaintop or in the valley, one truth always rings clear: The God who created us is for us. And he is sufficient for anything we walk through.

Whether you and your wife face financial setbacks, relational pain, sick kids, or the death of parents—a marriage of three can survive and thrive in the midst of the storm. But you will survive only if you and your wife step out of your selfishness and self-protection, and submit your wills to the lordship of Jesus Christ.

Minister to your wife's spiritual needs. Pray, study God's Word, and allow Jesus to stay in the middle of your marriage.

ENCOURAGING YOUR WIFE

During my freshman year of high school, report cards were distributed every six weeks. For the student doing a great job, that meant the opportunity for praise and encouragement was forthcoming at least every month and a half. For those who were bombing, it meant they had to face their parents, school counselors, and teachers on a regular basis for a little reality check. Guess which group I landed in? I earned twenty-seven Ds, six Fs, and three Cs that year. It was ugly.

One by one my teachers would come into the counselor's office and tell my parents how much of a failure I was. Except Mark Schwertley, my English teacher. He was a first-year teacher, and he loved kids. I'll never forget one quarter's parent-teacher conference. He slouched in his chair (much to the chagrin of my parents and the attending counselor), looked me in the eyes, and said, "Gary isn't doing too well in English, but I want to tell you all something. He is going to make it. I believe in him. There is something in Gary's eyes that tells me down deep there is a glimmer of hope."

Mark's comments led to three distinct reactions in those meetings. One, I would pretend to blow him off, yet underneath I loved his words because I was screaming out for someone's approval. Two, my counselor would roll her eyes and tell my parents, "College, for Gary, is a pipe dream. He'll be lucky to finish ninth grade, let alone the rest of high school." Three, my parents wanted to adopt Mark because he seemed like he was the only one in academia who believed in me.

I'm happy to say that Mark was right. I did graduate from high school and went on to graduate from the same university (Drake) that Mr. Schwertley attended. I earned three degrees and taught graduate school on the adjunct faculty for five years. Thanks, Mr. Schwertley! Today I love to credit his belief in me as one of the most significant crossroads of my life story.

How did this first-year English teacher make such a difference in my life? By following the same recipe that Barb told you to use in building a great marriage: encouragement.

She reminded you to be quick with hearty affirmations, to focus on your wife's strengths, and to be generous with appreciation. I love the definition of *encouragement:* "to give courage; to inspire with courage, spirit, or hope; to hearten."

You are called to be your wife's number one encourager. If she isn't getting it from you, then where is she going to get it? Think about it for a minute. Do your affirming comments far outweigh your neutral and negative comments? This direct question can be the measuring stick of how well you are either hitting or missing the mark. Barb wrote that most women fight discouragement continually. We know they are stretched in their roles as woman, wife, daughter, sister, friend, mom, worker, volunteer, etc. Let your voice be the one that rings in her ears: "Keep going. You can make it. You are worth it. You are the best. I believe in you. I love you. I need you."

LOVING YOUR BEST FRIEND

Early in our marriage Barb and I scraped together the down payment for our first house. It had eight hundred square feet and no hallway. A tiny bathroom connected the small bedrooms, which in turn were connected to the kitchen and living room. Our home was small, but our hopes were huge. This is the place to which we brought Sarah home from the hospital. It is the place that dozens of junior and senior high school kids from our church youth group (not all at once, of course) filled with laughter. It is the home in which early marital memories were established and the foundation for building a great marriage was laid.

That house was also the place from which Barb and I watched a sixty-year marriage finish well.

Cleve and Connie were our neighbors. We were young; they were old. We had a baby; they were childless. We had our future; they had their memories. We raced through life; they walked slowly. As different as our stages of lives were, we saw several similarities. Cleve and I loved our wives. And Connie and Barb were loyal to their husbands.

Barb and I had the honor of watching our friends finish well. When Connie died, Cleve followed her to heaven within days.

This dear couple had a profound impact on our marriage. Barb and I learned by watching them. Like hawks. We would catch glimpses of them walking down the street together hand in hand. At times we would see them smooch on the front porch. Our "Cleve and Connie sightings" communicated a powerful message to us as a young couple: Lifelong companionship is its own reward. "Barb, let's finish like those two" was my typical comment when we would catch them showing love toward each other. Something they did often and well.

At FamilyLife conferences Barb and I show a video in which a woman turns to her husband and simply says, "I just want to be . . . so old with you." They laugh through their tears, and no matter how many times I watch the video, I smile through wet eyes. That is how I want to finish with Barb. Just being "so old" with her.

Barb encouraged you in her chapter on friendship to step into your wife's world, open up about your day, and work on being best friends. Nothing too fancy, men. It simply means being one with each other and living out the interdependence that God designed for you to have. Does it mean you have to act like her female friends? Nope. She doesn't want that, and you don't want that either. To the contrary, it means you bring your God-designed masculinity to the relationship, softening it a bit. It demands that you step outside of yourself and not only tune in to your wife's world but also open your world to her. It means expressing love for your wife by reminding her that she is getting better and better every day.

The key to companionship in marriage is rock-solid commitment, security, and integrity. Barb and I saw it in Connie and Cleve. I saw it lived out in my own parents. At the end of the race I want our kids to say they saw it in Barb and me.

THE GREATEST MARRIAGE I EVER SAW

I want to wrap up my portion of this book by telling you about the greatest marriage I ever witnessed. It was my parents' marriage.

My parents met at a small private high school in Chicago in the 1930s. They courted for a few years and married in 1941. Dad headed overseas to serve in World War II, and after he returned home, over the next thirteen years, they had four kids. There was much laughter in John and Audrey Rosberg's home, but there were also painful times of illness and financial difficulties.

I learned about marriage not only by what my parents said but also by what they *did*. I watched my dad honor my mom above all others. I watched my mom stand by my dad through thick and thin. I drank from the well of security and commitment during our family's struggles with polio, cancer, and sudden heart attacks. I watched them grow deeper through the trials of life. I watched Mom come to a personal relationship with Jesus Christ during one of the greatest stresses of her life: the loss of the family business. I had the joy of leading my dad into a personal relationship with Jesus Christ during the celebration of his seventy-fifth birthday. I watched them dance in the kitchen without music and witnessed my dad's tender heart wipe away my mom's tears by just looking at her from across the room. I didn't see them start, but I saw them finish. And as a couple they finished strong.

Standing in a hospital room on February 3, 1996, I saw my mom release her husband of fifty-four years into the arms of our heavenly Father. As Dad gave up his fight with a brain tumor and congestive heart failure, he let go of his body and received his new body from the Lord.

About twenty minutes before Dad took his last breath, Mom and I were holding each of his hands as we prayed for him. Then Mom did something I will never forget. She stood up real tall, and as if she were speaking to no one in particular but anyone who had ears to hear, she proclaimed, "Gary, your father is a good man. He is an honest man. He is a loving man." To which I replied with tears streaming down my cheeks, "Mom, after fifty-four years of marriage, what more could anyone ask for?"

Moments later Dad died. The greatest man I ever knew was home with Jesus. I can't wait to see him on the other side.

Paul's words to the Romans echo in my ears as I write these last few paragraphs. "When we were utterly helpless, Christ came at just the right time and died for us sinners. Now, no one is likely to die for a good person, though someone might be willing to die for a person who is especially good. But God showed his great love for us by sending Christ to die for us while we were still sinners" (Rom. 5:6-8).

Jesus died for a good man named John Rosberg. He also died for you and me. All we need to do is to receive Christ. Mom's last words to Dad affirmed that he was a good man. She was right. Just as your kids and wife are looking on your life story, I was there observing my mom and dad's marriage. John Rosberg was a good man, and he had a great marriage. That, men, is what I seek for my own life story.

I pray you'll work to meet your wife's love needs and together pursue a great marriage.

CHAPTER 12

BARB'S FINAL WORD TO WOMEN

Recently Gary and I were broadcasting our weekly radio show from separate locations. I was in Des Moines at the WHO radio studio, and Gary was on location in Nebraska at a Promise Keepers event interviewing Coach Bill McCartney. During the interview Coach talked candidly of the hurt he had caused in his wife's life. His major regret was not allowing Lyndi to experience her own life dreams. Through intermittent tears, he spoke of wanting to turn things around, having made an intentional commitment to make her dreams a reality. Coach's heartache was exposed to the world.

When the interview concluded, Gary spoke to me over the airwaves and asked, "Barb, what do you think of what Coach just said?"

Emotional from the interview, I quickly said, "I'm waiting for my husband to ask me what my dreams are."

His tender voice responded, "Okay, Barb, what are some of your dreams?"

I couldn't resist. "Gary, honey, I think we ought to have another baby!" I heard his booming laughter at my joke erupt across the airwaves. Gary had fallen out of his chair, and my normally talkative husband was speechless!

Before Gary returned from the event, I thought seriously about what my dreams are. For the rest of that weekend I found myself staring out the kitchen window wondering if my goal of walking alongside my husband, helping him become effective in ministry, had caused me to abandon my dreams. I thought about it a lot, as I'm sure you've caught yourself doing as well.

My conclusion? Although I'm not ashamed to admit that I have an ambitious streak in me to push my life and influence to the uttermost, I have concluded that my greatest ambition is to be the best wife I can be, doing everything possible to meet Gary's love needs and to pursue a great marriage. Since I've had a husband committed to the same goal, that dream has become a reality. Our marriage hasn't held me back from my dreams. It's been the *reason* for them.

Many women reading these concluding pages could say the same thing. Your husband and your marriage have completed you in every sense of the word.

Many women, however, cannot say that. The chasm between you and your husband seems like too much to bridge. Hurt feelings, hurtful words, painful memories, and months of inattention have left you feeling not only as if the thrill is gone but also as if the hope is gone.

What you are facing is something I call "the test." I know of few marriages that haven't gone through "the test."

Like every married couple, Gary and I have had our share of normal ups and downs: illnesses, graduate school, new babies, times when we ignored each other's needs. But through it all we've been committed to facing these ups and downs together, as a team. With the help of God we have navigated dangerous passages and withstood many trials. And through each one we came out the other side with greater determination, devotion, and a deeper love because we took the precarious journey together. But none of them was "the test."

Then we hit it. The one trial that could have done us in.

Not long after Gary's dad died, we felt as if life crashed into us like the iceberg hitting the *Titanic*. Gary struggled with his tremendous grief and loss. Pressures from ministry demands delayed him from taking time to deal with some steps in the grief process. Over time it became painstakingly clear that Gary was in a depression. Because we were a committed team, however, I encountered this trial not as a bystander but as an active participant. It torpedoed both of our souls and then threatened our exposed hearts. At times we bled from the attack, vulnerable from being overworked and emotionally drained.

"The test" in our marriage had arrived.

Some days I went to work with Gary, and on other days he just wanted to stay home. During those dark hours I canceled everything on my calendar just to sit and hold him as he processed his grief. Neither of us could comprehend what was happening. Sometimes living a day at a time seemed like too much. We were reduced to living five minutes at a time!

Like you, I'm a woman who likes life with a semblance of security, so, to say the least, I was scared. This debilitating depression threw our family out of whack, and I felt absolutely helpless. But I needed some control. Publicly I increased my responsibilities in our business and ministry to compensate for Gary's absence. Privately I wept over the anguish and turmoil that Gary was going through. Our home had always been steeped in love, full of warmth and laughter. During Gary's depression, we still had our share of lighthearted moments, but mostly each day seemed like more than I could bear. I was walking my own tightrope. To be honest, at times I felt like dying and spiraling down into his private hell alongside of him.

Early one morning I was crying out uncontrollably in prayer. Memories of our love-filled home washed over me. All I could think of was wanting to go back in time to the way things had always been. A home in which Gary's loving arms had always waited to comfort and console. A home in which my tears would have been wiped away by his white handkerchief. "Oh, God, take me home!" I sobbed. Childhood memories of my mom's comfort flooded my mind, as did recollections of crawling up on my dad's lap, where I found the shelter of masculine protection. How I longed for my dad's shoulder on which to bury my head and weep. In my private agony I pleaded, "Please, God, strengthen my husband!" I was exhausted from fighting the battle with him. I felt broken and beaten down. It was at that moment that God's unfathomable love embraced me. He was my close companion in the midst of my battle. I understood God as if he were saying, "Let me be your husband, and I will wipe away your tears. Let me be like a mother, and I will comfort you. Come sit on my lap, and I will be like a father to you."

In the privacy of my dining room, as I knelt on our blue carpet, God met me and carried me as a gentle shepherd would carry a broken, wounded lamb. In that hour I transferred my needs onto the One who was meant to carry all of my burdens. Matthew 11:28-29 reminds us so clearly: "Come to me, all of you who are weary and carry heavy burdens, and I will give you rest. Take my yoke upon you. Let me teach you, because I am humble and gentle, and you will find rest for your souls."

For some reason, as God continued to purge the pain from Gary, I felt an unmistakable passion and deepened love for God. It took courage for Gary to walk through the valley of the shadow of death, but if there could be an even greater dimension of joy in going through this battle, it was that we went through this test together.

Going through that test was difficult for us. But our experience in that test gives us a foundation to go through any others that God may allow us to face. We have hope because we are reminded: "We can rejoice, too, when we run into problems and trials, for we know that they are good for us—they help us learn to endure. And endurance develops strength of character in us, and character strengthens our confident expectation of salvation. And this expectation will not disappoint us. For we know how dearly God loves us, because he has given us the Holy Spirit to fill our hearts with his love" (Rom. 5:3-5).

My perspective on trials has changed. In facing them, I'm not as fearful because I know they actually produce something good in my life. People continually ask Gary and me where we get our joy. If you didn't know us well, you would likely think we hadn't any burdens to bear. Well, now you know. Like you, we do have burdens. But we have much joy as well! If you see peace, life, and joy, it's because, just like you, we have a heavenly Father who provides shelter through the storms, a haven so safe and strong that no power on earth can conquer it!

Whether it's my marriage or yours, great marriages are often forged through trials. In your particular season of marriage, your life may be out of control. James 1:2-4, however, tells us, "Dear brothers and sisters, whenever trouble comes your way, let it be an opportunity for joy. For when your faith is tested, your endurance has a chance to grow. So let it grow, for when your endurance is fully developed, you will be strong in character and ready for anything" (James 1:2-4).

So don't look at your trials as an enemy. As you go through them hand in hand with your husband, strive to meet his top five love needs so you can have a great marriage!

But what of the normal times of marriage? If your marriage is void of major trial at this point in life, how can you work on getting your relationship ready to withstand the minor irritations or "the test" that may still be off in the future? I've read Gary's words, and he's coached you (and me) well. But let me add my own insights to each of your husband's top five love needs.

LOVE HIM UNCONDITIONALLY

At the heart of every man is the longing to be loved unconditionally. Unfortunately, we've been raised in a culture that is concerned more about image than authenticity. Even the smallest weakness in a man's younger years could have unwittingly conditioned your husband to put on a mask. And like the Phantom in *Phantom of the Opera,* he may still have a portion of his mask attached to cover hidden scars and old wounds that have never fully healed. The mask common to most men is worn to cover fear—*the fear of failing you.*

One essential role you play for your husband is to help him take off his mask. God has generously gifted you with the natural ability to be gentle and loving. Demonstrate these qualities by being transparent with your weakness to show him how to pry off a mask that may be there from earlier years. Past generations were not taught Transparency 101 in their homes. If your husband is acting as if nothing bad ever happened to him, he is singing the old familiar score of a *Phantom* tune.

Everyone goes through differing levels of pain, injury, and difficulty. And as you travel on those bumpy roads, make him feel comfortable being real with the mask off. Make him feel so comfortable that he'll never want to put it on again.

How? Four suggestions:

1. *Be a cheerleader.* Your perspective on life counts. It determines how safe your husband will feel in opening up. If you're tender and compassionate, your husband will feel free to talk about what's going on inside him. Life can bruise him, and disappointments can break him unless he feels your total support. He doesn't need a yes-woman, and he doesn't want a fake smile no matter what's happening. But when he knows you will cheer him on in good times and bad, the emotion you bring him can be exactly the energy he needs to pull himself up.

2. *Be tender.* Give your husband loads of tender moments before he starts the battle of his day. Wrap your arms around him while you are still in bed. Make him feel safe and secure in an embrace. It is a rare husband who does not long for those times with his wife.

3. *Read his moods.* Husbands have moods just as wives do, but your husband's masculinity serves to keep those moods somewhat hidden. Gary is a happy man. When he leaves for the office in the morning, he is at ease and open. A few hours later, however, I see him at the office and am at times taken aback when I see that his mood often shifts from positive to preoccupied and stressed. I always forget he's put on his battle fatigues and entered his war zone—not because his office is an unpleasant place, but because the work world is full of stress.

Study your husband, know him, and make sure you never use his moods as a weapon against him. When he realizes you're making an effort to love him unconditionally through his mood swings, he will be able to relax and return to the guy you recognized in the morning.

4. *Timing is everything.* Gary, like your husband, faces stress points in his work. Overloaded schedules, deadlines, financial pressures, as well as the normal stuff. If a colleague isn't sensitive to the heavy loads he's managing and pushes him to carry more, even Mr. Even Keel can break. As a wife, you need to be sensitive to the load your husband is carrying just as you need him to be considerate of your load. Tune in to him. Don't make the mistake of neglecting to think through what he's struggling with. You don't want to unintentionally dump on him something that can add weight to a world he feels he's already carrying.

It's a matter of timing. It doesn't mean you avoid issues with your husband when he gets home from work; it simply means that you hold some of them until after he has eaten and has had a chance to catch his breath. Then he will be more open to listening to you tell him the bank account is overdrawn, you had car trouble, or your teenage son spent another afternoon in the dean's office.

FULFILL HIS SEXUAL NEEDS

The surprise that sexual needs ranked number two is outweighed only by the fact that it wasn't also third, fourth, and fifth!

This need accentuates the differences between men and women, almost to the point of exasperation. Gary's right when he says men spell intimacy S-E-X and women spell it T-A-L-K.

You can help bridge these differences by communicating that your security in expressing your sexuality is based on the way he treats you outside of the bedroom. If your husband is interested in some sexual intimacy with you late at night, he needs to start tuning in to your mind and emotions as soon as he wakes up in the morning! Men need to hear that great sex is a product of the entire marriage relationship—how he treats you in every other room of the house. It's the environment of the marriage that makes you hot or leaves you cold with your husband.

Don't forget that most men find a great deal of their masculinity in their sexuality. The normal man longs for his wife to be open to his advances and respond to him in a positive way. Otherwise, if the rejection continues over time, he can close his spirit to you. To be honest, most of us wives don't have a clue how vulnerable our husbands are in sexual issues. I do know, however, that when I respond to my husband and enjoy his sexuality, I help increase his feelings of male security. A good sex life will often bring joy to him in all areas of his life. The converse is true too. A frustrating sex life that fails to understand his rhythm is an invitation to the devil to tempt your husband beyond what he can handle.

Most men long to give their wife pleasure, especially as they get older. Your husband may not tell you this, but it's a well-documented fact. If you're resisting your husband's sexual advances, not only will you miss out, but this attitude can really shut him down.

Ask God, "What is it that is blocking a healthy sex life?" He will gently show you. It may be a resentful attitude. Or there may be deeper issues that need to be resolved: past sexual behavior, adultery, abortion, or sexual abuse. Men and women who have faced these problems can attest to the serious impact on a person's capacity to enjoy a healthy sexual relationship. Left unattended, these issues can steal the joy of intimacy from your heart. If you have been wounded and hurt by someone, then take it to our heavenly Father. He is a wonderful Counselor, who longs for you to run into his arms and to be quieted from all those fears and guilt.

Do what you must to deal with the pain, and ask God to give you a brand-new start in the area of sex with your husband. If you have suffered from abuse, you may find help in Dan Allender's *The Wounded Heart* and Diane Langberg's *On the Threshold of Hope*.[1] Go through the books with a highlighter, and identify areas that you relate to your situation. Then give the book to your husband, and ask him to read what you have high-

---

[1]Dan B. Allender, *The Wounded Heart: Hope for Adult Victims of Childhood Sexual Abuse* (Colorado Springs, Colo.: NavPress, 1990); and Diane Mandt Langberg, *On the Threshold of Hope: Opening the Door to Hope and Healing for Survivors of Sexual Abuse* (Wheaton, Ill.: Tyndale, 1999).

lighted. Help him understand what you are going through. Don't go it alone.

The most important part of your relationship with your husband is your heart attitude toward him. If there is even a trace of unresolved anger, resentment, lack of forgiveness, or doubt, it will show up in your sexual relationship. Your attitude affects your ability to be open, trusting, and genuinely interested in your husband. The fact is, if you aren't relaxed and showing interest in him, he'll notice that something is wrong anyway.

Is anger or resentment building between you and your husband? Confess it, confide in him, and be done with it!

A few other tips:

- Never go to bed angry. Anger robs you of intimacy. If there is unresolved tension in your relationship, it will generally show up in the bedroom.
- Give your husband tips (outside the bedroom) about things that could use some modification in the bedroom: longer interludes with him, things you like, and things you would prefer to change.
- Confess any attitudes that are creeping in and robbing you of enjoying your husband. Before two hearts can touch, two hearts must be open and clean.
- Confront the darkness. More and more women confide that men want pornography. This must stop. Men are bringing darkness into their bed. They must see the value of keeping the marriage bed pure.
- Pray about your sex life. Inviting the originator of sex into that arena of marriage is awesome. What a great way to fully enjoy your husband.

ENJOY YOUR BEST FRIEND

When you have a secret to share, a burden to unload, or a special triumph, do you generally tell an acquaintance or your best friend? I tell my best friend, Gary.

Joy is fully experienced in marriage when you unlock the door between two hearts. True friendship with your husband will satisfy your heart and will give you hope for shared intimacy.

Remember that you and your husband will view friendship a bit differently. You probably value emotional intimacy in a friendship. Your husband needs you to have realistic expectations about what your friendship will be like. But beware. We can intentionally look to him to meet all of our emotional needs, and that feels smothering. He isn't made to meet all your friendship needs. You still need your female friends as well. But step closer to him, and build that foundation of friendship. Remember, it's hard for a man to open up. He fears looking inadequate and doesn't want to look bad to you. Be aware that he doesn't need your perfectionism. He needs a safety net that will allow him to be himself and know that you will love him deeply—no matter what.

Satisfy your husband's friendship needs by joining in his work-related activities and his recreation. He may love to hunt, fish, golf, jog, or go to ball games. He appreciates it when you take an interest in his world. Doesn't that make sense? Gary and I have learned to step into each other's varied interests. I have joined him in downhill skiing, snorkeling, and swimming with stingrays. We are even planning to swim with dolphins in the near future. When I'm around Gary, I wind up trying things that I would never choose on my own, but I do them simply because it's such fun for us! What can you do to enter your husband's world and develop your friendship?

ENCOURAGE HIM

Gary shared in chapter 1 that several years ago we lost half of our income after one phone call. My opportunity to encourage my husband was put to the test. As he told me the story, I listened for the details. When he finished, all I could think was, *Man, he has integrity. I love it!*

When I think about being married to a man with integrity, I feel like a very wealthy woman! I'll take that kind of character in my husband over anything money can buy. All I knew was that God had always taken care of us and that he would continue to provide in the future. Gary's obedience was my assurance. Regardless of the spiritual implications to our financial need, Gary still needed my reinforcement that I believed in him. And I assure you he got it!

Your words mean so much to your husband as he walks through times of uncertainty. Regularly assure your husband that no matter what happens, you will stay close to him. He can never hear enough praise from you. Say encouraging things to him, such as: "I'm proud of you." "I'm so glad I'm married to you." "I see God working through

you." "I admire your [name a virtue]." Show him how much you love
him, not for what he earns, but for his character and presence in your
life.

BUILD SPIRITUAL INTIMACY

I long to be loved and tenderly led to the Cross by my husband. But, like
you, I sometimes resist that leadership and want to control my life. When I
choose to lead when I should follow, I'm opting for second best. I get out
of balance like an overloaded washer and bring tension into our marriage.

I want to live my life with God as my first priority. God should always
be my Father, my Husband, and my Best Friend. Why? Because I know
that only he can meet some of my deepest needs. God created those
needs, and only a perfect God can satisfy them. When I am experiencing
God's unconditional love, he fills me to overflowing. Who benefits the
most besides me? Gary.

Don't make the mistake of making your husband sit on a throne that
only God should fill. Continue to learn the secret of living your life with
an audience of One.

If your husband is struggling in an area, pray for him, talk to him if he
is open to that, and then let God work in his heart. God will gradually
open his spiritual eyes as you obey the scriptural command to win him
by a "gentle and quiet spirit" (1 Pet. 3:4). You are a major part of the
equation to help your husband move your family in the right direction.
But you can't do it with a baseball bat. You have to let God do it in his
good timing.

THE FOUR P'S = POWER

Meeting any or all of your husband's love needs also means not trying to
do it under your own power. It can't be done. I've discovered four things
I can do to make sure it's God's power doing the work, not mine. I call
them my "four Ps." They aren't radically different from anything you've
heard before, but they work!

Personal, daily time reading the Word. I love *The One Year Bible,* published
by Tyndale. It provides daily readings from the Old and New Testa-
ments, Psalms, and Proverbs. Find a place where you can go to hide
away from it all and spend time with God and his Word. Then apply

what the Scriptures are teaching you by responding to your husband in a godly way.

Prayer. Don't miss a day. I call out to the Lord in thoughts—and sometimes out loud—many times during the day. If you want to truly meet your husband's love needs and have a great marriage, then you must humble yourself and turn toward the infinite wisdom of a powerful God. Begin every prayer with words of thanksgiving and praise for what he has done in your life.

Partner with a friend. When I'm wading through high waters, I am quick to call my prayer partners. Julie Pigneri and Pat Holmertz are just as quick to respond, either in person or over the phone. This partnership with other women of kindred hearts really works!

Past provision of God. When discouragement stabs you out of the dark, thank God for how he has worked in the past. Neither you nor I know what the future holds, but we know the One who does. He promises to never leave us or forsake us. And remember, he is the best promise keeper.

My parents taught me a great deal in creating a thirst for God. Jack and Colleen Bedford provided a home steeped in the love of family, and for that I am so grateful. Their fifty-nine-year commitment to marriage established my foundation and solidified my belief in the safety and permanence of marriage. From the time I was an infant, my dear mother prayed for the man I would marry. Those prayers contributed to shaping Gary into the wonderful man that he is today.

My dad, a former marine, always made sure our home was shipshape. He set tough rules to make sure that his daughter was being honored. I'll never forget the day when I brought Gary to meet my parents; I was nineteen years old. I told my dad I was going to go to church that evening alone. He was walking through the living room, and my proclamation of independence made him stop in his tracks.

He glared at Gary and said, "No daughter of mine is going to church alone!" With no place to hide, Gary reluctantly volunteered. That was the last place he wanted to go. Dad got Gary in church, and God did the rest. That night I watched and listened as Gary learned for the first time of the unconditional love of our heavenly Father. Most people were scared of my dad's tough side, but I saw right through to his wonderful, tender heart. He is still one of my heroes.

A great marriage isn't a dream; it's a choice. Meeting your husband's love needs isn't an option; it's a must! It's deciding together that from this day forward your relationship is going to change. It's choosing to meet these top five love needs and going beyond these five to all the rest. Most of all, the great marriage is a committed team of three. When you and your husband acknowledge God and put him first in everything you do, he promises to bless your marriage.

As Gary and I work to meet each other's love needs and pursue a great marriage, I pray to see you along that path pursuing yours.

APPENDIX

The findings here represent the categorical data that emerged from our survey of 700 couples in 8 cities. We gave each husband and each wife a list of 20 needs and asked them to rank them in order of importance.

HUSBANDS' NEEDS

1. Unconditional love and acceptance

2. Sexual intimacy

3. Companionship

4. Encouragement and affirmation

5. Spiritual intimacy

6. Trust

7. Honesty and openness

8. Communication and emotional intimacy

9. Family relationships

10. To be desired

11. Career support

12. To provide and protect

WIVES' NEEDS

1. Unconditional love and acceptance

2. Communication and emotional intimacy

3. Spiritual intimacy

4. Encouragement and affirmation

5. Companionship

6. Family relationships

7. Honesty and openness

8. Nonsexual touch

9. Security and stability

10. Romance

11. Trust

12. Understanding and empathy

HUSBANDS' NEEDS

13. Personal time

14. Understanding and empathy

15. Admiration

16. Security and stability

17. Significance

18. Romance

19. Domestic support

20. Nonsexual touch

WIVES' NEEDS

13. Sexual intimacy

14. Personal time

15. To be desired

16. Domestic support

17. To provide and protect

18. Significance

19. Admiration

20. Career support

ABOUT THE AUTHORS

Dr. Gary and Barbara Rosberg are America's Family Coaches—equipping and encouraging America's families to live and finish life well. Having been married for over twenty-five years, Gary and Barbara have a unique message for couples. They have conducted conferences on family and relationship issues in over one hundred U.S. cities. They are on the national speaking teams for FamilyLife's marriage conferences and FamilyLife's "I Still Do" arena events for couples. Gary also has spoken to thousands of men at Promise Keepers' stadium events and to parents and adolescents at Focus on the Family's "Life on the Edge Tour" conferences.

Together Gary and Barbara host *America's Family Coaches LIVE,* a nationally syndicated daily radio program. On this live call-in program heard in cities all across the country, they coach callers on many family-related issues. Gary and Barbara also host a Saturday radio program on the award-winning WHO Radio.

Gary, who earned his Ed.D. at Drake University, has been a marriage and family counselor for more than fifteen years. He has written two best-selling books: *Dr. Rosberg's Do-It-Yourself Relationship Mender* (Tyndale and Focus on the Family), which deals with closing the loop of conflict in interpersonal relationships, and *Guard Your Heart* (Multnomah), which helps men stand strong in the midst of temptations. Gary coaches CrossTrainers, a men's Bible study and accountability group of more than six hundred men.

Barbara joined Gary in writing a special chapter for *Guard Your Heart* and in writing a study entitled *Improving Communication in Your Marriage* (Group Publishing) for FamilyLife's HomeBuilders Couples Series. In addition to speaking to families, Barbara coaches and encourages women through A Woman's Legacy, a series emphasizing the incredible value and worth of a woman.

The Rosbergs live in West Des Moines, Iowa, and are the parents of two daughters: Missy, a college student studying communications, and Sarah, who lives in West Des Moines with her husband, Scott.

For more information on the ministries of America's Family Coaches, contact:

America's Family Coaches
2540 106th Street, Suite 101
Des Moines, Iowa 50322
1-888-ROSBERG
www.americasfamilycoaches.com